A WOMAN'S VOICE IN BAROQUE MUSIC: MARIANE VON ZIEGLER AND J. S. BACH

Christiane Mariane von Ziegler

Frontispiece to Jacob Friedrich Lamprecht, *Sammlung der Schriften und Gedichte welche auf die Poetische Krönung Der Hochwohlgebohrnen Frauen, Frauen Christianen Marianen von Ziegler gebohrnen Romanus, verfertiget worden* (1734). Universitätsbibliothek Leipzig (8-B.S.T.393).

A Woman's Voice in Baroque Music: Mariane von Ziegler and J. S. Bach

MARK A. PETERS
Trinity Christian College, USA

ASHGATE

Published by
Ashgate Publishing Limited
Gower House
Croft Road
Aldershot
Hampshire GU11 3HR
England

Ashgate Publishing Company
Suite 420
101 Cherry Street
Burlington, VT 05401-4405
USA

Ashgate website: http://www.ashgate.com

British Library Cataloguing in Publication Data
Peters, Mark A., 1975–
  A woman's voice in baroque music: Mariane von Ziegler and J.S. Bach
  1. Ziegler, Mariane von – Criticism and interpretation 2. Bach, Johann Sebastian, 1685–1750.
  Cantatas 3. Cantatas, Sacred – Texts – History and criticism 4. Cantatas, Sacred – History
  and criticism 5. Lutheran Church – Liturgy – History – 18th century
  I. Title
  782.2'4'092

Library of Congress Cataloging-in-Publication Data
Peters, Mark A., 1975–
  A woman's voice in baroque music: Mariane von Ziegler and J. S. Bach / Mark A. Peters.
      p. cm.
  Includes bibliographical references (p.   ) and index.
  ISBN 978-0-7546-5810-8 (alk. paper)
  1. Bach, Johann Sebastian, 1685–1750. Cantatas. 2. Ziegler, Mariane von. 3. Women
  poets, German–18th century. I. Title.
  ML410.B1P425 2007
  782.2'4092–dc22

                                                                                            2007035685

ISBN 978-0-7546-5810-8

Printed and bound in Great Britain by TJ International Ltd, Padstow, Cornwall.

For Don O. Franklin,
with gratitude and admiration

Contents

List of Figures

List of Tables

List of Music Examples

Acknowledgements

Thank you to Don O. Franklin for his advice and encouragement throughout this project and for the many hours he spent commenting on its many incarnations. For their helpful comments on, and criticisms of, the manuscript at various stages, I would like to thank David Brodbeck, Stephen Crist, Tanya Kevorkian, Robin Leaver, Mary Lewis, and Martin Petzoldt. My work on the Ziegler/Bach cantatas has also benefited from discussions with a great number of scholars, of whom I would particularly like to thank Alfred Dürr, Hans-Joachim Schulze, and Joshua Rifkin. Thank you also to my editor, Heidi May, for her many helpful insights.

Research for this book was conducted at the Bach-Archiv in Leipzig, the Bach-Institut in Göttingen, the Herzog August Bibliothek in Wolfenbüttel, the Library of Congress (European and Performing Arts Reading Rooms), the Niedersächsische Staats- und Universitätsbibliothek in Göttingen, the Stadtbibliothek in Leipzig, and the Universitätsbibliothek Leipzig. Thank you to the many kind staff members who facilitated my work in these places. Special thanks also to Jim Cassaro of the University of Pittsburgh music library and to Marci Frederick, Tippi Price, and Ingrid Boyer of the Trinity Christian College library.

For providing financial support for this project, I am grateful to Trinity Christian College for Summer Research Grants (2005, 2006, 2007), a Research Fellowship (2006–07), and an Interim Research Release (2007). Thank you also to the Center for West European Studies at the University of Pittsburgh for funding my research in Germany.

Thanks to my wife, Candace Peters, for her love, support, patience, and laughter. Thanks also to the many colleagues, friends, and family members who provided encouragement for, and at times relief from, the project. And a special acknowledgement to my children, Jared, Elyssa, Josiah, and Samuel, who love music and books and who had such helpful comments as: "Push the right buttons" (on the computer), "Why are you writing that book?" "Maybe you could write another book next year," and "What book?"

List of Abbreviations

Liturgical Occasions

Liturgical occasions involving a number designation are distinguished between a day "of" or a day "after" by means of number placement. A number before the liturgical occasion indicates a day "of," while a number after the liturgical occasion indicates a day "after." For example:

1 Advent	First Sunday of Advent
2 Christmas	Second Day of Christmas
Epiphany 1	First Sunday after Epiphany
Trinity 1	First Sunday after Trinity

Scoring Designations

The following abbreviations are used in the text and in music examples and tables. In such listings, instruments playing in unison with one another are indicated by a slash (/). E.g., "V I/V II/Va" indicates strings in unison, while "V I, V II, Va" indicates three separate parts.

A	alto	T	tenor
B	bass	Timp	timpani
Bc	basso continuo	Tr	trumpet (tromba)
Cor	corno	Tr da tir	tromba da tirarsi
Fl	flauto traverso	Trb	trombone
Fl picc	flauto piccolo	V	violin
Ob	oboe	V conc	violin concertate
Ob d'am	oboe d'amore	Va	viola
Ob da cacc	oboe da caccia (taille)	Vc	violoncello
mm.	measures	Vc picc	violoncello piccolo
S	soprano		

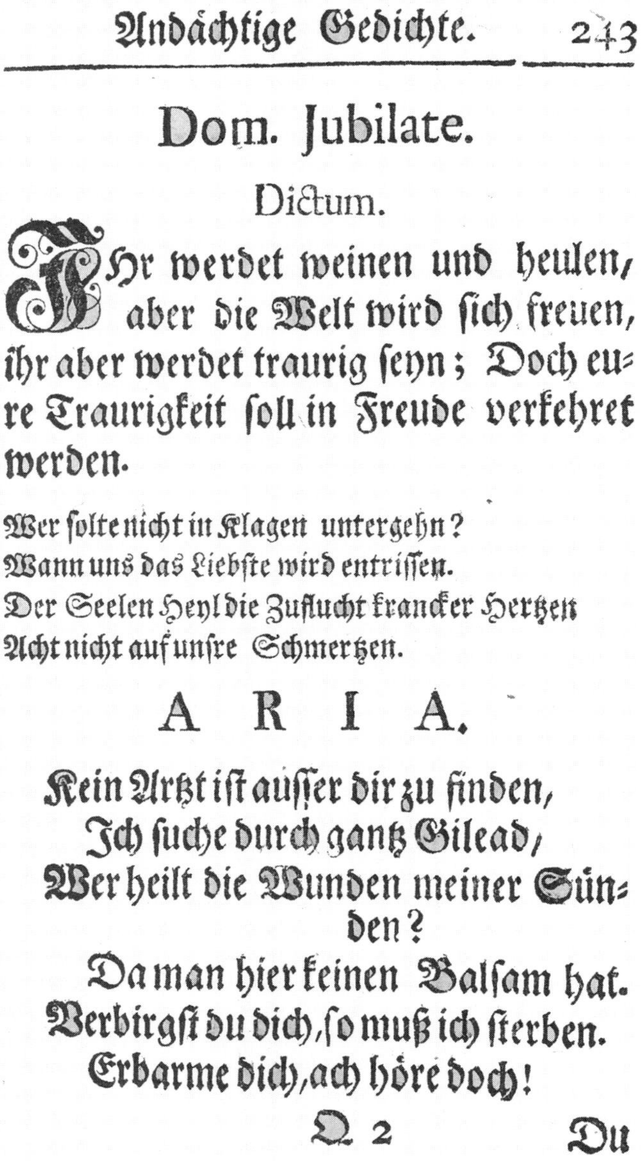

Andächtige Gedichte.   243

Dom. Jubilate.

Dictum.

Ihr werdet weinen und heulen, aber die Welt wird sich freuen, ihr aber werdet traurig seyn; Doch eure Traurigkeit soll in Freude verkehret werden.

Wer solte nicht in Klagen untergehn?
Wann uns das Liebste wird entrissen.
Der Seelen Heyl die Zuflucht krancker Hertzen
Acht nicht auf unsre Schmertzen.

A R I A.

Kein Artzt ist ausser dir zu finden,
Ich suche durch gantz Gilead,
Wer heilt die Wunden meiner Sünden?
Da man hier keinen Balsam hat.
Verbirgst du dich, so muß ich sterben.
Erbarme dich, ach höre doch!

Q 2   Du

Figure I.1   Opening text of *Ihr werdet weinen und heulen* (BWV 103). In Christiane Mariane von Ziegler, *Versuch in gebundener Schreib-Art* (1728). Herzog August Bibliothek Wolfenbüttel (Lo 8318).

Introduction:
Mariane von Ziegler and J. S. Bach

As Leipzig town cantor, Johann Sebastian Bach was responsible for the performance of a sacred cantata for each Sunday and feast day in the Lutheran liturgical year, about 60 annual performances in all. His schedule, therefore, in his early Leipzig years was intense. For a typical Sunday, not only did Bach compose the cantata, but he also arranged for its parts to be copied and directed its rehearsals and performances. And once these Sunday performances were completed, Bach began anew preparing the next Sunday's cantata. This schedule only intensified with the addition of feast days which did not fall on a Sunday. Consider, for example, the year 1724 and Bach's first Christmas in Leipzig: Christmas, like Easter and Pentecost, was a three-day feast in the Lutheran year, so it required three cantatas. Bach was therefore responsible for three Christmas cantatas: Saturday 25 December; Sunday 26 December; and Monday 27 December. This was closely followed by a cantata for New Year's Day, Saturday 1 January, and then for the Sunday following New Year's Day, 2 January. Adding Epiphany on Thursday 6 January, and the next Sunday, 9 January, Bach was required to provide seven cantatas in this 16-day period.

Not surprisingly, the composer was exceedingly practical in his approach to cantata performance during his first year in Leipzig (Jahrgang I). If he had already composed a sacred cantata suitable for a particular liturgical occasion, he used it. Bach, therefore, reperformed 22 pre-Leipzig cantatas during his first year in Leipzig, usually with no more than minor changes. For four other cantatas, Bach based the music on secular cantatas he had composed in Cöthen. Of the 62 cantatas Bach performed during his first year in Leipzig, only 36 were newly composed (see Appendix C for a list of Bach's cantata performances during his first two years in Leipzig).

But practicality was superseded by artistic ambition in Bach's second Leipzig year (Jahrgang II): Bach composed a new cantata for every Sunday and feast day from 11 June 1724 to 25 March 1725, 40 cantatas in all. During this period, Bach systematically pursued the composition of chorale cantatas, a particular sub-genre of the cantata based on the Lutheran chorale and employing both chorale texts and melodies. Although he had composed only one chorale cantata before this time, his Mühlhausen cantata BWV 4, *Christ lag in Todesbanden*, Bach's penchant for the methodical exploration of a delineated compositional approach, evident in such other major works as his *Well-Tempered Clavier* and later *Art of Fugue*, seems to have led him in 1724 to this intense focus on the chorale and its various possibilities for cantata composition.

However, Bach did not follow through on his chorale cantata project for the entire Jahrgang. While he continued composing chorale cantatas up to Lent (a period during which no cantatas were performed in Leipzig) and for the Annunciation to Mary (a feast day which occurs during Lent), Bach did not write any more chorale cantatas during this year. When he resumed his cantata performances at Easter 1725, he returned to the general text type of Jahrgang I.

Although there has been much speculation over the cessation of Bach's Jahrgang II chorale cantata cycle, the precise reasons behind it are yet unknown. One possible scenario has been offered by Hans-Joachim Schulze, who speculates that Bach's librettist for the chorale cantatas was Andreas Stübel, the conrector emeritus of the Thomasschule who possessed both a solid theological background and ample poetic experience. Stübel died on 31 January 1725 after only three days of illness. From the existence of a printed text booklet for the five cantatas performed from 28 January to 25 March 1725, it is evident that Stübel could have written the texts for these cantatas before his death. If Stübel was indeed the librettist for the chorale cantatas, this explains both why they would have continued until 25 March and also why Bach composed no additional chorale cantatas after this date in Jahrgang II.[1]

With the coming of Easter on 1 April 1725 and his resumption of cantata composition and performance, Bach returned to his Jahrgang I practices. On Easter Sunday, he performed the so-called Easter Oratorio (BWV 249) *Komm, eilet und laufet*, a parody of the secular cantata BWV 249a, as well as his chorale cantata from Mühlhausen, BWV 4. In addition to parody and reperformance in this period, Bach composed three cantatas, BWV 6, 42, and 85, which were textually and musically similar to his post-Easter cantatas of Jahrgang I.

But having temporarily returned to his Jahrgang I practices, Bach instead completed his second Jahrgang by composing nine cantatas to texts by a single librettist. His choice of librettist is particularly surprising: an unknown Leipzig poet with no published writings, one ten years Bach's junior at only 30 years of age, one in no way officially connected to the church, one with no formal theological training, and—most surprising of all—a woman: Christiane Mariane von Ziegler (1695–1760).

While not yet known as a poet, Ziegler was anything but anonymous in the city of Leipzig. She had been born into the wealthy and influential Romanus family, and her father, Franz Konrad Romanus, had been installed as one of Leipzig's mayors shortly after his daughter's sixth birthday in 1701. The family's ongoing prominence in Leipzig was not based, however, on Romanus's continued position as mayor. On the contrary, Romanus was arrested without stated charge in 1705 and imprisoned without trial until his death in 1746. All the more striking about this situation is the fact that Romanus's family seems to have been little affected by his absence: they continued to enjoy prestige in the city and live in the elaborate house Romanus had built during his brief tenure as mayor (see Chapter 1 below, Figure 1.2).

But neither her family's political intrigue and wealth nor her own experience of being married and widowed twice by the age of 27 would have attracted Bach's

---

1   Hans-Joachim Schulze, "Texte und Textdichter," in *Die Welt der Bach Kantaten*, Vol. 3, *Johann Sebastian Bachs Leipziger Kirchenkantaten*, ed. Christoph Wolff, 109–25 (Stuttgart, 1999), 116. While Bach did make sporadic attempts in later years to fill in the chorale cantatas that were missing from the cycle, he never completed this project. See Table 8.9, "Chorale Cantatas (later additions)," in Christoph Wolff, *Johann Sebastian Bach: The Learned Musician* (New York, 2000), 280.

attention to Ziegler's poetic gifts. Ziegler would not publish any poetry under her own name for another three years, with no evidence of her future successes of publishing four books, being inducted into Leipzig's Deutschen Gesellschaft, and being crowned poet laureate anywhere in view. However, we must remember that, in 1725, Bach himself was relatively unknown. While we are tempted from our twenty-first century perspective to see the great composer setting texts by Germany's first female poet laureate, we must recognize the local and temporary nature of the cantatas' creation.

So while the interaction between Ziegler and Bach may be judged to be outstanding and the results thereof (the nine sacred cantatas, BWV 103, 108, 87, 128, 183, 74, 68, 175, and 176) exemplary, at the time it seems that the town composer needed some new cantata texts in a hurry and somehow connected with an amateur poet who agreed to try her hand at writing them. Although the precise details of the Ziegler/Bach collaboration are not documented, Hans-Joachim Schulze speculates that the two were introduced by a mutual friend, Maria Elisabeth Taubert. The first of the nine cantatas was performed just a few days after the birth of Bach's son Christian Gottlieb, for whom Taubert served as godmother.[2] Friendly relations are also evident between the Bach and Romanus families themselves, as Ziegler's aunt served as godmother for Bach's daughter Elisabeth Juliana Friederica in 1726.[3] But even though both composer and poet were prominent in Leipzig for years to come, Bach evidently never set another of Ziegler's texts after May 1725 and there is no evidence of any ongoing relationship between the two.

The fact that Bach did not set any of Ziegler's later cantata texts (she published a completed yearly cycle in 1729) should not come as a surprise, since Bach clearly never intended to use Ziegler's texts for anything more than the completion of his second Jahrgang. The cycle came to a close on Trinity Sunday, 27 May 1725, with the final Ziegler/Bach cantata, BWV 176, *Es ist ein trotzig und verzagt Ding*. Beginning the next week, with the first Sunday after Trinity, Bach appears to have either reperformed his own compositions or performed cantatas by other composers. And while Bach did briefly resume regular cantata composition at the beginning of the ensuing liturgical year—Christmas Day, 25 December 1725, to Epiphany 3, 27 January 1726—he continued the year rather by performing cantatas of his cousin Johann Ludwig Bach of Meiningen before returning to a somewhat regular schedule of cantata composition during the Trinity season of 1726.

The end of the Ziegler cantatas thus marked the cessation of Bach's steady composition of sacred cantatas. He apparently never again resumed the intense schedule of cantata composition which he pursued during his first two years in Leipzig. Remarkable in themselves for their many points of textual and musical interest, Bach's Ziegler cantatas are further striking when considered in light of this

---

2   Hans-Joachim Schulze, "Neuerkenntnisse zu einigen Kantatentexten Bachs auf Grund neuer biographischer Daten," in *Bach-Interpretationen*, ed. Martin Geck (Göttingen, 1969), 23–24.

3   Arnold Schering, *Johann Sebastian Bach und das Musikleben Leipzigs im 18. Jahrhundert*, Vol. 3 of *Der Musikgeschichte Leipzigs* (Leipzig, 1941), 323.

chronology. They essentially represent not only the completion of Bach's second Jahrgang, but also the culmination of his regular schedule of cantata composition.

The story of this book, then, is the story of a "great" composer setting texts by a "great" poet, but before either were considered "great." The details of their personal relationship are evidently mundane, and the musical results of their collaboration were eminently practical: specific pieces for the services and liturgical occasions of a one-month period of time in Leipzig's principal churches. We can speculate that neither composer not poet perceived these cantatas as spectacular, and neither of their future careers seems to have been greatly affected by this collaboration.

But even given these caveats, the story of these cantatas is truly remarkable. Through them a woman's voice was heard in the Lutheran liturgy, a turn of events unthinkable at the time when considering the spoken word. Furthermore, this woman went on to be one of Germany's preeminent poets and one of its most outspoken advocates for women's rights to a public voice. In considering the composer, these cantatas reflect a new freedom and inventiveness, the expansion and exploration of a striking compositional voice. While representing only one month in two remarkable artistic lives, the Ziegler/Bach cantatas deserve detailed attention by scholars and performers alike.

The goal of the present volume is to offer the first in-depth study of Ziegler, her cantata texts, and their settings by J. S. Bach. In order to achieve this goal, it approaches the cantatas from a number of different perspectives, including historical, liturgical, textual, and musical. These various approaches are focused around the concept of voice, a prevalent trope in Ziegler's own writings, both secular and sacred. In employing various ideas of voice as an organizing principle, I particularly focus on Ziegler's belief that the voice, or speech, stands as a metaphor for all human expression.

Chapter 1, "Woman's Voice: Mariane von Ziegler as Poet," presents an account of Ziegler's life within the context of women's rights to expression in early eighteenth-century Germany. This account addresses a lacuna in both literary and musicological scholarship by presenting the first detailed biography of Ziegler. As its title implies, this biography not only relates the details of Ziegler's life and works, but also does so within the context of Ziegler's defenses of women's rights to a voice. Ziegler believed that women, like men, had a right to be heard, a right to be involved in public discourse both through speech and through writing.

Given the societal prohibitions against women's public self-expression, and particularly against women speaking in the church, it is remarkable that Ziegler provided cantata texts for the Lutheran liturgy in Leipzig. The singularity of this occurrence is emphasized by the fact that these are not only Bach's only settings of texts by a female poet, but also the only known liturgical cantata texts by a woman to be performed in the Lutheran church of eighteenth-century Germany. Chapter 2, "Anonymous Voice: Mariane von Ziegler's Sacred Cantata Texts," addresses textual characteristics of Ziegler's cantatas within such a context, arguing for the special nature of Ziegler's texts both theologically and poetically. The title "Anonymous Voice" draws attention to the fact that Ziegler would not have been publicly recognized as librettist when these cantatas were first performed.

Growing out of the textual features of the cantatas, and particularly Ziegler's proclivity for biblical quotation, Chapter 3 explores the Vox Christi, the literal words of Jesus in biblical quotation, in the Ziegler/Bach cantatas. Its title, "Divine Voice: The Significance of the Vox Christi for Ziegler and for Bach," highlights the Vox Christi as the divine voice, one that held special significance and authority in orthodox Leipzig, as well as the fact that the Vox Christi held particular, albeit different, significance for both Ziegler as librettist and Bach as composer. For Ziegler, the words of Jesus in biblical quotation lent authority to her cantata texts and thus to her voice as a female librettist. For Bach, they provided special compositional impetus, opportunities both to identify with existing Lutheran traditions of setting the Vox Christi and to create new and innovative movements.

Chapter 4, "The Composer's Voice: Bach's Compositional Procedures in the Ziegler Cantatas," focuses even more closely on Bach's compositional choices in the Ziegler cantatas. In surveying his treatment of movement ordering, aria forms, recitative, and scoring, I argue that the special nature of Ziegler's texts contributed to Bach's particular musical choices. Given the high number of innovative movements and striking compositional procedures in these nine cantatas, I further argue that these works demonstrate a particularly fertile compositional period within Bach's cantata output.

In light of the special textual and musical features of Bach's cantatas to Ziegler texts, I conclude my study by arguing for a reconsideration of Ziegler as cantata librettist, particularly in relation to her collaboration with Bach. Chapter 5, "Woman's Voice Restored: The Reception of the Ziegler Cantatas and Their Significance in Bach's Output," addresses and reconsiders two commonly-stated issues in scholarly reception of the Ziegler/Bach cantatas: the textual differences between the cantatas as set by Bach in 1725 and published by Ziegler in 1728 and the fact that Bach never set another Ziegler text after May of 1725. In light of new perspectives on both these issues, I call for a reconsideration of Ziegler and her nine cantatas set by Bach on the basis of their textual and musical features and historical significance.

While this book is not accompanied by sound recordings, I encourage the reader to listen to the nine Ziegler/Bach cantatas throughout your engagement with this volume. Listening to individual movements as I discuss them in Chapters 3 and 4 will help to illumine the discussion there. Furthermore, I hope a familiarity with the sound of the nine cantatas will contribute to your understanding and enjoyment of the book as a whole, just as I hope your reading of the book will further your understanding and enjoyment of the cantatas.

Figure 1.1   Christiane Mariane von Ziegler, 1736. Herzog August Bibliothek
              Wolfenbüttel (A 24792).

Chapter 1

Woman's Voice:
Mariane von Ziegler as Poet

Itzo wird es mir erlaubet seyn, für mich und die wenigen meines Geschlechtes zu reden.
(Even so it will be allowed for me, and for the least of my gender, to speak.)
Christiane Mariane von Ziegler, *Vermischete Schriften* (1739)

In her *Moralische und vermischte Send-Schreiben* of 1731, Christiane Mariane von Ziegler (1695–1760) stated—in opposition to the norms of early eighteenth-century German society—that learning was not a difficult task for a woman. Women, Ziegler argued, possessed the same patience and diligence on which men prided themselves, and if a woman studied from her youth she could achieve the same levels of learning as a man. Ziegler presented "three learned heroines" as illustrating her point: the Dutch poet, artist, philosopher, and scholar of ancient and modern languages, Anna Maria van Schurman (1607–78); the French novelist and salon hostess, Madeleine de Scudéry (1607–1701); and the French author, editor, and translator, Anne Dacier (1651–1720).[1]

Ziegler could have mentioned other learned women in German-speaking lands, as well, such as Maria Sibylla Merian (1647–1717), who published and illustrated several books in the field of natural history; and Maria Winkelmann Kirch (1670–1720), an astronomer who discovered a comet in 1702 and published several of her writings, including an essay on the conjunction of Jupiter and Saturn (1712). Indeed, a number of women in seventeenth- and eighteenth-century Europe were notable for achieving erudition and making significant contributions in both the arts and sciences. Such women, however, were exceptions to established gender norms. They generally came from elite or noble families, often with an intellectual father who encouraged his daughter's learning or with tutors hired for a brother's education. And even so, such women were criticized for what was considered a "transgression" into the field of male learning.

Hence Ziegler's argument for better, and more widespread, education of women and her assertion of women's educability. Ziegler herself had the advantage of a solid education in the home, as well as the leisure to pursue intellectual interests afforded to her as the member of a wealthy, upper-class family. Even so, her accomplishments in the field of literature were remarkable, as was her continued defense of women's rights to be educated and to publish their literary works.

---

1   Christiane Mariane von Ziegler, *Moralische und vermischte Send-Schreiben, An einige Ihrer vertrauten und guten Freunde gestellt* (Leipzig, 1731), 7–9.

This chapter presents an account of Ziegler's life and works within the context of women's rights to self-expression in early eighteenth-century Germany. After providing context on gender norms, particularly as they related to women's education and writing, the chapter continues with a chronological overview of Ziegler's life within the context of her published writings (for an annotated list of Ziegler's works, see Appendix A). The detailed discussion of Ziegler's works focuses particularly on her treatment of women's issues and her defenses of women's rights. This biography illuminates our understanding both of Ziegler and of women in German society by detailing the life and works of yet another "learned heroine" of the early eighteenth century.

Women and Men in Eighteenth-Century Germany Society

In contrast to learned women such as van Schurman, Merian, Kirch, and Ziegler, the public life of most women in early eighteenth-century Germany was one of silence. Society allowed women little opportunity for public expression, with public life being the domain of men, domestic life the domain of women, and little communication between the two. The association of women with silence took as its basis the writings of Martin Luther, who did not allow women to speak in the church.[2] But it went further and denied women any public voice, either in speech or in writing.

Eighteenth-century German society was indeed defined by clear-cut gender norms. Men were viewed as being by nature active, rational, powerful, the bread winner, the public figure; women, on the other hand, were perceived as being by nature passive, emotional, weak, and dependent.[3] A man's social position was associated with his productive role in the community, his ability to provide materially for his wife and family. A woman's social position, on the other hand, was determined by her marital status and her domestic roles. As the eighteenth century progressed, more authors spoke in terms of a female "profession" in the home as wife, mother, and housekeeper, thus reinforcing the exclusion of women from public and professional roles outside the home.[4]

While Enlightenment thinkers in early eighteenth-century Germany promoted women's equality with men, such equality lacked practical application. The Enlightenment revolutionized western intellectual life by establishing the (male) individual as the source and purpose of knowledge. Women, however, became the "other" to this male "self." Enlightenment thinkers exalted women above the cultural and political world of men, relegating them to the "higher" sphere of morality and intuition. All women were grouped together under the idea of "woman," the opposite

---

2   See "Ein Brief D. Mart. Luthers Von den Schleichern und Winkelpredigern, 1532," in *D. Martin Luthers Wercke*, Vol. 30, 510–27 (Weimar, 1910), 524. English translation, "Infiltrating and Clandestine Preachers, 1532," in *Luther's Works*, American Edition, vol. 40, trans. and ed. Conrad Bergendoff, 379–94 (Philadelphia, 1958), 390–91.

3   Helen Watanabe-O'Kelly, "What Difference Does Feminism Make to the Study of German Literature?" in *Gendering German Studies: New Perspectives on German Literature and Culture*, ed. Margaret Littler, 2–11 (Oxford, 1997), 3.

4   Peter Petschauer, "Eighteenth-Century German Opinions about Education for Women," *Central European History* 19 (1986): 268–69.

of man. Men of the Enlightenment insisted that treating women with courtesy, decency, and respect was a hallmark of a civilized society. But rather than facilitating equal opportunity, insistence on women's special kind of excellence reinforced their limited social roles.[5]

The field of learning served to enforce the gendered separation of society by excluding women from academic institutions and insisting upon a different type of learning for women. Initially the Enlightenment contributed favorably to women's learning, as women benefited from the belief that their intellectual faculties equaled those of men and from a general focus on improved education. More women were taught to read and write, as literacy rates increased dramatically in the seventeenth and eighteenth centuries. Enlightenment thinkers believed that education was the key to the creation of a new social (male) being, devoid of old prejudices and saturated in new reason. Women were seen as having an important role as the educators of these new men during the impressionable years in which their minds would be shaped.[6] Women were, therefore, to have some level of education in order to prepare them to be better mothers and educators for their children, as well as to be more intellectually stimulating partners for their husbands.[7]

But while Enlightenment ideals served to improve education for women, they also enforced a double standard for men's and women's learning. When applied to a man, the adjective "gelehrt" (learned) indicated participation in a scholarly occupation, professional or academic, for which the subject possessed an academic degree. But the term "gelehrt" was used much more loosely for women, being applied to any woman who possessed an unusually high level of education. A "gelehrt" woman was certainly not expected to possess an academic degree or to participate in the same fields or levels of scholarship as a "gelehrt" man:

> Women and girls should not really be learned; they should only taste the fruits of the useful and beautiful subjects and not be at all concerned with the "strict," the "higher" sciences. The female "learning" … therefore relates to only a portion of knowledge and is also there differentiated from the nature and intensity of men's learning.[8]

---

5   Elizabeth Fox-Genovese, "Women and the Enlightenment," in *Becoming Visible: Women in European History*, 2nd ed., ed. Renate Bridenthal, Claudia Koonz, and Susan Stuard (Boston, 1987), 251–52, 263–65.

6   Martine Sonnet, "A Daughter to Educate," in *A History of Women in the West, III. Renaissance and Enlightenment Paradoxes*, trans. Arthur Goldhammer, ed. Natalie Zemon Davis and Arlette Farge (Cambridge, MA, 1993), 107–08.

7   Susanne Kord, "Erudite Woman/Gelehrte," in *The Feminist Encyclopedia of German Literature*, ed. Friederike Eigler and Susanne Kord (London, 1997), 125.

8   "Mit derartigen Methoden führen vor allem die frühen Wochenschriften einen kleinen Feldzug für die weibliche Bildung. Dabei wird immer wieder betont: Frauen und Mädchen sollen nicht eigentliche Gelehrte werden; sie sollen nur die Früchte der nützlichen und der schönen Wissenschaften genießen und mit den 'strengen,' den 'höheren' Wissenschaften überhaupt nicht befaßt werden. Die weibliche 'Gelehrsamkeit' … bezieht sich also nur auf einen Teil der Wissenschaften und ist auch dort nach Art und Intensität von der Gelehrsamkeit der Männer unterschieden." Wolfgang Martens, *Die Botschaft der Tugend: Die Aufklärung im Spiegel der deutschen Moralischen Wochenschriften*, 2nd ed. (Stuttgart, 1971), 525–27.

All translations are my own unless otherwise noted.

Education for most women was not academic, but rather centered in the home and focused on practical affairs and domestic responsibilities, things that a girl could learn from her mother. Outside of reading and writing, what women were allowed to study was closely scrutinized, with subjects thought to be too abstract—such as classical languages, rhetoric, theology, and philosophy—being excluded.[9] A good example of stipulations placed on German women's learning is the *Frauenzimmerlexikon* of 1715 by Gottlieb Siegmund Corvinus ("Amaranthes").[10] In the foreword to this compendium of popularized and easily accessible information designed for women, Corvinus listed subjects on which women should not spend much time: "mathematics, philosophy, the sciences, government, criticism, philology, poetry, languages, higher theology, law, and medicine."[11] Unlike men, women were not expected to engage in serious study or to delve too deeply into any one subject area.

Lack of in-depth education for most women contributed to the silencing of their voices in the public sphere. Not only were they excluded from speaking through public office, the church, and the university, but they were also discouraged from formal literary pursuits. Although many eighteenth-century German women enjoyed a good literary education, writing was intended solely as a domestic pastime. Women were neither expected nor encouraged to publish their writings. They were, therefore, not taught the mastery of rhetoric and grammar or the rules of poetry that were generally passed on through the study of Latin. Furthermore, much of the German poetry published in the eighteenth century was philosophical and didactic, dependent to a large extent on a level of intellectual training that women did not possess.[12]

Women were further limited in what literary genres were deemed suitable for them, things such as letters, devotional literature, and domestic manuals. Female authors, should they publish their writings, were to limit themselves only to what was considered appropriate for female readers. In the field of poetry, women generally wrote only occasional pieces in honor of such family and social occasions as baptisms, birthdays, weddings, deaths, and exchanges of presents. Such poetry was designed for particular private occasions and not for publication.

Women who attempted to exceed these bounds by publishing their writings were subjected to severe criticism. As late as 1792, Marianne Ehrmann described thus the fate of female writers in Germany:

---

9   Sonnet, "A Daughter to Educate," 101–07.

10   Amaranthes [Gottlieb Siegmund Corvinus], *Nutzbares, galantes und curiöses Frauenzimmer-Lexicon* (Leipzig, 1715; rev. ed. 1739).

11   "Mit solchen Weibes-Personen aber, die sich in der Mathematic, Philosophie, scientifica, Staats-Kunst / Critic / Philologie, Poesie, Sprachen / der höheren Theologie, Jurisprudentz und Medicin allzusehr vertiefft haben, wird wohl niemanden viel gedienet seyn." Qtd. in Jean M. Woods, "Das 'Gelahrte Frauenzimmer' und die deutschen Frauenlexica 1631–1743," in *Res Publica Litteraria: Die Institutionen der Gelehrsamkeit in der frühen Neuzeit*, Vol. 2, ed. Sebastian Neumeister and Conrad Wiedemann (Wiesbaden, 1987), 582.

12   See Heide Wunder, *He Is the Sun, She Is the Moon: Women in Early Modern Germany*, trans. Thomas Dunlap (Cambridge, MA, 1998), 110–11; and Ruth-Ellen Boetcher Joeres, "The German Enlightenment (1720–1790)," in *The Cambridge History of German Literature*, ed. Helen Watanabe-O'Kelly, 147–210 (Cambridge, 1997), 194.

I for my part do not advise any woman, unless fate has selected her for it through a combination of many circumstances, to venture into *this* career. First, it would lead our sex as a whole too far from our destiny, and second, it is connected with so many difficulties, which barely *one* woman in a hundred is able to surmount! Considering the difficulty of attaining artistic prowess and the loss of one's peace of mind, this is really the saddest female occupation on earth. To produce art, to be able to write *well* and *usefully*, is such an infinitely demanding task, and the many public attacks, the bitter criticism, the prejudice directed at woman's writings, the jealousy which tries to besmirch them, the personal attacks against woman writers, usually denying them all domestic virtues—taken together, these far outweigh the little bit of glory and satisfied vanity.[13]

Criticism of women writers often came in the form of a personal attack having nothing to do with the quality or content of what was written. On the whole there was nothing subversive about the work of female writers in eighteenth-century Germany. Although many deplored the injustice of women's condition, they generally did not question societal norms. A woman author's liberating act, and the act that drew criticism, was merely to write, regardless of what she wrote.[14]

In light of such gender norms, the call for women to have a greater public voice often took the form of calls for better education and for the opportunity to publish their writings unhindered. One of the most voluble spokespersons for women's rights to a voice was Leipzig poet Mariane von Ziegler. From 1725 to 1740, Ziegler vigorously, and publicly, defended not only women's rights in general, but in particular their rights to improved education and to literary enterprise. The freedom that Ziegler sought was truly the freedom of a voice, the freedom to express herself in published writing. She repeatedly challenged male hegemony in the field of literature, asserting women's equal intellectual ability and right and calling for women's equal opportunity.

Ziegler thus did not accept the common state of affairs in which the husband was the public voice, while the wife was to be silent. Although she did not challenge the traditional Lutheran domestic role of women, she believed (like Luther himself, but unlike the majority of her male contemporaries) that this social structure did not rest on a difference in ability or intelligence between the sexes. Ziegler repeatedly argued that women possessed the same intellect that men did, but were not privileged with the same level of education. In one of her best-known poems, "Das männliche Geschlechte, im Namen einiger Frauenzimmer besungen," Ziegler mocked men who were haughty about their own abilities and stated that all humans were by nature the same:

Die Männer müssen doch gestehen,	Men must truly confess,
Daß sie wie wir, auch Menschen sind.	That they as we are also humans.
Daß sie auch auf zwey Beinen gehen;	That they also walk on two legs;
Und daß sich manche Schwachheit findt.	And that some weakness is found in them.

---

13   Qtd. (in English translation) in Jeannine Blackwell and Susanne Zantop, *Bitter Healing: German Women Writers 1700–1830: An Anthology* (Lincoln, NE, 1990), 9.

14   Claude Dulong, "Conversation to Creation," in *A History of Women in the West, III. Renaissance and Enlightenment Paradoxes*, trans. Arthur Goldhammer, ed. Natalie Zemon Davis and Arlette Farge (Cambridge, MA, 1993), 411–14.

Sie trinken, schlafen, essen, wachen.	They drink, sleep, eat, wake.
Nur dieses ist der Unterscheid,	Only this is the difference,
Sie bleiben Herr in allen Sachen,	They remain lord in all things,
Und was wir thun, heißt Schuldigkeit.	And what we do is called duty.[15]

Ziegler further argued in her *Moralische und vermischte Send-Schreiben* that the senses and reason were also equally present in both sexes: "We [women] likewise bring five senses into the world as others [men] do; understanding and reason are distributed by nature among the sexes, and memory is also granted by her as part of our dowry."[16]

A special attention to the five senses is characteristic of Ziegler's poetry. By focusing on the senses, and particularly on those having to do with verbal communication, she emphasized what for her represented the equality of the sexes: a voice. The state of affairs wherein men were verbal and women silent was not acceptable for Ziegler. The voice represented for her the right of self-expression, to which all persons, male or female, should have equal access. The story of Ziegler's life is the story of the repeated call that women's voices be heard.

Christiane Mariane von Ziegler, *née* Romanus, came from a wealthy and prominent family of Leipzig lawyers (see Table 1.1 for a chronological overview of Ziegler's life). Her ancestor, Franz Romanus, had been ennobled in 1616 as "von Muckershausen" after purchasing the "Lehngut Muckershausen."[17] Mariane's father, Franz Konrad Romanus, was born in Leipzig on 7 March 1671. His father, Kaspar Theophilus Romanus, was a doctor of law and an assessor on the law faculty of the University of Leipzig; his mother died a few days after his birth. Franz Konrad followed in the family tradition by studying law at the University of Leipzig. He also studied in Dresden at the school of Count Wolf von Beichling, who in 1700 became chief counselor to the head of the Elector of Saxony's Privy Council. Upon his appointment, Beichling sought a man for the Leipzig town council who would unswervingly support the party of the Elector. He found such a man in his former student, Franz Konrad Romanus.[18]

On 29 August 1701, at only 30 years of age, Romanus was installed as one of Leipzig's mayors in place of the recently deceased Adrian Steger. Romanus quickly became a man of great influence, a man who was hated and feared by some while admired and praised by others. His position was always clear: he would do whatever

---

15 Christiane Mariane von Ziegler, *Vermischete Schriften in gebundener und ungebundener Rede* (Göttingen, 1739), 70.

16 "Wir bringen ja eben sowohl fünff Sinnen mit auf die Welt, wie jenes [Geschlecht], Verstand und Vernunfft werden unter beyderley Geschlechten von der Natur ausgetheilet, und das Gedächtnis wird uns zur Mitgifft von Ihr mit angerechnet." Ziegler, *Moralische und vermischte Send-Schreiben*, 8.

17 Katherine R. Goodman, *Amazons and Apprentices: Women and the German Parnassus in the Early Enlightenment* (Columbia, SC, 1999), 103.

18 Gustav Wustmann, "Der Bürgermeister Romanus," in *Quellen zur Geschichte Leipzigs: Veröffentlichungen aus dem Archiv und der Bibliothek der Stadt Leipzig*, Vol. 2, ed. Gustav Wustmann, 263–352 (Leipzig, 1895), 264–67.

Table 1.1   Mariane von Ziegler: a chronology

28 June 1695	Born, Leipzig
29 August 1701	Father, Franz Konrad Romanus, installed as Leipzig mayor
1701–04	Romanus house built in Leipzig
16 January 1705	Franz Konrad Romanus arrested and imprisoned for life without trial
Summer 1711	Marries Heinrich Levin von Könitz
1712	First daughter born
c. 1712	Heinrich Levin von Könitz dies
22 January 1715	Marries Georg Friedrich von Ziegler from Eckartsleben
12 February 1716	Second daughter born
c. 1716–22	Follows husband on military campaigns during Saxony's war with Sweden; husband and daughters die
13 July 1720	Visits father in Königstein (only recorded visit)
1722	Returns to Leipzig residence
3 February 1724	Johann Christoph Gottsched arrives in Leipzig
14 April 1725	Birth of J. S. Bach's son, Christian Gottlieb, for whom Maria Elisabeth Taubert, mutual friend of the Bach and Romanus families, stands as godmother
22 April–27 May 1725	First performances of Bach's nine sacred cantatas to Ziegler texts
1725–26	Publication of Gottsched's *Die vernünftigen Tadlerinnen*, to which Ziegler contributes under the names "de Rose," "Silere," and "Clarimene von Lindenheim"
April 1726	Ziegler's aunt stands as godmother for Bach's daughter Elisabeth Juliana Friederica (b. 5 April 1726 in Leipzig)
1728	Publishes *Versuch in gebundener Schreib-Art*, containing revised versions of cantata texts set by Bach
1728	Publication of G. P. Telemann's *Der getreue Music-Meister*, containing a secular cantata to a Ziegler text, *Ich kann lachen, weinen, scherzen*
1729	Publishes *Versuch in gebundener Schreib-Art, anderer und letzter Theil*
August 1730	Elected first female member of Deutschen Gesellschaft in Leipzig
15 November 1730	Gives inaugural speech to Deutschen Gesellschaft
1731	Publishes *Moralische und vermischte Send-Schreiben, An einige Ihrer vertrauten und guten Freunde gestellt*

continued

Table 1.1   *continued*

12 May 1732	Wins Deutschen Gesellschaft prize for poetry for her "Der Sächsischen Unterthanen getreue Wünsche und frohe Hoffnung bey dem glücklichen Antritt des grossen Stuffen-Jahres Gr. Königl. Majest. in Pohlen und Churfürstl Durchl. zu Sachsen"
Summer 1732	Laura Bassi earns Ph.D. in physics from University of Bologna; Ziegler publishes poem in her honor
1733	Named on subscriber list for first edition of Telemann's *Tafelmusik*
17 October 1733	Crowned imperial poet laureate by philosophical faculty of the University of Wittenberg
29 October 1733	Coronation ceremony in Romanus house
1734	Publication of *Sammlung der Schriften und Gedichte welche auf die Poetische Krönung Der Hochwohlgebohrnen Frauen, Frauen Christianen Marianen von Ziegler gebohrnen Romanus, verfertiget worden*, edited by Johann Friedrich Lamprecht
7 October 1734	Wins Deutschen Gesellschaft prize for poetry for her "Die Zufriedenheit eines Landes, das nach einem schweren Kriege durch den Frieden wieder erfreuet wird"
1735	Publishes translation of *Der Mad. Scudery Scharfsinnige Unterredungen, von Dingen, Die zu einer wohlanständigen Aufführung gehöhren*
1735	Romanus house sold to city councilor Friedrich Benedict Ötel, who permits Ziegler and her mother to continue residence
1736	Publication of Sperontes, *Die Singende Muse an der Pleisse*, containing poem satirizing women who aspire to learning, "Ihr Schönen, höret an"
1736	Publication of Luise Gottsched's drama *Die Pietisterey im Fischbein-Rocke; Oder die Doctormäßige Frau*, satirizing women who aspire to learning (published anonymously)
1737–43	Publication of Johann Friedrich Gräfe, *Sammlung verschiedener und auserlesener Oden* (four volumes); first volume dedicated to Ziegler; remaining three contain musical settings of nine Ziegler poems by Gräfe, Hurlebusch, de Giovannini, and C. P. E. Bach
1738	Sidonia Hedwig Zäunemann crowned poet laureate by University of Göttingen
11 June 1738	Gottsched submits resignation as Senior of Deutschen Gesellschaft
20 June 1738	Deutschen Gesellschaft accepts Gottsched's resignation; Ziegler among signatores
1739	Publishes *Vermischete Schriften, in gebundener und ungebundener Rede*

Table 1.1   *concluded*

30 March 1739	Mother, Christiane Marie Romanus, dies at age 63
1 December 1739	Applies for Leipzig citizenship; resides at Haus zur Weißen Taube, a short distance from the Romanus house
14 September 1741	Marries Wolf Balthasar Adolph von Steinwehr (1704–71), member of Deutschen Gesllschaft and professor of history and natural law in Frankfurt an der Oder; moves from Leipzig to Frankfurt an der Oder
20 December 1743	Steinwehr establishes a Deutsche Gesellschaft in Frankfurt an der Oder
1744	Publishes translation of *Des Abtes Trublet Gedanken über verschiedene Sachen, welche zur Gelehrsamkeit und Sittenlehre gehören*
14 May 1746	Father, Franz Konrad Romanus, dies in the prison Königstein at age 75
1 May 1760	Dies in Frankfurt an der Oder at age 64

was in the best interest of the Elector and would make money for himself.[19] Romanus's pretensions were embodied in his grand new house in the Baroque style, built between 1701 and 1704 by Leipzig town architect Johann Gregor Fuchs (shown in Figure 1.2). Romanus not only brought on criticism through the extravagance of the house itself, but he also angered local guildsmen by employing outside artisans to do the work.[20]

Romanus's ambitions, however, proved to be short lived. On 16 January 1705, armed police officers entered the Romanus house and placed Franz Konrad under arrest. He was imprisoned in the Pleissenburg and later moved to the Sonnenstein and finally the Königstein. Although a commission to investigate Romanus's misdeeds continued for several years, his case was never brought to trial and the precise charges against him are yet unknown.[21] It does appear that Romanus diverted to himself funds from the Leipzig citizens that were intended for the Elector, but Romanus's downfall likely resulted more from his greed for greater power. The Elector, possibly in recognition of Romanus's ambitions and unscrupulous nature, did nothing to intervene on the mayor's behalf. The commission investigating Romanus after his imprisonment concluded only that it was not known whether all of his criminal activities had yet been discovered and that further examination of the case was required.[22] If such further inquiry did take place, its results were not recorded. Romanus remained imprisoned in the Königstein without trial for forty-one years until his death on 14 May 1746.

---

19   Wustmann, "Der Bürgermeister Romanus," 268.

20   Goodman, *Amazons and Apprentices*, 104.

21   The most thorough examination of Romanus's case appears in Wustmann, "Der Bürgermeister Romanus." Although the charges against Romanus were still not clear, Wustmann concluded that it was fortunate for the city of Leipzig that Romanus never regained his freedom (351).

22   Wustmann, "Der Bürgermeister Romanus," 306.

Figure 1.2   Copperplate engraving of Romanushaus, Leipzig. Amsterdam: Petrus Schenk, 1704. Stadtgeschichtliches Museum Leipzig (Mü.III/44 b).

Despite Franz Konrad's downfall, his family continued to enjoy respect and prestige in Leipzig, as well as the favor of Count Johann Friedrich von Flemming, the Saxon court's powerful governor in the city. Romanus himself also received ongoing support from some Leipzig citizens who did not believe in his guilt. As late as 1734, Jacob Friedrich Lamprecht lauded Romanus's "vigorous zeal for the establishment of his home city, his insight into the art of government, his immense understanding of law, and his mayorship characterized by intelligence." He continued by praising Romanus's nobility, his zeal, his honor, and his example to and tender love for his daughter.[23]

After Franz Konrad's imprisonment, the Romanus family continued to live in their newly-built house, which his wife, Christiane Marie Romanus, paid off with 28,000 Thaler from her dowry. There is no evidence that the family's social status declined as a result of Franz Konrad's misdeeds, and Ziegler never seems to have felt a need to hide her identity as a Romanus (most of her publications include her maiden name). Ziegler also seems not to have harbored any bitterness against the Elector, who had allowed her father to fall. She wrote an ode in honor of his birthday in 1732 and another mourning his death in 1733.[24]

If Ziegler did experience any distress over the imprisonment of her father, it was nothing compared to what she would suffer in the years 1711 to 1722. During this period, she was married and widowed twice and bore two daughters, both of whom also died. Ziegler was first married in the summer of 1711, at the age of 16, to Heinrich Levin von Könitz. In 1712, they had a daughter, whose name and birth date are unknown. Von Könitz died shortly thereafter, and Mariane married Georg Friedrich von Ziegler from Eckartsleben on 22 January 1715. She bore another daughter on 12 February 1716. Although little is known about this period of Ziegler's life, it appears that she traveled with her husband, a military captain, on Saxony's campaigns against Sweden in the Great Northern War (1700–21). At some point in the late 1710s, her husband and two daughters died. Ziegler returned by 1722 to her

---

23 "Wofern es eine Ehre giebt, von edlen, klugen, und um das gemeine Beste verdienten Voreltern abzustammen, so hat die Frau von Ziegler die gerechteste Ursache dieselbe zu fordern. Ihr berühmter Vater, der gepriesene Romanus, ertheilet Ihr schon allein dieses Recht. Sein munterer Eifer für das Aufnehmen seiner Vaterstadt, seine Einsicht in die Staatskunst, seine ungemeine Rechtsgelehrsamkeit, seine mit Klugheit bekleidete Bürgermeisterstelle, sind solche wahre Vorzüge, welche zugleich seine unvergleichliche Tochter erheben." Jacob Friedrich Lamprecht, "Vorrede" to *Sammlung der Schriften und Gedichte welche auf die Poetische Krönung Der Hochwohlgebohrnen Frauen, Frauen Christianen Marianen von Ziegler gebohren Romanus, verfertiget worden,* ed. Jacob Friedrich Lamprecht (Leipzig, 1734), ii.

24 "Der Sächsischen Unterthanen getreue Wünsche und frohe Hoffnung bey dem glücklichen Antritt des grossen Stuffen-Jahres Gr. Königl. Majest. in Pohlen und Churfürstl. Durchl. zu Sachsen," in *Zwo Schriften, welche In der Deutschen Gesellschaft zu Leipzig, auf das Jahr 1732. die Preise der Poesie und Beredsamkeit erhalten haben* (Leipzig, 1732), rev. ed. in Ziegler, *Vermischete Schriften,* 227–35; and "Gedicht auf das Absterben Königs Friedrich August von Polen und Kurfürsten von Sachsen," *Neue Zeitungen von gelehrten Sachen* 19 (1733): 261–64, rev. ed. in *Vermischete Schriften,* 235–38.

mother's home in Leipzig, where she quickly assumed the role of an aristocratic widow free from economic concerns.

Contemporary Descriptions of Ziegler

Ziegler was buoyed after the deaths of her husband and daughters by both her poetic undertakings and her indomitable spirit, the latter of which also contributed greatly to her literary success. All contemporary descriptions of Ziegler's personality relate that she was energetic and extroverted, possessing a lively wit. One account by Ziegler herself is particularly significant, as it demonstrates Ziegler negotiating her position as a woman in a male-dominated world. In response to a male acquaintance's request for a portrait, a medium that emphasizes the physical, Ziegler sent him a "picture in rhymes" instead, thus emphasizing the intellectual and artistic:[25]

Mein Freund, o! thu dir nicht Gewalt;	My friend, oh, I do not take you by force;
Kennst du mich gleich nicht von Gestalt,	You know nothing of my form,
Deswegen fasse keine Grillen;	Therefore I do not grasp at a whim;
Den Kummer will ich dir bald stillen.	I will quickly halt your grief.
Ich setze schon die Feder an.	I already apply the quill.
Mit dieser wird dir kund gethan:	With this I will have given you notice:
Du sollst mein Bild in Reimen lesen,	You shall read my picture in rhymes,
Mein Ansehn und mein ganzes Wesen.	My appearance and my whole disposition.
Ich bin nicht klein, ich bin nicht groß,	I am not small, I am not large,
Ich geh bedeckt und niemals bloß.	I go covered and never bare.
Mit aufgeräumten frohen Minen	With a cheerfully happy mien
Such ich der ganzen Welt zu dienen.	I seek to serve the whole world.
Ich bin nicht starck; ich bin nicht schwach;	I am not strong; I am not weak;
Mein Fuß ist schnell, kein Ungemach	My foot is quick, no hardship
Setzt meine Seel aus ihren Schranken;	Places my soul out of its boundaries;
Mein fester Sinn pflegt nicht zu wanken.	My fixed mind takes care not to waver.
Ich liebe Kunst und Wissenschaft,	I love art and learning,
Und lache wenn man sich vergafft.	And laugh when one makes a joke.

The most detailed description of Ziegler comes from Christian Gabriel Fischer, who spent an evening at Ziegler's home when he visited Leipzig in 1731. Fischer's description also addresses gender issues, particularly in relation to Ziegler's widowhood and marriageability. But it goes further and provides a fascinating description of Ziegler's appearance, personality, and activities:

> She is yet a young widow, but may, due to many circumstances, have difficulty remarrying. Among other things, her conduct is almost more than feminine and her spirit much too lively and clever than that she should submit herself to a common male intellect. Of shape is she not unpleasant, but somewhat thick-boned, mature, plain of face, smooth of forehead, lovely eyes, healthy and somewhat brunette in color, her age about thirty-six

---

25 Ziegler, *Vermischete Schriften*, 293–94. This interpretation of the poem is given by Sunka Simon in "'Als sie ihr Bildness schildern sollte': Die sprachliche Struktur der Innen- und Aussenporträts in der Lyrik Christiana Mariana von Zieglers," *Daphnis* 19 (1990): 247–65.

years, free in speech, but clever and well-mannered, in social intercourse more friendly, amusing, and humorous than serious. In short, there is nothing constrained in her manner. She takes part in everything, she plays quite a lot of musical instruments and sings along, she shoots with rifles, pistols, and crossbow en compagnie. She speaks French, and is particularly strong in the German style and in poetry, in which Hr. Mag. Corvinus instructed her in her youth. But presently she needs no instructor, as her writings and those samples whereof I am witness demonstrate.[26]

Jacob Friedrich Lamprecht, writing in 1734, focused more on Ziegler's virtue, generosity, and intelligence, as well as her endurance through suffering:

Never has a lady been truly more qualified to gain approval and respect through her generosity and intelligence than Frau von Ziegler. Her exceptional merits give her a lofty status above countless of her gender: she strives to be great through virtue as well as affability. Her acquired skill serves only to her betterment, and if she reminds herself of the same it so happens only in order not to deprive herself of that happily fortunate contentment which a mature knowledge is necessarily in the habit of following. No-one could appear whom she had offended through arrogance, frivolity, scorn, and selfishness: countless on the other hand would be found whom she has given occasion to admire her through generous gifts. All of these virtues still lift up a steadfast disposition, which does not exist through an illusion; but which was toughened through so much endured misfortune and won the victory over all adverse circumstances.[27]

---

26 "Noch ist es eine junge Wittibe, die aber wegen vieler Umbstände schwerlich heyraten dörffte. Unter andern ist ihre Conduite fast überweiblich und ihr Geist viel zu munter und aufgeweckt, als daß sie sich gemeinem männlichen Verstande unterwerfen sollte. Von Gestalt ist sie nicht heßlich, aber etwas starck von Knochen, gesezt, plat von Gesicht, glatt von Stirn, schönen Augen, gesund und etwas brounett von Farbe, ihres Alters etwa 36 Jahre, von Reden frey, aber gescheid und artig, im Umbgang mehr freundlich, lustig und schertzhafft als gravitätisch. Kurtz, es ist an ihr nichts gezwungenes. Sie macht alles mit, sie spielet auff allerhand musikalischen Instrumenten und singt dabey, sie schießet mit Büchsen, Pistolen und Armbrüsten, *en compagnie*. Sie sprichte frantzösisch, absonderlich ist sie starck in dem deutschen Stylo und in der Poesie, wozu sie Hr. Mag. Corvinus in der Jügend angeführet. Jetzt aber braucht sie keine Anführer, wie aus ihren Schrifften und denen Proben, wovon ich Zeuge bin, erhellet." Qtd. in Albert Predeek, "Ein vergessener Freund Gottscheds [Christian Gabriel Fischer]," in *Beiträge zur Deutschen Bildungsgeschichte: Festschrift zur Zweihundertjahrfeier der Deutschen Gesellschaft in Leipzig 1727–1927* (Leipzig, 1927), 121.

27 "Niemals ist wohl eine Dame fähiger gewesen, durch Großmuth und Klugheit sich Beyfall und Ehrfurcht zu erwerben, als die Frau von Ziegler. Ihre ausnehmende Vorzüge geben Ihr einen erhabenen Rang über unzählige von Ihrem Geschlechte: gleichwohl bestrebet Sie sich bloß durch Tugend und Leutseligkeit groß zu seyn. Ihre erworbene Geschicklichkeit dienet allein zu Ihrer Verbesserung, und wenn Sie sich ja derselben erinnert, so geschiehet es nur, um sich nicht derjenigen glückseligen Zufriedenheit zu berauben, welche einem reifen Erkenntniße unaufhörlich zu folgen pfleget. Niemand wird auftreten können, welchen Sie durch Hochmuth, Leichtsinnigkeit, Verachtung, und Eigennutz beleidiget hätte: Unzehlige hingegen werden zu finden seyn, denen Sie durch großmüthiges Bezeigen Gelegenheit genug Sie zu bewundern gegeben hat. Alle diese Tugenden erhebet noch ein standhaftes Gemüthe, welches nicht etwa in einer Einbildung bestehet; sondern das durch so viel erduldetes Unglück abgehärtet ist, und über alle wiedrige Zufälle den Sieg erhalten hat." Lamprecht, "Vorrede" to *Sammlung ... auf die Poetische Krönung Der ... Ziegler*, iv–v.

Taken together, the descriptions by Ziegler, Fischer, and Lamprecht present a picture of Ziegler as not only lively and fun-loving, but also steadfast and virtuous. Her strong personality and resiliency in the face of attack certainly contributed to her positive public role as defender of women's rights to a public voice.

Early Poetry, c. 1722–26

Having returned to Leipzig in 1722 after the deaths of her husband and daughters, Ziegler turned to poetry for consolation. Her early poetic endeavors came about in relation to her interactions with three prominent Leipzig men: Gottlieb Siegmund Corvinus ("Amaranthes"), Johann Sebastian Bach, and Johann Christoph Gottsched. Her interactions with Corvinus and Gottsched not only encouraged her immersion in the study and writing of poetry, but also contributed to the development of her ideas about women's roles in intellectual and literary enterprise which would define her later public discourse.

In the description of Ziegler cited above, Christian Gabriel Fischer stated that she was "particularly strong in the German style and in poetry, in which Hr. Mag. Corvinus instructed her in her youth." Gottlieb Siegmund Corvinus (1677–1746) was a Leipzig lawyer who published poetry under the name "Amaranthes." While any specific details of the relationship between Corvinus and Ziegler are unknown and particular poems that Ziegler may have written under Corvinus's tutelage unidentifiable, Corvinus stated in 1739 that Zeigler had begun to write poetry soon after her marriage to Georg Friedrich von Ziegler.[28] It is, therefore, likely that she studied with him at this time, perhaps after her return to her mother's home in 1722 and before Johann Christoph Gottsched's arrival in Leipzig in 1725.

In addition to providing her with instruction in poetry, Corvinus influenced and encouraged Ziegler as a vocal defender of women's ability and right to learn. Corvinus is best known for his *Nutzbares, galantes und curiöses Frauenzimmer-Lexicon* of 1715, in which he sought to provide women with a compendium of practical knowledge including entries on French court gallantry, orthodox religion, practical household tips, and famous women from mythology and history. Furthermore, Corvinus argued vehemently for women's educability and aimed to remove any obstacles for women who wanted to advance their learning. The *Frauenzimmer-Lexicon* was limited in the type and extent of knowledge for women, as Corvinus did not expect them to pursue serious or in-depth study particularly in fields dominated by men. However, the volume was significant in promoting the idea that women be educated at all. In both providing Ziegler with examples of learned women from history and promoting women's rights to education, as well as by providing her with poetic instruction, Corvinus surely stimulated Ziegler's thoughts about women's rights to education and literary enterprise.

Ziegler's first public poetic undertaking, although it was anonymous at the time, was also a unique one in her literary career. In 1725, Ziegler provided town cantor

---

28   Amaranthes, *Frauenzimmer-Lexicon* (1739), 1749–50. For more on Corvinus's *Frauenzimmer-Lexicon*, see Goodman, *Amazons and Apprentices*, 11–39.

Johann Sebastian Bach (1685–1750) with texts for nine sacred cantatas which he set to music for performance in Leipzig's two main churches, the Thomaskirche and Nicolaikirche. These cantatas were first performed on the Sundays and feast days of the post-Easter season, 22 April to 27 May 1725.

While the precise details of the collaboration between Ziegler and Bach are not documented, Hans-Joachim Schulze has speculated that the two were introduced by a mutual friend, Maria Elisabeth Taubert. The first of the nine cantatas was performed just a few days after the birth of Bach's son Christian Gottlieb (14 April 1725), for whom Taubert served as godmother.[29] Friendly relations evidently continued between Bach and the Romanus family, as Ziegler's aunt—wife of town councilor Carl Friedrich Romanus—served as godmother for Bach's daughter Elisabeth Juliana Friederica in 1726.[30] Furthermore, in her 1729 poem "Zu einer Garten-Musik" Ziegler mentions Bach as a possible composer upon hearing a beautiful overture (the other composers Ziegler mentions are Georg Philipp Telemann and Georg Friedrich Handel).[31]

That the collaboration between Ziegler and Bach was significant for poet and composer alike will be evident throughout the remaining chapters of this volume. It provided Ziegler with her first public literary enterprise and the opportunity, as a woman, to "speak" in the church through her cantata texts. Ziegler is the only woman known to have provided poetic texts for the Lutheran liturgy in eighteenth-century Germany. For Bach, these cantatas proved to be particularly rich musical endeavors, ones in which he experimented with a number of compositional techniques. But while both composer and poet were prominent in Leipzig for years to come, Bach evidently never set another of Ziegler's texts after May 1725 and there is no evidence of any ongoing relationship between the two.

While in music history Ziegler is linked with Bach, in literary history her name generally appears in conjunction with Johann Christoph Gottsched (1700–66), one of the leading literary figures of early eighteenth-century Germany. Ziegler and Gottsched collaborated and supported each other's efforts for more than a decade, as both sought to promote women's roles in German literature with the ultimate goal of advancing German language and culture.

Ziegler likely became acquainted with Gottsched shortly after his arrival in Leipzig on 3 February 1724. Gottsched had just fled his native Königsberg because of the impending threat of conscription into the Prussian army, and he quickly became involved with Leipzig's literary scene. Gottsched soon began a literary enterprise in which Ziegler would prove to be an important collaborator, the moral weekly *Die vernünftigen Tadlerinnen*, which appeared each week throughout the years 1725 and 1726. This weekly was in the tradition of the English *The Tatler* (1709–11) and *The Spectator* (1711–12, 1714), which had been imitated in German-speaking lands

---

29   Hans-Joachim Schulze, "Neuerkenntnisse zu einigen Kantatentexten Bachs auf Grund neuer biographischer Daten," in *Bach-Interpretationen*, ed. Martin Geck, 22–28 (Göttingen, 1969), 23–24.

30   Arnold Schering, *Johann Sebastian Bach und das Musikleben Leipzigs im 18. Jahrhundert*, Vol. 3 of *Der Musikgeschichte Leipzigs* (Leipzig, 1941), 323.

31   Christiane Mariane von Ziegler, *Versuch in gebundener Schreib-Art, anderer und letzter Theil* (Leipzig, 1729), 297.

by the Swiss *Die Discourse der Mahler* (1721–23) and the Hamburg *Der Patriot* (1724–26). Such moral weeklies were an outgrowth of Enlightenment thought, which stressed a more active interest in the welfare of others and in the individual's capacity and duty to improve his surrounding world. The moral weekly as a genre became the most widely read literature in early eighteenth-century Germany.[32]

Gottsched's *Die vernünftigen Tadlerinnen* followed the moral weekly tradition in its overriding themes: the desirability of leading a satisfying, well-balanced life; the necessity of a practical philosophy; the encouragement of a secular literature, both critical and imaginative; and the role and education of women.[33] It also followed the moral weekly tradition in its writing style, which was popular, light, and easily accessible, addressed to a middle-class readership of men and women.[34] However, *Die vernünftigen Tadlerinnen* was unique both in addressing the role and education of women more extensively than its predecessors and in being published under the ruse of female editorship. The first issue stated that the tone of the weekly would be conditioned by the fact that it was written by women, and that its style would therefore not be studied but would rather flow from natural understanding. While *Die vernünftigen Tadlerinnen* did much to highlight and encourage women's education and literature, the four editors were in fact men writing under female pseudonyms: Phyllis = Johann Friedrich May (1697–1762), Iris = Johann Georg Hamann (1697–1733), Clio = Lucas Geiger (1683–1750), and Caliste = Johann Christoph Gottsched. While the first three men seem to have lost interest in the project fairly quickly, Gottsched continued the weekly for two years, maintaining all four pseudonyms as the others dropped out.[35]

In presenting the weekly from the perspective of female authorship, Gottsched aimed to demonstrate the cleverness of women, provide examples of how well women could write when adequately educated, and encourage female writers in their own efforts. Gottsched thus constructed "woman" as the representative of, and catalyst for, a new civil society based on Enlightenment thought. Through such an idea of "woman" Gottsched defended his beliefs that the enlightenment of each individual could eliminate evil and that German culture, language, and literature could be elevated, as France's had, through the inclusion of women in social discourse. Katherine R. Goodman has summarized Gottsched's aims in the weekly thus: "*Die vernünftigen Tadlerinnen* constructed ideal female voices to serve as enlightened examples of what actual women might become, with the ultimate goal of elevating German national culture and challenging the intellectual hegemony of the French and the English."[36]

---

32   Marvin Bragg, *From Gottsched to Goethe: Changes in the Social Function of the Poet and Poetry* (New York, 1984), 18–19.

33   P. M. Mitchell, *Johann Christoph Gottsched (1700–1766): Harbinger of German Classicism* (Columbia, SC, 1995), 11.

34   Eric A. Blackall, *The Emergence of German as a Literary Language: 1700–1775*, 2nd ed. (Ithaca, NY, 1978), 50.

35   Gottsched explained the extent of the others' involvement, as well as the fact that all the editors were men, in the final issue of the weekly, 27 December 1726. See Goodman, *Amazons and Apprentices*, 65–69.

36   Goodman, *Amazons and Apprentices*, 93.

In order for women to be involved in such a social discourse, Gottsched argued, they had to receive better education. While Gottsched, like Corvinus, was not arguing for a university education or anything other than a domestic role for women, he advocated a good elementary education for all girls and the possibility of somewhat more in-depth study for exceptional women. In addition, *Die vernünftigen Tadlerinnen* encouraged women's literary enterprise by providing positive examples of women's writing and encouraging women to write. The promotion of female authors supported Gottsched's goals of linguistic reform, as he argued for the cultivation of a "natural" style (embodied by women) as opposed to a "learned" style (embodied by men), set a practical example of fluid German style free from foreign words, and encouraged women to write in a good, accessible style.[37]

Despite its primarily male authorship, *Die vernünftigen Tadlerinnen* included many contributions from women. In its final issue, after identifying such contributors as Mariane von Bressler, Gottsched refered to "another noble lady [who] altered her hand and name a good ten times, even giving herself some masculine names, only in order not to be considered by me to be the same correspondent all the time."[38] Eugen Wolf identified this woman as Mariane von Ziegler, writing under the pseudonyms "de Rose," "Silere," and "Clarimene von Lindenheim."[39] Given Gottsched's description, it appears that Ziegler also contributed to the weekly under other names which have not yet been identified. While her writings in *Die vernünftigen Tadlerinnen* were anonymous, Ziegler's involvement with the weekly was known to some extent, as confirmed by the references to Ziegler's contributions to the weekly by Johann Friedrich Lamprecht in 1734 and by Gottlieb Siegmund Corvinus in 1739.[40]

In Ziegler's contributions to *Die vernünftigen Tadlerinnen* one finds a microcosm of her later writings, and particularly of her arguments for women's rights to education and to involvement in public discourse through literary enterprise. Ziegler stated here many of the main themes that she would later elaborate: the equality of men and women in creation, the need for better education for women, that women speak naturally more eloquently than men, and that women should be allowed to write poetry without being hindered by men.

Ziegler's first known poem in *Die vernünftigen Tadlerinnen* provides a good example of her themes in this period. The poem is entitled "Vertheidigung unsers

---

37 See Goodman, *Amazons and Apprentices*, 72–75.

38 "So viel ist gewiß, daß ein andres vornehme Frauenzimmer ihre Hand und Namen wohl zehnmal verändert, ja sich wohl einen männlichen Namen gegeben, um nur von mir nicht allezeit für dieselbe Correspondentinn gehalten zu werden." *Die vernünftigen Tadlerinnen, anderer Jahr-Theil 1726* (Leipzig, 1727; reprint Hildesheim, 1993), 415.

39 Eugen Wolff, *Gottscheds Stellung im Deutschen Bildungsleben*, vol. 2 (Kiel & Leipzig, 1897), 117–19. Ziegler published two poems under the pseudonym "de Rose" (Vol. 1, no. 52, 26 December 1725 and the appendix to Vol. 2, 18 February 1726) and one under "Clarimene von Lindenheim" (appendix to Vol. 2, 18 February 1726). In addition, the weekly makes another reference to "Clarimene von Lindenheim" (Vol. 2, no. 3, 18 January 1726) and one to "Silere" (Vol. 1, no. 34, 22 August 1725) and includes three lines from a Ziegler poem as the opening motto for one issue (Vol. 2, no. 49, 6 December 1726).

40 Lamprecht, "Vorrede" to *Sammlung ... auf die Poetische Krönung Der ... Ziegler*, vii; Amaranthes, *Frauenzimmer-Lexicon*, 1749–50.

Geschlechts wider die Mannspersonen" ("Defense of Our Sex against Men") and was written in response to a poetry contest announced by the weekly on 4 July 1725 on the subject of "Vertheidigung des weiblichen Geschlechts gegen die Beschuldigungen der Mannspersonen" ("a defense of the female sex against the accusations of men").[41] In her letter introducing the poem, Ziegler, writing under the name "de Rose," explained that she would not undertake a complete defense of the female sex against men but would rather address solely the point of women's ability to write poetry. She based her defense of women's poetry on the voice, asserting that women naturally spoke more eloquently than men:

Natur gilt mehr als Kunst! der feste Satz bestehet,	Nature gilds more than art! the firm principle states,
Kein Salomon ist so, wie Lilien angekleidt: …	No Solomon is clothed like the lilies: …
Uns Weiber mag man wohl dergleichen Lilien nennen,	One may well call us women these lilies,
Das männliche Geschlecht gleicht jenes Königs Pracht:	And compare the male sex to that king's splendor:
Indem sie nimmermehr der Einfalt Prunk erkennen,	While they never recognize the simple pomp,
Womit uns die Natur vor ihnen reich gemacht.	Whereby nature makes us rich over them.
Das Frauenzimmer weiß ohn allen Zwang zu denken,	A woman knows how to think without any constraint,
Dieß zeigt ihr Reden an, dieß zeigt die Dichterey.	Her speech indicates this, as does her poetry.

After further defending women's natural fluidity of speech, Ziegler went on to accuse men of purposely hindering women from writing poetry. She asserted that women have by nature an inclination toward poetry, and that such natural poetry is preferable to the bombastic, contrived poetry of men. Ziegler concluded by asserting that women's poetry exceeded that of men:

Wir rühmen uns allein natürlich schöner Sachen,	We pride ourselves in just naturally beautiful things,
Und folgen so im Vers, als Reden, dieser Spur.	And follow this path in verse as in speech.
Kein Rolandsschwerdt soll uns den Vorzug streitig machen:	No sword of Roland shall dispute our advantage,
Wo ihr nicht zeigt: die Kunst sey mehr, als die Natur.	Unless you show that art is more than nature.

In addition to providing examples of women's poetry, Ziegler's arguments in this and her other poems in *Die vernünftigen Tadlerinnen* buttress those of Gottsched. Ziegler and Gottsched clearly aided each other through their collaboration in the

---

41   Gottsched, ed., *Die vernünftigen Tadlerinnen*, Vol. 1, no. 52 (26 December 1725), 411–15.

weekly, with Ziegler supporting Gottsched's literary ideals and providing exemplary samples of women's writing and Gottsched encouraging Ziegler's literary efforts and providing a publication venue for them.

In the 27th issue of *Die vernünftigen Tadlerinnen*, Gottsched stated thus his goal of elevating German culture through women's writings:

> I burn with envy when I read the French poems of Madame [Antoinette] Deshoulières, and as a result consider that Germany does not yet have that which one can set up against the French in these passages. We do have here and there small samples which show sufficient understanding and liveliness … . But where do we have a new book, which was completed by a single woman poet? And as long as this does not take place, we German nymphs (what a shame this is!) ever still allow the French women to have the advantage.[42]

Through her talent and initiative, as well as Gottsched's support, Ziegler became one of the primary responders to this summons. From 1728 to 1739, she published three volumes of her own poetry and one of letters, thus directly answering Gottsched's call for complete books by a German female author.

Versuch in gebundener Schreib-Art (1728)

In her collaborations with Corvinus, Bach, and Gottsched in the mid-1720s, Ziegler had operated within realms deemed acceptable for a woman by presenting her poetry anonymously and in association with prominent men. However, Ziegler soon challenged male privilege in the public forum as she began to publish books of her poetry under her own name and unedited by a man. In her first volume, the *Versuch in gebundener Schreib-Art* of 1728, Ziegler entered the public discourse as a female poet who vigorously defended women's rights to education and public literary enterprise. Ziegler clearly recognized the challenge her volume posed to the male-dominated literary establishment, stating in her dedication that some people might think it unusual that one "who was only born to female occupations" should thus be entering the field of men's learning.[43]

The content and presentation of Ziegler's *Versuch in gebundener Schreib-Art* are particularly striking when compared with a volume published in Leipzig only 13

---

42 "Ich brenne vor Neid, wenn ich die französischen Gedichte der Madame Deshoulières lese, und dabey bedenke, daß Deutschland noch nichts aufzuweisen habe, was man den Franzosen in diesem Stücke entgegen setzen könnte. Wir haben zwar hie und da kleine Proben, die Verstand und Lebhaftigkeit genug zeigen … . Allein wo haben wir ein neues Buch aufzuweisen, welches von einer einzigen Poetinn verfertiget worden? Und so lange dieses nicht geschiehet, müssen wir deutschen Nymphen (welch eine Schande ist das!) den Französinnen noch immer den Vorzug lassen." Gottsched, *Die vernünftigen Tadlerinnen, erster Jahr-Theil 1725*, 211.

43 " … andern theils aber möchte IHNEN dieses vollendes als was seltsames und ungewöhnliches vorkommen / daß eine solche Person / welche nur zu weiblichen Geschäfften gebohren worden / und daher dem männlichen Geschlechte in ihren Wissenschafften / worinnen sie gleichsam das Bürger=Recht alleine erhalten / keinen Eintrag thun solte / …" Ziegler, Dedication to *Versuch in gebundener Schreib-Art* (Leipzig, 1728), iv–v.

years earlier by Sophie Regina Gräf, the *Liebes-Opffer, d. i. Poetische Applicationes derer Sonn- und Fest-täglichen Evangelien*.[44] Gräf's volume, although significant as a complete poetic collection published by a woman, conformed to the expectations for women in German society at the time. Not only was the work published anonymously, but the title page and foreword also both stated that it was published without the author's knowledge or consent. The poetry was collected and introduced by an anonymous man ("N. N."). It was entirely sacred in its nature, with the volume including primarily a series of devotional poems based on the Sundays and feast days of the church year. Unlike Ziegler's sacred cantatas, these poems were intended for personal devotion, not for public use. In a brief foreword, "N. N." made every effort to defend Gräf's piety and to emphasize the fact that she had no desire to publish the poetry or to practice poetry as an art, but that the poems grew simply out of her love for God.

In her *Versuch in gebundener Schreib-Art*, Ziegler deliberately went against the societal conventions to which Gräf conformed. Ziegler defended such a decision in the volume's foreword, which opened with the statement that as long as women have produced books almost no women's writing has appeared that has not been edited by a man. Ziegler, however, attested that she was publishing her volume without any advice or editing from men. She did so not because she believed her writings to be superior to those of women who had been edited by men, but because she wished to present natural rather than contrived poetry. As in her poem in *Die vernünftigen Tadlerinnen* (26 December 1725), Ziegler equated women with nature and men with artifice, stating again "Natur geht über Kunst" ("Nature is superior to art"). She further recalled her earlier poem by attesting to women's priority over men in speech and questioning why such skill did not carry over into women's writing:

> However, I have thought about this many times with amazement, how it yet must happen that in such a case a woman, both in the court and also in well-established cities, has the glory with applause by all that even the most learned of men has, often speaking better than they; yet in writing it is not so for them, but ten women's quills do not come up to the writing of one leading man in learning (I would not say in learned, but merely proper, things). The answer to this is evident already in my recitation itself, since when a woman studies, she could then easily surpass men also in writing, in that an unlearned men seems to write just as badly as the same woman, and then I suppose that the foundation of a good writing must without fail be skill in the art of speech.[45]

---

44   *Eines andächtigen Frauenzimmers S. R. G. Ihrem JESU im Glauben dargebrachte Liebes-Opffer, d. i. Poetische Applicationes derer Sonn- und Fest-täglichen Evangelien zu Ihrer eigenen Erbauung und Vergnügung Ihrer Seelen abgefasset, Und Ohne Dero Wissen zum Druck befördert von N. N.* (Leipzig, 1715).

45   "Indeß habe ich vielmal der Sache mit Verwunderung nachgedacht, wie es doch zugehen müsse daß da das Frauenzimmer, so wol bey Hofe, als auch in woleingerichteten Städten, den Ruhm mit Beyfall aller, auch sogar derer gelehrtesten Männer hat, oft besser als jene zu reden / dennoch im schreiben es mit ihnen gar nicht fort wolle, sondern zehn Weiber=Federn nicht an die Schrifft eines einigen in der Gelehrsamkeit angeführten Mannes, ich will nicht sagen in gelehrten, sondern bloß ordentl. Sachen reichen. Die Antwort hierauff stehet zwar dem Ansehn nach schon in meinen Vortrage selbst / weil, wenn das Frauenzimmer studierete, es auch das Mannsvolck alsdenn im schreiben leicht übertreffen könte, indem ein

Ziegler further challenged societal norms of what was appropriate for a female writer through her volume's contents. Rather than devotional poetry, such as that which appears in Gräf's volume, Ziegler's poetry is primarily secular, often satirical, and at times even bawdy. Of the 352 pages of poetry in *Versuch in gebundener Schreib-Art*, only 41 contain sacred poetry. As opposed to the pious spirit and devotional poetry expected from German women, Ziegler wrote in her foreword:

> If it would appear odd to several readers, that I have thrown in among these my poems many joking thoughts, then I know of nothing else to bring forward in my defense, than that I am of the absolute opinion, that one must not all the time demand from a lady a serious and Catonic face, particularly since my temperament and lively disposition would certainly not allow, when I view a hypocritical larva before my face, and with each occurrence to portray the world with downcast eyes and sighing gestures.[46]

While Ziegler's *Versuch in gebundener Schreib-Art* was thus revolutionary for a German woman, it was rooted in another tradition of women's writing, that of the French gallant poets of the previous century. In her foreword, Ziegler mentioned with approbation Madeleine de Scudéry, La comtesse de la Suze (Henriette de Coligny), Anne Dacier, and Antoinette Deshoulières. She further identified with the French salon culture by stating that much of her training had come through interactions in well-mannered and sensible society, which she considered to be a fine school for a rightly ordered life. Likewise, many of her poems focus on good behavior in society: she criticized one woman who was a busy body (227) and another who talked too much in a company (235), and she praised gallant conversation (231). In her satires, Ziegler mocked both men and women for various faults. Furthermore, her cantatas and poetic epistles in this volume focus more on the artful expression of sentiment than the narration of action and often have a conversational quality common within the French gallant tradition.[47]

A number of poems in Ziegler's *Versuch in gebundener Schreib-Art* also address specific issues of women in society. In a birthday poem for Count von Flemming (3–7), Ziegler acknowledged and defended her invasion of male territory with her verse:

---

ungelehrter Mann eben so schlecht zu schreiben scheinet, als ein dergleichen Frauenzimmer, und also wohl der Grund von einer guten Schrifft die Gelehrsamkeit in der Sprach=Kunst ohnfehlbar seyn muß." Ziegler, "Vorbericht" to *Versuch in gebundener Schreib-Art*, iii–iv.

46 "Wolte es etlichen Lesern seltsam vorkommen, daß ich unter diese meine Gedichte viel schertzhaffte Gedancken mit geworffen, so weiß ich zu meiner Vertheidigung nichts anders vorzubringen, als daß ich der völligen Meynung bin, man müsse von einer Dame nicht allezeit ein ernsthafftes und Catonisches Gesichte begehren, zumahl da mein Temperament und aufgewecktes Wesen gar nicht zulassen würde, wann ich eine Gleißnerische Larve vor das Antlitz nähm, und bey jeder Begebenheit mich mit niedergeschlagnen Augen und seufftzenden Geberden der Welt darstellte." Ziegler, "Vorbericht" to *Versuch in gebundener Schreib-Art*, xxi.

47 See Goodman, *Amazons and Apprentices*, 141–42.

Was dünckt Dich, Grosser Graf? mein matt und weiblich Singen,	What do you think, great count, of my feeble and female songs?
Magt sich, es ist zu frey, an Deine Tafel hin,	They venture (it is too freely) there to your table,
Allwo Dir Männer nur gebeugt ihr Opfer bringen,	Where only men bow to bring their offerings to you:
Zu deren Orden ich nicht mit zu zehlen bin.	I am not to be numbered with them in their order.
Doch mein Beginnen ist nicht strafbar zu benennen,	Yet my beginning is not to be called criminal:
Schau nur, Erhabner Graf, die Pierinnen an,	Look only, esteemed count, upon the Muses,
Und sag, ob wir uns nicht darzu mit stellen können?	And say whether we may not place ourselves with them.

Many of the poems in the volume celebrate a life of independence from men's control, and the "Lob der Poesie" links this independence directly to her own artistic drives and aspiration (34–35). Issues of women's writing are further addressed by both Ziegler and Breslau poet Mariane von Bressler (1693–1726) in a series of poetic epistles between the two (55–58, 82–91, 123–30) and in Ziegler's poem mourning Bressler's death (22–25). Ziegler also praised historical and mythical heroines, beginning with the Amazons, while calling for the acknowledgement of contemporary women, in her "Ob Einer Dame erlaubet In Waffen sich zu üben" (42–43):

Wer will nicht nach Verdienst die Amazonin preisen?	Who would not praise the merits of the Amazons,
Die noch die heutge Welt muß heldenmüthig heissen?	Whom the present world must yet call heroic?
In Männer-Hertzen wohnt nicht Hertz und Muth allein,	Heart and courage dwells not only in men's hearts:
Das Frauenzimmer kan auch Heroinen seyn.	Women can also be heroes.

Ziegler thus attacked the male literary establishment through the use of her own name, the insistence that no man had edited her work, the secular nature of her poetry, and her defense of women's rights. Ziegler clearly recognized the challenge her work posed to accepted gender norms and sought to temper her publication and its defense of women's rights. In her dedication, she attested that her poetry was innocent and that she was not seeking the same glory that men achieved in the field of literature. Furthermore, the dedication was to a powerful man, Count Ernst Christoph von Manteufel, cabinet minister and privy council to the Elector of Saxony, whom she petitioned for understanding and protection. In her foreword, she further appealed to her tragic biography as the basis for her poetry: "I did not know how a woman, who like me had had the misfortune to be widowed twice already in her youth, could while away her sad time other than through a soothing verse."[48] In

---

48   "Hiernechts wüst ich nicht, wie ein Frauenzimmer, das gleich mir das Unglück gehabt, in ihren jungen Jahren, schon zweymahl zur Wittbe zu werden, ihre traurige Zeit vergönnter,

the conclusion to her foreword, Ziegler directly addressed would-be critics, attesting that she was "only a lowly woman" and that this was merely an attempt ("Versuch") in the art of poetry. She further welcomed any suggestions from those who would point out her failures and thereby assist her poetic endeavors.[49]

Despite Ziegler's attempts to avoid negative criticism, responses to her *Versuch in gebundener Schreib-Art* were mixed. Evidence that the volume was well received in certain circles is found in the announcement of this and later of her books in the *Neuen Zeitungen von gelehrten Sachen*, as well as in Ziegler's own comments in the foreword to her ensuing volume (where she modestly attributed this success to blind luck) and a poetic epistle to Barthold Heinrich Brockes thanking him for his positive response.[50] However, Ziegler's 1729 foreword also attested to the nature and extent of the negative criticism her first volume had received, particularly in relation to her position as a woman publishing her own poetry. She refered to:

> that abusive part of the world that would twist our thoughts out of an adverse nature and oppose an innocent and reasonable joke, wishing to teach us a bashful character and spoil the joy of poetry; there are many bold and nonsensical writers who would allow the world to fly into a worthless and naive jumble, wherein they attack all performances, positions, and offerings of woman authors through their ready hypocrisy, in order to bring people into an unrighteous and scandalous suspicion.[51]

Rather than responding directly to her critics, Ziegler decided the best rejoinder would be a second volume of poetry, which she published the following year.

Versuch in gebundener Schreib-Art, anderer und letzter Theil (1729)

In its nature and its contents, Ziegler's *Versuch in gebundener Schreib-Art, anderer und letzter Theil* can be seen as something of a retreat. Ziegler's foreword to this new volume lacked any of her earlier defense of women's rights to be educated or to publish their writings, and very few of her poems dealt with such topics.

---

als durch einen stillen Vers vertreiben könte." Ziegler, "Vorbericht" to *Versuch in gebundener Schreib-Art*, x.

49   Ziegler, "Vorbericht" to *Versuch in gebundener Schreib-Art*, xxiii.

50   Leipzig, *Neuen Zeitungen von gelehrten Sachen* 14 (8 January 1728): 31–32; 15 (16 May 1729): 359–60; 16 (5 October 1730): 712. Ziegler, "Vorbericht" to *Versuch in gebundener Schreib-Art*, ii–iii, 280–82.

51   " ... die allzu wunderlichen und Lästerungs=vollen Urtheile der Welt, als welche unsre Gedancken auf eine gantz widrige Art zu verdrehen gewohnet ist, und offtermahls, entweder aus Schmähsucht, oder einer Unbesonnenheit, den aller unschuldigsten und vernünfftigsten Schertz, mit aller Macht und Gewalt, ich weiß nicht, zu was, machen will, uns allerdings ein schüchternes Wesen beybringen, und die Lust zum Dichten rechte sehr vergällen; Ja es unterstehen sich auch vielmahl verwegne und unbesonnene Federn nichtswürdige und einfältige Mische in die Welt fliegen zu lassen, worinnen sie der in angestellten Gesellschafften sich befindlichen Frauenzimmer Aufführung, Stellung und Geberden durch ihre gar angeschickte Hechel ziehen, um das Volck auf den ungerechten und schändlichen Argwohn zu bringen." Ziegler, "Vorbericht" to *Versuch in gebundener Schreib-Art, anderer und letzter Theil*, vii.

Furthermore, Ziegler stated that a woman who writes is constantly reminded that she and all women are the weaker vessels (261) and also that men simply own the advantage in the field of poetry and do not allow women to be heard (441–42). But while attacks from critics on her first volume may have discouraged Ziegler and temporarily quieted her vigorous advocacy of women's rights, her 1729 *Versuch* may be seen as Ziegler's effort to refine, and gain respect for, her own public voice. In contrast to her previous publication, Ziegler's 1729 *Versuch* included primarily sacred poetry, considered more appropriate for a German woman. Furthermore, the improved quality of her poetry and prose gives evidence of intense study, and the more serious nature of the volume's secular poetry exhibits Ziegler's efforts to establish a respected voice in the public forum.

Ziegler's efforts to respond to her critics and also gain more respect as a woman poet most clearly evidenced by her greater inclusion of sacred poetry. As opposed to only 41 pages of sacred poetry and 311 of secular in her previous volume, her 1729 *Versuch* contained 256 pages of sacred poetry and 187 of secular. Ziegler's approach to her sacred poetry was also more systematic in her second volume. Its 64 liturgical cantatas, when added to the nine cantatas set by Bach and published in her 1728 *Versuch*, completed an entire yearly cycle of texts for the Lutheran church year.

Ziegler explained in her foreword that the impetus for her second volume came from these sacred cantatas. She refered to a government official who had written her in response to her first volume to express his approval of it and state that he would like to see the poetic texts completing the liturgical year (iii–iv). Ziegler took up this challenge, becoming the only woman to publish a complete cycle of liturgical cantata texts.

But while such a focus on sacred poetry would have been considered more acceptable for a woman, Ziegler subtly challenged male dominance through her choice of genre. Rather than devotional poetry to promote personal piety, such as that in Gräf's *Liebes-Opffer*, Ziegler published texts intended for public use in the church, a place where women were to be silent. The cantatas were based on the Gospel readings of the church year and employed the text types common in sacred cantatas: Bible verse, chorale, recitative, and aria. Furthermore, Ziegler gave instructions in her foreword to composers who might wish to set the texts to music. Clearly the poet was seeking a wider public hearing through these texts. While the realization of a public voice thus became more subtle in her 1729 *Versuch*, Ziegler's beliefs about women's rights to such a voice had not changed.

In addition to this new treatment of sacred poetry, Ziegler seems to have altered her approach to secular poetry in response to her critics. Ziegler still included many humorous poems and joking thoughts, but the bawdy references of the first volume are absent from the second. She still expressed concern for good manners, such as in her "Die verderbten Sitten der Menschen" (375–86), but did so without her earlier mocking tone. She further stated in her foreword that all joking thoughts were included for the more serious purpose of helping people to recognize and amend their own shortcomings (ix–x). In general, Ziegler's manner in her 1729 *Versuch* was both more refined and more earnest.

Ziegler's most significant, albeit most subtle, response to her critics was the greater linguistic purity and higher quality of both her prose and poetry in the *Versuch in gebundener Schreib-Art, anderer und letzter Theil.* The prose of her foreword is much more fluid and readable, and her poetry is more varied and engaging in its use of language, meter, and syllabification. Through her intense study and practice of poetry in the intervening year, Ziegler sought to fashion a voice worthy of the public forum. Ziegler herself gave testimony to her intense efforts throughout the volume. In a poetic epistle to a friend, she wrote:

Du fragst darinnen mich, was meine Muse macht?	You ask of me what my Muses are doing?
Die sitzet, liebstes Kind, und dichtet Tag und Nacht.	They sit, dear child, and write poetry day and night.[52]

And in her foreword, Ziegler related her diligent study of and commitment to poetry to her hopes that the second volume would be even better received than the first:

> I cannot myself discern whether my Muse has improved within the time since I laid my first *Versuch* before the eyes of the world, and now come closer to that aim which has until now extended my joy and desire for poetry; yet—since one can, in that art and learning after which we indeed keenly and anxiously strive, through daily and constant practice, length of time, sustained patience, and doubling of strength of disposition and body come to cultivate from day to day a better insight, and the human understanding must probably strengthen itself through incessant reflection—I flatter myself still that this, my second volume, may therefore hold a slight advantage over the first, since I have devoted more time and effort to these poems than I did to the first.[53]

Ziegler's more serious study of poetry is further reflected by her insights into the poetic art. She bemoaned the many writers who would venture glibly into poetry without true understanding and stated that the writing of poetry should be based upon the ability to discern between good and evil, between true and false thoughts. Ziegler further stressed the extensive learning required to write poetry and cited Johann von Besser's comparison of poetry to an artful and complex tapestry which must be woven out of the arts and sciences. As an example, Ziegler observed how much study was required just to achieve a basic outline of mythology, which she considered only the "smallest part of learning which relates to poetry" (xi–xiii).

---

52 Ziegler, *Versuch in gebundener Schreib-Art, anderer und letzter Theil*, 413.

53 "Ob meine Muse sich binnen der Zeit, als ich meinen ersten Versuch der Welt vor Augen legte, gebessert, und demjenigen Ziel, welches mir die Lust und Begierde zur Dicht=Kunst bißher ausgestrecket, nunmehr näher gekommen, kan ich selbst nicht wissen, doch da man in derjenigen Kunst und Wissenschafft, nach welcher wir recht eyfrig und bemüht streben, durch tägliche und beständige Ubung, Länge der Zeit, anhaltende Gedult und Verdoppelung der Gemüths= und Leibes=Kräffte eine bessere Einsicht, von Tag zu Tag zu überkommen pfleget, und der menschliche Verstand durch unaufhörliches Nachsinnen sich vermuthlich verstärcken muß; so schmeichle ich mir dennoch damit, daß dieser, mein anderer, Theil vor dem erstern deswegen einen, obgleich kleinen Vorzug erhalten möchte, weil ich auf Verfertigung dieser letztern Gedichte mehr Zeit und Mühe als auf die erstern, verwendet." Ziegler, "Vorbericht" to *Versuch in gebundener Schreib-Art, anderer und letzter Theil*, viii–ix.

Ziegler's study is further reflected by the many poems in the volume which address specific literary themes. These include "An einen vornehmen und gelehrten Mann in H[amburg (Brockes)]" (280–82), "Über den allzugrossen Mißbrauch der edlen Poesie" (323), "Über des Herren Brockes Sinn- und geistreiche Schriften" (341–47), and "Über des Herrn von Canitz Gedichte" (424–26).

Despite her intense study of poetry during the preceding year and her obvious interest in the nature and practice of poetry, Ziegler concluded the foreword to her *Versuch in gebundener Schreib-Art, anderer und letzter Theil* by declaring this to be the end of her poetic art. She stated that although she had greatly loved her "diversion into masculine endeavors," she did not wish to become like a starving man who comes to a full meal and gorges himself far past being satisfied. After having spent so much time on poetry, particularly in the previous year, Ziegler simply stated that she wished to have more hours each day to devote to music (xiv).

Ziegler elaborated upon her intentions in the volume's final poem, "Abschied an die Poesie" ("Farewell to Poetry," 438–43). The poem begins by stating the reasons for her departure from poetry, with strophe 2 particularly citing the extensive amount of time and effort the art required:

Ich bin, ihr könnt es sicher glauben,	I am—you can surely believe it—
Des lieben Dichtens müt und satt,	Full and satisfied of beloved poetry,
Es pflegt uns nur die Zeit zu rauben,	It tends only to rob us of time,
Und macht den Kopff recht mürb und matt,	And makes the head truly worn out and dull,
Das viele Grübeln schwächt die Geister,	The much brooding weakens the spirit,
Man ist, läst man zu tieff sich ein,	One is—if one allows oneself to become involved too deeply—
Warhafftig selbst nicht mehr sein Meister,	Truly no more his own master,
Der man doch immer solte seyn.	Which one should yet always be.

In addition to such explanations of poetry's overwhelming demand on her time, some of Ziegler's later statements imply that she was affected by the negative criticism of her first volume. For example, Ziegler stated in the ninth strophe that no amount of effort would bring her to poetic greatness:

Was würd es, sagt es mir, wohl nützen?	Tell me, what would be the advantage?
Wenn ich in euren Reyhen blieb	If I remain in your numbers
Zeit meines gantzen Lebens sitzen,	Sitting during the time of my entire life,
Und immer während säng und schrieb;	And ever more sang und wrote;
Ihr könnt bey so gestalten Sachen,	You could with such type things—
Wenn ich mich auch beswchwatzen ließ,	If I also let myself be coaxed—
Dennoch aus mir kein Bildnüß machen,	Yet out of me make no portrait,
Das einer *Sappho* ähnlich hieß.	That could be called similar to a Sappho.

The effect of negative criticism is felt even more strongly in strophes 11 and 12, where Ziegler stated that the Muses simply prefered men's literary endeavors to women's and that men, therefore, always had the advantage in the field of poetry:

Ihr werdt es doch nicht übel nehmen,
Wenn ich, wiewohl gantz leiß und still,
Um euren Chor nicht zu beschämen,
Euch was ins Oehrgen sagen will:
Nicht wahr? ihr seyd, gesteht es immer,
Dem Männer Volck weit mehr geneigt,
Und holder, als dem Frauenzimmer,
Wie die Erfahrung täglich zeigt.

Der Vorzug ist sehr groß zu nennen,
Hört nur der Männer Flöten an,
Ihr selbst müst es mir bekennen,
Daß man nichts netters hören kan.
Was zeigen sie vor Kunst? vor Griffe?

Sie sind an Geist und Feuer reich,
Und wenn man sich zu todte pfieffe,
So spielt man ihnen doch nicht gleich.

Yet you would not take it as evil,
If I—how well completely soft and quiet,
In order not to shame your choir—
Wish to say something in your ears:
Not true? You are, it is always confessed,
Much more inclined toward men,
And sweeter, than toward women,
As experience daily shows.

The advantage is very great to name,
Only the men's flutes are heard,
You yourselves must confess it to me,
That one can hear nothing nicer.
What do they display for art? for graspings?

They are rich in spirit and fire,
And if one would pipe oneself to death,
Even so one could not play like them.

While Ziegler stated in her foreword that she anticipated writings from other female authors and that she had no doubt that these would exceed her own, her final poem gives rather little hope. After a year of intense work refining her own poetic voice and producing a significant volume of poetry, Ziegler seems to have lost some of her belief that a woman's voice could be heard in the public forum. But despite this apparent discouragement and the declaration of her farewell to poetry, Ziegler actively pursued her literary work throughout the 1730s and soon renewed her call for a public voice for women.

Induction into the Deutschen Gesellschaft in Leipzig (1730)

In the foreword to her *Versuch in gebundener Schreib-Art, anderer und letzter Theil*, Ziegler thanked those learned men who had encouraged her poetic endeavors (xiv). While such men apparently included Flemming and Brockes, the primary one was likely Johann Christoph Gottsched. Katherine Goodman sees Gottsched's influence in Ziegler's second volume, not only in the more purposeful treatment of themes, but also in the linguistic purity of the poetry and prose. It is possible that Ziegler's intense study of poetry during this time occurred under Gottsched's tutelage.[54]

Gottsched's encouragement and promotion of Ziegler's literary endeavors moved from the private to the public sphere when on 16 November 1730 the *Neuen Zeitungen von gelehrten Sachen* announced:

> The Deutschen Gesellschaft in Leipzig has recently conferred, through unanimous choice and of their own motion, a place among their members upon an astute and eloquent lady,

---

54   Goodman, *Amazons and Apprentices*, 150–51.

Madame Christiane Mariane von Ziegler, née Romanus, on the basis of her reputation in her poetry and prose writings which have been published to date."[55]

Ziegler was not only the first woman to be named a member of the Deutschen Gesellschaft in Leipzig, but also the only woman to ever participate actively in the society. Her induction seems to have heartened Ziegler in her literary pursuits, while also leading to the inclusion of a woman's voice in one of Leipzig's learned societies.

Upon his arrival in Leipzig in 1724, Gottsched had been employed by the University of Leipzig history professor Johann Burkhard Menke as librarian and tutor for Mencke's son. Gottsched quickly became involved in the Deutsch-übende Gesellschaft, of which Mencke was founder and head. In 1727 Gottsched became the society's director and reorganized it as the Deutschen Gesellschaft.[56] Under Gottsched's leadership, the society continued to pursue the cultivation and improvement of the German language and also worked for the reform of German literature and theater. The Deutschen Gesellschaft's statutes of 1727 included the following statement:

> One should be diligent at all times about the purity and correctness of speech; that is, not only to avoid all foreign words, but also all incorrect expressions and dialects in German; so that one writes neither Silesian nor Meissen, neither Franconian nor Lower Saxon, but pure high German; so that one can understand it in all Germany.[57]

The Deutschen Gesellschaft thus encouraged the awareness and cultivation of German as a means of literary expression and thereby strongly influenced German literature of the eighteenth century. The ideals of the society were promoted through weekly meetings in which members presented their new, unpublished literary works in both poetry and prose, and also through the society's publications.

By sponsoring Ziegler's inclusion as the first female member of the Deutschen Gesellschaft, Gottsched sought to promote her as an example of his belief, expounded first in *Die vernünftigen Tadlerinnen*, that German culture would be elevated when women were drawn into social discourse. Ziegler's role in the Deutschen Gesellschaft was an active one. Throughout the 1730s, she participated in, and at times hosted, the

---

55   "[Der Deutschen Gesellschaft in Leipzig] hat neulich einer scharffinnigen und beredten Dame, Frauen Christianen Marianen von Ziegler, geb. Romanus, in Ansehung ihrer in gebundener und ungebundener Schreib=Art, zeither ans Licht gestellten Schrifften, durch einhellige Wahl und aus eigener Bewegung eine Stelle unter ihren Mitgliedern zuerkannt." *Neuen Zeitungen von gelehrten Sachen* 16 (16 November 1730): 816.

56   Dietmar Debes, Foreword to *Bibliotheca Societatis Teutonicae Saeculi XVI–XVIII: Katalog der Büchersammlung der Deutschen Gesellschaft in Leipzig*, ed. Ernst Kroker, 2 vols. (Munich, 1971), vii–ix.

57   "Man soll sich allezeit der Reinigkeit und Richtigkeit der Sprache befleißigen; d.i., nicht nur alle ausländische Wörter, sondern auch alle Deutsche unrichtige Ausdrückungen und Provinzial-Redensarten vermeiden; so daß man weder Schlesisch noch Meißnisch, weder Fränkisch noch Niedersächsisch, sondern rein Hochdeutsch schreibe; so wie man es in ganz Deutschland verstehen kann." Qtd. in Eric A. Blackall, *The Emergence of German as a Literary Language*, 107–08.

weekly meetings of the society as well as more informal gatherings of the society's members. She won the Deutschen Gesellschaft's annual prize for poetry in both 1732 and 1734, and she contributed poems to the society's publications.

Ziegler's participation in the Deutschen Gesellschaft thus led to her revived focus on women's role in public discourse. Not only was Ziegler's poetic voice promoted through the society's publications, but her literal voice was also heard in the society's meetings. In addition to her regular involvement in the society's discussions, two of Ziegler's formal speeches to the society are recorded, her inaugural speech of 15 November 1730[58] and her undated "Abhandlung, ob es dem Frauenzimmer erlaubet sey, sich nach Wissenschaftern zu bestreben" ("Treatise on whether a woman should be permitted to pursue learning").[59] In these speeches, Ziegler not only gave an example of a woman's voice within the context of a learned society of men, but also renewed her public defense of women's rights to participation in the public forum. She called on the members of the Deutschen Gesellschaft to aid her in this defense and to protect and defend her from negative criticism.

Ziegler's "Abhandlung, ob es dem Frauenzimmer erlaubet sey, sich nach Wissenschaftern zu bestreben" particularly addresses topics of women's roles in public discourse, defending women's rights to education and literary enterprise. Ziegler opened her speech by recognizing her unique position as a woman in a society of learned men and by defending her right to speak in the Deutschen Gesellschaft on the basis of her membership and her identification with the society's aims:

> Those who usually attribute an innate stupidity to the female sex should discourage me from calling such a number of prestigious and learned men into my chamber. However, it multiplies my strength of spirit many times, and their presence stimulates my senses. What should I fear? I am since long before marked in the register of their learned names. I likewise make the effort to elevate the worth of the German language. I train to speak and to write German after their taste. I judge myself after the prescribed rules; in short: my intentions agree with theirs completely. All of these preceding circumstances grant me the freedom to disclose my thoughts to them without fear.[60]

---

58 "Antrittsrede der Hoch=Wohlgebohrnen Frauen Christianen Marianen von Ziegler, geb. Romanus, aus Leipzig," in *Der Deutschen Gesellschaft in Leipzig Gesammlete Reden und Gedichte, Welche bey dem Eintritte und Abschiede ihrer Mitglieder pflegen abgelesen zu werden*, ed. Johann Christoph Gottsched, 287–95 (Leipzig, 1732); rev. ed. in Ziegler, *Vermischete Schriften*, 381–89.

59 Reprinted in Ziegler, *Vermischete Schriften*, 394–99.

60 "Die sonst dem weiblichen Geschlechte angebohrne Blödigkeit sollte mich abhalten, eine solche Anzahl ansehnlicher und gelehrter Männer in mein Zimmer zu bemühen. Allein es verdoppeln sich vielmehr die Kräfte des Geistes, und ihre Gegenwart ermuntert mein Nachsinnen. Was sollte ich fürchten? Ich bin ja vorlängst in das Register ihrer gelehrten Namen eingezeichnet. Ich bemühe mich ebenfalls, den Werth der Deutschen Sprache empor zu bringen. Ich übe mich, nach ihrem Geschmacke Deutsch zu sprechen und zu schreiben. Ich richte mich nach den vorgeschriebenen Regeln; kurz: Mein Absichten stimmen mit den ihrigen vollkommen überein. Alle diese angeführten Umstände ertheilen mir die Freyheit, ihnen meine Gedanken ungescheuet zu eröffnen." Ziegler, *Vermischete Schriften*, 394.

Rather than continuing with an attack on men who would criticize women's pursuit of learning, such as those found in her *Versuch in gebundener Schreib-Art*, Ziegler bemoaned the fact that most women were not interested in bettering themselves through education:

> It would only remain to wish that more of my sex would have such zeal, and endeavor to cast aside the foolishness for which one can rightly blame them, and listen with delight. Yet with this remembrance almost all courage escapes me. I see with the utmost perception how much they allow themselves to deviate more and more from the path of true goodness. They regularly dress merely for their sensual presentation and manage the blithe penchants of their disposition only too well: and so they can never come to a sensible reflection. The unspeakable degeneration, my sirs, truly stirs the inmost regions of my soul. How gladly I wish for you, most lost women, to remove the corrupt senses and to see you in more fortunate circumstances! O that I could stir your hearts for you by means of my regret, so much do I feel over your weaknesses![61]

Ziegler went on to defend women's ability to learn and stated that no law prevented women from pursuing wisdom: "No clever person will maintain that there is a lack of ability in every woman to grasp more than one commonly claims for her sex. One can also quote no law which excludes a woman from pursuing the wisdom which one can acquire through education."[62] After this brief defense of women's education, Ziegler attacked those critics who denied women's rights to pursue learning or to publish their literary works:

> Yet it is deplorable that as quickly as a noble impulse toward this or that science is expressed by one woman or another; as quickly as the quill is seized in poetry or prose to demonstrate their ability, it must be seen that hard judgments, corruption, disgrace, and the most delicate encounters be exposed. Thus prestigious and learned men are often not at all afraid to talk at length in their blind zeal about them in a laughable way. They

---

61   "Es wäre nur zu wünschen, daß mehre unter meinem Geschlechte von solchem Eifer eingenommen würden, und sich bestrebeten, die Thorheiten, so man ihnen mit Recht vorwerfen kann, abzulegen und der Vernungt Gehör zu geben. Doch bey dieser Erinnerung entfällt mir fast aller Muth. Ich sehe mit der äussersten Empfindung, wie sehr sich dieselben vielmehr angelegen seyn lassen, von der Bahn des wahren Guten immer mehr abzuweichen. Sie trachten gemeiniglich bloß ihren sinnlichen Vorstellungen, und ihrer wohllüstigen Gemüthsneigung Genüge zu leisten: Und so können sie niemals zu einer vernünftigen Ueberlegung kommen. Der unaussprechliche Verfall, meine Herren, rühret mir wahrlich das Innerste der Seelen. Wie gerne wollte ich euch, verirrtes Frauenzimmer, den verderbten Sitten entziehen, und euch in glückseligern Umständen sehen! O könnte euch das Leidwesen, so ich über eure Schwachheiten empfinde, das Herze rühren!" Ziegler, *Vermischete Schriften*, 394–95.

62   "Kein Kluger wird behaupten, daß es allem Frauenzimmer an Fähigkeit mangele, mehr zu fassen, als man gemeiniglich von ihren Geschlechte fordert. Man wird auch kein Gesetze anführen können, welches die Weiber ausschliesset, der Weisheit nachzugehen, die man durch Wissenschaften erlangen kann." Ziegler, *Vermischete Schriften*, 396.

criticize the perfidious blather of women and yet fall into it themselves, since careful remarks fail them.[63]

Ziegler then addressed women's writing, declaring her innocent intentions and noble aims; calling on women authors to pursue writing; and calling on the members of the Deutschen Gesellschaft to support female writers:

> Women do not seek to obtain offices and positions of honor with their quill; they do not write out of any greed; they are not blinded by the taste for glory to dispute their right of preference with learned and famous men; innocence lays the foundation of their efforts, and the noble aim to become wiser and more mature is their final purpose. By these notions I have not been able to abstain from encouraging myself and others and from admonishing to an unmovable steadfastness. I advise you, my sisters, to let yourselves be led in the way of true wisdom with fearless courage and sincere hearts. Proclaim your intentions along with mine, so you may confidently learn and write. Do not allow the many troubles to hinder you from pursuing your course to the end. One will not with serious judgments force you to swerve from sensible pursuits. But if my admonitions could not bring you to other thoughts, then I turn to desire the best from you, my sirs. You will lay to rest all my sisters' fears when they wish to be instructed, how they can lay aside the opinions of some learned men who maintain that women should not be allowed to train in learning like the male sex, even though they possess just as much ability to do so.[64]

Ziegler finally positioned her comments within the context of contemporary German society. While she did not challenge the traditional domestic role of women,

---

63   "Doch ist zu beklagen, daß so bald sich nur ein edler Trieb zu der und jener Wissenschaft, bey einem oder dem andern Frauenzimmer äussert; so bald es die Feder ergreifet, in gebundener oder ungebundener Schreibart seine Fähigkeit zu zeigen, es sich harten Urtheilen, Lästern, Schmähen, und den empfindlichsten Begegnungen ausgesetzet sehen muß. So gar angesehene und gelehrte Männer scheuen sich nicht, ihren blinden Eifer oft lächerlicher Weise darüber auszulassen. Sie tadeln das niederträchtige Gewäsche der Weiber, und verfallen doch selbst darein, weil es ihnen an gründlichen Einwürfen fehlet." Ziegler, *Vermischete Schriften*, 396.

64   "Das Frauenzimmer trachtet ja nicht mit ihrer Feder Aemter und Ehrenstellen zu erhalten: Sie schreiben aus keiner Gewinnsucht: Sie sind nicht von abgeschmacktem Ehrgeize verblendet, gelehrten und beruhmten Männern den Vorzug streitig zu machen: Die Unschuld leget den Grund zu ihren Bemühungen; und die edle Absicht, weiser und gesetzter zu werden, ist ihr Endzweck. Bey diesen Vorstellungen habe ich mich nicht enthalten können, mich selbst und andere zu ermuntern, und zu einer unbeweglichen Standhaftigkeit zu ermahnen. Ich rathe euch, meine Schwestern, euch mit unerschrocknem Muthe und aufrichtigen Herzen auf den Weg der Wahren Weisheit leiten zu lassen. Stimmen eure Absichten mit den meinigen überein, so könnt ihr getrost lernen und schreiben. Lasset euch viele Verdrüßlichkeiten nicht hindern, den Lauf nach dem Ziele zu vollführen. Man wird euch bey ernstlichen Verrichtungen nicht zwingen, die vernünftigen Ergetzlichkeiten zu verschweren. Können aber meine Ermahnungen euch nicht auf andere Gedanken bringen, so wende ich mich um eures Besten willen zu ihnen, meine Herren. Sie werden alle Furcht meiner Mitschwestern verjagen, wenn sie dieselben belehren wollen, wie sie die Meynungen einiger Gelehrten widerlegen können, welche behaupten, daß es dem Frauenzimmer nicht erlaubet sey, sich wie das männliche Geschlechte in Wissenschaften zu üben, ob es gleich vielen an der Fähigkeit dazu nicht fehlet." Ziegler, *Vermischete Schriften*, 397.

she stated that such a role did not preclude a woman from pursuing learning. She wished, too, that learned women in Germany would be honored like they were in other lands:

> I know well that one tends to say that a woman should make use her mind's capability on the judicious maintenance of her household, to raise her children virtuously, to make herself skillful in baking, sewing, cooking, and other woman's work; thereby would the republic be filled with well-trained and efficient wives, on whom men could rely completely. All these rules have their reason; but I also know that they do not go against those which the woman who is led to learning would know. A sensible woman can run her household and child-raising well and still have several hours left to turn to the reading of good books. For my part, I believe that their acquired understanding would make a sensible woman yet more skillful to live up to her duties. In other nations, it is known that women who take up learning are entitled to a special preference. Should the fair sex then be reprehensible in Saxony, one might rather wish to be born a foreigner.[65]

Ziegler's involvement with the Deutschen Gesellschaft, which continued until she left Leipzig in 1741, thus helped to renew her vigorous defense of women's rights to learning and to literary enterprise. Buoyed by her active involvement in this literary society, Ziegler quickly published her third volume, the *Moralische und vermischte Send-Schreiben* of 1731.

Moralische und vermischte Send-Schreiben (1731)

In her *Moralische und vermischte Send-Schreiben*, Ziegler artfully combined the very different approaches to defending women's rights she had employed in her earlier publications. This volume manifests both the vocal treatment of women's issues that characterized her contributions to *Die vernünftigen Tadlerinnen* and her *Versuch in gebundener Schreib-Art* and the refined expression and fluid style of her *Versuch in gebundener Schreib-Art, anderer und letzter Theil*. After having worked so hard to improve her writing in the face of negative criticism, Ziegler shook off such criticism and applied her refined skills once again to defending women's rights to education and literary enterprise.

---

65   "Ich weis wohl, daß man zu sagen pfleget, das Frauenzimmer sollte die Fähigkeit ihres Verstandes auf die Kluge Einrichtung ihrer Haushaltung anwenden, die Kinder tugendhaft erziehen, sich im Backen, Nähen, Kochen und anderer Frauenzimmerarbeit geschickt machen, damit die Republik mit wohl erzogenen und wirthlichen Weibern angefüllet würde, und sich die Männer auf dieselben völlig verlassen könnten. Alle diese Regeln haben ihren Grund; ich weis aber auch, daß sie gegen die nichts ausrichten, welche das Frauenzimmer zu Wissenschaften angeführet wissen wollen. Eine vernünftige Frau kann ihrer Haushaltung und Kinderzucht wohl vorstehen, und dennoch dabey einige Stunden auf Lesung guter Bücher wenden. Vor mein Theil glaube ich, daß ihre erlangte Erkenntniß sie noch geschickter machen werde, den Pflichten einer vernünftigen Frau nach zu leben. Von den Ausländern ist es bekannt, daß sie denjenigen Frauenspersonen einen besondern Vorzug zugestehen, die sich auf Wissenschaften legen. Sollte denn das angenehme Geschlechte deswegen in Sachsen verwerflich seyn; so möchte man wünschen, bey den Ausländern gebohren zu seyn." Ziegler, *Vermischte Schriften*, 397–98.

Having written her farewell to poetry in 1729, Ziegler turned instead to prose expression in the form of letters. Like devotional poetry, the letter as a literary genre was closely associated with female writers in seventeenth- and eighteenth-century Europe. Women were viewed as exemplary letter writers, since the form required no special training and ostensibly did not aim at publication or fame. While German female writers of this period gained a degree of literary esteem through their letters, the private nature of this genre did not allow for significant public recognition or involvement in public discourse.[66] As she had done with sacred poetry in her 1729 volume, Ziegler here adopted a genre considered appropriate for a woman, the letter, and employed it to challenge male dominance by presenting it in published form.

The groundbreaking nature of Ziegler's *Moralische und vermischte Send-Schreiben* was not lost on contemporary critics. A review of the volume appearing in the 156th issue of *Actorum Eruditorum* in 1731 stated: "One must give the author the credit that she is the first among the Germans to venture on the task of clever and ethically-related letters."[67] While many French women had published collections of letters, Ziegler was the first German woman to do so. Ziegler stated in her foreword that she was hesitant to be the first German woman to publish a volume of letters, especially since the first person to do a thing is often harshly judged. However, she concluded that such an effort would serve to forge the path for other female writers whose efforts, she believed, would exceed her own (vi–viii).

While recognizing the significance of her collection for German literature, Ziegler also admired the accomplishments of French women and particularly praised the letters of Anne Thérèse de Lambert (1647–1733). French salon culture thus continued to influence Ziegler's writing, as is also evident through her many letters proclaiming principles for well-mannered interaction in society (for example, 162–66, 217–21, 264–68). However, Ziegler went beyond such topics and treated a broad range of subjects. Her 100 letters discuss such topics as how to raise well-behaved children (32–36), that a man should not spend too much money on books (36–40), the importance of being joyful despite bad weather (138–42), the state of Leipzig's churches (142–46), and the importance of being satisfied with one's present condition (296–300). Ziegler explained in her foreword that these letters were based on drafts of letters she had sent in the past, but that she had altered them by removing any personal references and focusing on their moral messages.

Within the variety of topics in *Moralische und vermischte Send-Schreiben*, Ziegler took many opportunities to defend women's rights and to fashion a context for a woman's voice within German society. One subtle way in which she did this was through the assertion of her own voice and opinions, often in opposition to those of men. Ziegler removed all personal references in her letters, and the original

---

66 See Helga Möbius, *Woman of the Baroque Age*, trans. Barbara Chruscik Beedham (Montclair, NJ, 1982), 151; Jo Catling, "Introduction" to *A History of Women's Writing in Germany, Austria and Switzerland*, ed. Jo Catling, 1–10 (Cambridge, 2000), 7–8; and Joeres, "The German Enlightenment," 161–63.

67 "Man muß der Verfasserin den Ruhm beylegen, daß sie unter den Deutschen die erste sey, welche sich an sinnreiche und die Sitten=Lehre betreffende Briefe gewagt." Qtd. in *Neuen Zeitungen von gelehrten Sachen* 17 (9 August 1732): 567–68.

recipients are not known. However, she did specify on each whether the recipient was a man or a woman. The letters contain many examples of Ziegler addressing a man, recalling an opinion which he had expressed to her, and disagreeing with it. Ziegler thus set herself up as a woman whose opinions could equal and even exceed those of men.

Ziegler further included a number of letters which dealt specifically with issues of women's rights, particularly those of education and writing. In addressing the education of women, Ziegler did not advocate university education but rather a better education within the home. Her account of the gendered division of learning is, however, ironic in tone:

> It is well known to you that the woman at the very least grieves herself to cultivate the same subjects [that is, academic education], since she is discouraged from them by other female and more necessary deeds, and it is not her place to mingle in the business of the learned world.[68]

Ziegler further described the kind of education available to women, and its shortcomings, thus:

> Our sex is not granted to visit the lecture halls of learned men, and are closed off from the profit of their careful teachings; we must unfortunately make do only with the mere reading of their writings, and so much which we could retrieve from this council is left shut to our strength of understanding, since often no-one explains the seemingly dark passages, nor can we discover a true understanding of their words.[69]

Within such a context, Ziegler strongly advocated better education for women and pleaded with her readers to encourage women in their pursuit of learning. In a letter encouraging a mother to allow her daughter to be educated, Ziegler countered what she considered to be the two primary arguments against women's learning, that it was too difficult and that a woman's household duties did not allow her the time to study. Ziegler blamed the supposed difficulty of study on men's jealousy and their desire to discourage women from learning. She instead asserted the equality of women and men in their creation, thus stating that that women could rival men in the ability to learn:

> The difficulty which one wishes to make of this rests primarily with the male sex, who ever wish to possess for themselves something special and disapprove when the female

---

68   "Es ist Ihnen ja wohl bekannt, daß die Damen um dergleichen Sachen sich am allerwenigsten zu bekummern pflegen, weil sie andere weibliche und nöthigere Verrichtungen hiervon abhalten, und es ihres Amtes nicht ist, sich in die Geschäffte der gelehrten Welt einzumischen." Ziegler, *Moralische und vermischte Send-Schreiben*, 52–53.

69   "Unserm Geschlechte ist nicht vergönnt, die Hör=Säle gelehrter Männer zu besuchen, und ihre gründliche Lehren sich zu Nutze zumachen; wir müssen uns leider nur mit blosser Durchlesung ihrer Schrifften behelffen, und so viel uns unsere Kräffte des Verstandes zulassen, Raths daraus erhohlen, worbey uns niemand, die öffters dunckel scheinenden Stellen erkläret, noch den wahren Verstand ihrer Worte entdecket." Ziegler, "Vorbericht" to *Moralische und vermischte Send-Schreiben*, v.

sex desires to climb up after them; their supposed privilege, which they seek to maintain over us, is therefore really a secret jealousy. Granted, that it is very difficult to achieve, to plumb the depths of wisdom and pursue the heights of the sciences, they must even so consider that we possess even the same diligence and patience which they pride themselves to cultivate. When a woman from her youth devotes herself to the study of the same learning and reflects on such things, why should she not receive the same benefit which those of the male sex obtain? We bring just as well five senses into the world, as they do; understanding and reason are distributed by nature among both sexes, and memory is also granted by her as part of our dowry. We have body and soul in common with them, and the power of judgement is not a special legacy which the creator granted them in advance, but he also allowed us to inherit it.[70]

After giving examples of learned women (van Schurman, Scudéry, and Dacier), Ziegler went on to address the issue of the time education required. Ziegler again did not debate the domestic role of women, but she did argue that such a role did not prohibit women's learning:

As far as the other point is concerned, which many say in their peculiar thoughts, that women were singularly and only merely placed in the world to turn themselves around in the house and kitchen each day, and to devote their hours only to these, it serves to briefly state that any woman must accept the housekeeping, the management of which is the necessary duty that belongs to our sex; however, as it appears to me, it also requires neither long time nor art to educate oneself. The day has many hours, and each one of them need not be the same as the other.[71]

---

70 "Die Schwürigkeit, so man Ihnen hierinnen machen will, rühret wohl am meisten von dem Männlichen Geschlechte her, dieses will immer etwas besonders vor sich alleine behalten, und siehet gar nicht gerne, wann Ihnen das Weibliche Geschlechte nachklettern will; Ihr vermeyntes Vorrecht, welches sie vor uns zu behaupten suchen, würcket also eine heimliche Eyfersucht. Gesetzt, daß es manchen schwer und selbst sauer ankömmt, die Tieffe der Weißheit zu ergründen, und den Höhen der Wissenschafften nachzugehen, so müssen sie bedencken, daß wir eben denjenigen Fleiß und Gedult besitzen, welcher beyder Sie sich zu rühmen pflegen. Wenn ein Frauenzimmer von Jugend auf sich der Erlernung dergleichen Gelehrsamkeit weyhet, und solchen Betrachtungen oblieget, warum solte es nicht eben denjenigen Vortheil erhalten, den das Männliche Geschlechte erlanget? Wir bringen ja eben sowohl fünff Sinnen mit auf die Welt, wie jenes, Verstand und Vernunfft werden unter beyderley Geschlechten von der Natur ausgetheilet, und das Gedächtniß wird uns zur Mitgifft von Ihr mit angerechnet. Wir haben Leib und Seele mit Ihnen gemein, und die Beurtheilungs-Krafft ist gar kein besondres Vermächtniß, welches Ihnen der Schöpffer zum voraus zugedacht, massen selbiger uns auch darvon mit erben lassen." Ziegler, *Moralische und vermischte Send-Schreiben*, 7–8.

71 "Was aber den andern Punct anbelanget, da viele in den wunderlichen Gedancken stehen, das Frauen-Volck wär einig und allein bloß deswegen in die Welt gestellt worden, damit sich selbiges in Hauß und Küche täglich herum drehte, und seine Stunden nur darzu verwendete, so dienet hierauf kürtzlich, daß sich ein iedwedes Frauenzimmer allerdings der Wirthschafft annehmen müsse, massen deren Besorgung mit unter die nothwendigsten Pflichten unsers Geschlechtes gehöret; allein wie mich bedüncket, so gehöret weder lange Zeit noch Kunst darzu, dieselbe zu erlernen. Der Tag hat viel Stunden, und bey dem einen muß das andere nicht versäumet werden." Ziegler, *Moralische und vermischte Send-Schreiben*, 8–9.

In addition to defending women's learning, Ziegler argued for women's rights to literary expression. She advised that all women should be trained in the art of writing (48–52) and discussed her own writings (109–14). She further highlighted her position, and rights, as a female writer by giving her opinions on many literary topics, including the use of satire (1–5), learned writing (308–12), translating (315–20), writing poetry, (357–60) and writing letters (414–16). As in her *Versuch in gebundener Schreib-Art, anderer und letzter Theil*, Ziegler's dedicated study of writing is thus reflected in her many literary themes. The difference in her *Moralische und vermsichte Send-Schreiben* is that such themes were now presented within the context of women's rights to better education and to literary enterprise. Far from retiring from the field of literature as she had promised at the end of her previous volume, Ziegler broke new ground as the first German woman to publish a book of letters while promoting her ideas about women's education and literature within a new context.

Ziegler's Salon: Poetry and Music

Another way Ziegler continued her literary endeavors and influence was through the salon she hosted in the Romanus house throughout the late 1720s and 1730s, further evidence of her ongoing interest in French salon culture. Originating among the Parisian aristocracy in the seventeenth century, the French salons were designed as one of the few places where men and women could socialize together and exchange ideas. Polite and polished conversation and fine manners were central to the salon culture, as was proper treatment of women (embodied particularly in the salon hostess).[72]

Salons in general, and Ziegler's salon in particular, were thus closely related to gender norms. On the most basic level, Ziegler's salon provided Leipzig with a venue for women's active participation in culture, both musical and literary. Like its French models, Ziegler's salon was based on well-mannered social interaction between men and women. Contemporary descriptions of the salon emphasized this interaction, and particularly women's roles in the company. Christian Gabriel Fischer, on his 1731 visit to Leipzig, spent an evening at Ziegler's salon. On this occasion, the salon had a literary focus and included extemporized poetry by each member of the company of six men and three women. Fischer was particularly amazed by each woman's skill and imagination in poetry, as well as by their lively thoughts and stimulating conversation. He especially noted Ziegler's role in the group, praising her well-mannered conduct, her learning, her poetic skill, and her lively temperament.[73]

---

72 Dulong, "Conversation to Creation, 397–405.

73 Qtd. in Albert Predeek, "Ein vergessener Freund Gottscheds," 121–23. Another contemporary description of Ziegler's salon by Johann Ernst Philippi recounts similar elements, including dinner, card playing, a sizable group of both men and women (here about ten persons), an emphasis on proper manners and speech, and extemporized poetry. See Johann Ernst Philippi, "Sottises galantes, oder Galante Thorheiten, angezeiget in einem Sendschreiben an … Gottsched … von Carl Gustav," (Lübeck, 1733); 3rd ed., in *Cicero: Ein*

Ziegler's salon thus provided an important venue for women's participation in cultural life. Furthermore, the salon allowed Ziegler a particularly active individual role in societal life. She was not just a participant in this cultural sphere, but, as salon hostess, served as an important leader within the group. In relation to the musical performances in her salon, this meant that Ziegler was the primary arbiter of taste. In her letter to a Kapellmeister in another city, she thanked her correspondent for the pieces of music he sent and stated that she would "as quickly as possible have them performed in my chamber."[74]

Ziegler herself was a practiced musician, playing transverse flute, recorder, lute, and clavier, and also singing. Her great love for music and its central role in her salon are documented in her own writings, such as the "Antwort-Schreiben" which appeared in her 1728 *Versuch in gebundener Schreib-Art*:

Du weist, daß mich nichts mehr als die Music kan laben,	You know that nothing can refresh me more than music.
Denn dieses Element ernehret Seel und Geist.	For this element nourishes the soul and spirit.
Es kan mir in der That kein größer Dienst geschehen,	Indeed, no greater service can be done for me
Als wenn ich, wie du selbst davon kanst Zeuge seyn,	Than when I, as you yourself can witness,
Vom lieben Noten-Volck mich soll umringet sehen,	See myself surrounded by dear musicians,
Ich räumte, gieng es an, ihm alle Zimmer ein.	I would, were it possible, give up all my rooms to them.[75]

In the foreword to the same volume, Ziegler further refered to "master virtuosi, who often while they are here and passing through grant me the honor of their encouragement."[76] In a letter published in her *Moralische und vermischte Send-Schreiben* of 1731, Ziegler asked an unidentified Kapellmeister that she be notified if any musical position should become available in his city and made reference to the concerts in the Romanus house: "I have many of these same needy ones, who ardently sigh after a promotion. You would make me very obliged thereby, since I recognize that through their aid and reinforcement my concerts have proved to be pleasing to me."[77]

---

großer Wind=Beutel, Rabulist, und Charletan; Zur Probe aus Dessen übersetzter Schutz=Rede (Halle, 1735), 327–56.

74   " … und werde selbige so bald es möglich in meinen Zimmer aufführen lassen, …" Ziegler, *Moralische und vermischte Send-Schreiben*, 392.

75   Ziegler, *Versuch in gebundener Schreib-Art*, 148. Translation in Hans Joachim Kreutzer, "Bach and the Literary Scene in Eighteenth-Century Leipzig," in *Music and German Literature: Their Relationship since the Middle Ages*, ed. James M. McGlathery, 80–99 (Columbia, SC, 1992), 87.

76   " … Herrn Virtuosen, die mir zum öfftern bey ihren Hierseyn u. Durchreisen die Ehre ihres Zuspruchs gönnen … ." Ziegler, "Vorbericht" to *Versuch in gebundener Schreib-Art*, xiii.

77   "Ich habe viele dergleichen Bedürfftige, welche nach der Beförderung sehnlich seuffzen. Sie würden sich mich dadurch sehr verbindlich machen, weil ich unterschiedenen,

While revealing details about the musical aspects of her salon, Ziegler's writings about music—particularly two letters in her *Moralische und vermischte Send-Schreiben*—also served to further advance her defense of women's rights. In one letter, Ziegler addressed women's roles in music by discussing her own musical training and practice and encouraging a mother to comply with her daughter's request to learn the transverse flute. In recounting the instruments she played, Ziegler especially defended her own playing of the flute, an instrument which was uncommon among German women and generally associated with men. Ziegler argued for the flute as an appropriate instrument for women on the basis of both her own love for the instrument and the example of French women:

> Those instruments which must borrow their sound and amenity from the human breath and our moved tongue are always strongly held by me in far higher esteem. They are, of course, harder for a woman to learn than the other stringed instruments; but my uncommon inclination to them and this accompanying zeal have helped to lighten the difficulty concerned and clear all hindering obstacles from the path … . If you wish to make a remark to me that this instrument is not at all proper for a lady, since it appears to be characteristic of men, then I give you the firm assurance that most of the French women—of both the upper and middle class—which have always found approval with all reason, and pass for galant and well-mannered creatures in the whole world, serve the so-called traversiere greatly … . Decide for yourself from there, and after especially long reflection, not to stop your daughter from learning this pleasant and not too common instrument, that I might obtain for myself a fellow traveler.[78]

By adopting and mastering what was considered a man's instrument, Ziegler challenged male privilege in a particular sphere, that of the flute.

In another letter to an unnamed man, Ziegler did not address as directly the role of women in music, but did assert even more firmly women's rights in the musical realm. Ziegler began the letter by emphasizing her status as an amateur musician: she did not consider herself a virtuoso, needed not support herself financially through music, and performed only for personal enjoyment and edification. But Ziegler went

---

die durch Ihren Beystand und Verstärckung meiner Concerte sich mir gefällig erwiesen." Ziegler, *Moralische und vermischte Send-Schreiben*, 395.

78 "Diejenigen Instrumenten, so von dem menschlichen Athem, und unsrer gerührten Zunge ihren Klang und Annehmlichkeit erborgen müssen, von mir allezeit in weit höhern Werth nicht unbillig gezogen worden. Sie sind freylich einem Frauenzimmer schwerer zu erlernen, als die andern Saiten-Spiele; Alleine meine ungemeine Neigung darzu und der diese begleitende Eifer hat mir die darbey besorgende Schwürigkeit erleichtern helffen, und alle hinderliche Steine aus dem Wege geräumet … . Wolten Sie mir aber einen Einwurff machen, ob schickte sich dergleichen Instrument gar nicht vor eine Dame, weil es dem männlichen Geschlechte eigenthümlich zu seyn schiene, so gebe ich Ihnen die theure Versicherung, daß die meisten von denen Frantzösichen Frauenzimmer so wohl adelichen als bürgerlichen Standes, welche doch jederzeit bey allen Rationen Beyfall gefunden, und vor galant und artige Geschöpffe in der gantzen Welt paßiren, sich der so genannten Traversiere starck bedienen … . Entschliessen Sie sich nur daher, und sonder langes Besinnen, Ihr Fräulein zu Erlernung dieses angenehmen und nicht allzugemeinen Instruments anzuhalten, damit ich an selbiger eine Mitgefehrtin bekomme." Ziegler, *Moralische und vermischte Send-Schreiben*, 407–09.

further by boldly asserting her musical opinions, including ones that differed from those of her correspondent. This is significant because the unnamed recipient of the letter is not only a man, but also a Kapellmeister. In response to some pieces of music he sent her, Ziegler wrote:

> It appears to me as if the two trios which you have enclosed were transcribed for me to enjoy on the traverso, and that before they were undoubtedly set for the oboe; yet it could be that I am mistaken. I will request this of you, that if you should again send me a package of music, that you may not trouble with the transcription, since I am of the firm opinion that a piece which is taken away from its characteristic instrument loses in the transfer a large part of its refinement. The enclosed overture combined with a fugue, which reflects a steady and true construction in nearly all voices, is very beautiful; the art here praises the master, just as do both concertos: but I would rather see how they would be set more tenderly and more cajoling, and not so seriously.[79]

Ziegler not only displayed here a profound musical understanding, but also provided musical instruction to a man who was an expert in his field. She thereby challenged, and even reversed, societal norms through writing about music.

Ziegler's salon thus provided her not only with a venue to participate in Leipzig's literary and musical cultures, but also with the opportunity to influence and control artistic taste on a local level. While contemporary accounts represented the gatherings as light-hearted affairs centered around dinner, poetry, and music, they also attested to Ziegler's central role as hostess and to her lively personality. Through Ziegler's influence, therefore, the Romanus house became a hub of intellectual life for higher Leipzig society and a place where women could be active participants in such a society. It further provided women, and particularly Ziegler, with a venue in which their opinions, their poetry, and their music could be heard.

Coronation as Poet Laureate (1733)

While Ziegler's salon continued to provide her with intellectual and artistic involvement on a local level, her renown would soon reach much further. In defending women's rights to learning and literary enterprise in the foreword to her 1728 *Versuch in gebundener Schreib-Art*, Ziegler had bemoaned the fact that learned

---

79 "Mir bedüncket, als wären die zwey Trio, so Sie mit beygelegt, mir zu Gefallen auf die Traversiere übersetzet worden, und zuvorhero ohnfehlbar auf die Hautbois gesetzt gewesen; doch kan es auch seyn, daß ich mich irre. Ich will Sie indessen ersuchen, daß, wenn Sie mir eine Compagnie von Noten-Völckern wiederum einschicken solten, Sie sich nicht mit der Ubersetzung bemühen dürfften, weil ich der sichern Meynung bin, daß einem Stücke, welches von seinen eigenthümlichen Instrumente in die Versetzung verfällt, der gröste Theil der Annehmlichkeit benommen werde. Die beygelegte Ouverture, so mit einer Fugue vergesellschafftet ist, welche beynahe von allen Stimen eine beständige und getreue Gefehrtin abgiebet, ist sehr schön; die Kunst lobet hier den Meister, dergleichen die beyden Concerten ebenfals thun: allein ich hätte lieber gesehen, wann selbige zärtlicher und schmeichelhaffter, und nicht so ernsthafft, gesetzet wären." Ziegler, *Moralische und vermischte Send-Schreiben*, 392–93.

women in German-speaking lands were not recognized as in other countries. While citing examples of how such women were honored in France and Italy, Ziegler argued that learned women should be duly praised and that a German woman could even be named poet laureate, an honor hitherto reserved exclusively for men.[80] Only five years later, Ziegler herself became the first German woman to achieve this honor: she was crowned imperial poet laureate by the philosophical faculty of the University of Wittenberg on 17 October 1733. Ziegler received the laurel wreath from the hand of Johann Gottlieb Krause, dean of Wittenberg's philosophical faculty, during a ceremony attended by members of the faculty as well as by J. C. Gottsched and other members of the Deutschen Gesellschaft.

The significance of crowning a woman poet laureate was not lost on Krause, as the diploma he presented to Ziegler makes clear. After a discourse upon the relation of poetry to philosophy (the background for the honoring of a poet by a philosophical faculty), Krause stated:

> I desire therefore, that it be known by each and every person, that I elevate and appoint the noble Frau Christiana Mariana von Ziegler, *née* Romanus, who is famed not less on account of her writings than on account of her gender, on the strength of the imperial might and authority, which I presently occupy, and in the name of my faculty, to imperial poet laureate, through the presentation of the laurel wreath and ring, and order that she be recognized by all as an imperial poet laureate.[81]

Not only did Krause praise Ziegler for her accomplishments as a woman ("who is famed no less on account of her writings than on account of her gender"), but he also defended her equal status with male poet laureates ("other poet laureates in all places"):

> I testify no less, that she has the absolute freedom to presume to all the rights, privileges, and honors to which the other poet laureates in all places have been entitled as their due under and by the law. Since we find, after further consideration in the frequently discussed fruits of her enlightened spirit, the most apt proofs of her strengths in her poetry, and that she is therefore worthy of the laurel crown and all freedoms and honors, which are associated with them.[82]

A second certificate from Krause lauds Ziegler within the context of the gender equality of all learned and honorable persons:

---

80   Ziegler, "Vorbericht" to *Versuch in gebundener Schreib-Art*, xv-xvii.

81   "Ego igitur CHRISTIANAM MARIANAM DE ZIEGLER GENTE ROMANAM Heroidem, non minus scriptorum, quam generis, celebritate illustrem, auctoritate ac potestate Imperatoria qua in præsentia fungor, nomine Ordinis mei, a me, Laureæ Coronæ impositione, Annulique traditione, Poëtriam laureatam ab omnibus salutari, ..." In Lamprecht, ed., *Sammlung ... auf die Poetische Krönung Der ... Ziegler*, 6.

82   "... atque agnosci jubeo, & potestate plena præditam esse testor, omnibus ac fingulis ornamentis, insignibus, privilegiis, prærogativis, exemptionibus, libertatibus, concessionibus, honoribus, favoribus, & indultis, utendi, fruendi, potiundi, & gaudendi, quibus ceteri Poetæ Laureati, ubivis locorum & Gymnasiorum promoti, gaudent, fruuntur, & utuntur, consuetudine, & de jure." In Lamprecht, ed., *Sammlung ... auf die Poetische Krönung Der ... Ziegler*, 6.

Glory approaches the arts, and it cannot be otherwise, than that the conferring of honor which embroiders learning and makes others beloved, must be especially advantageous to the republic. This inspires the noble disposition to emulation, and from there it applies all powers and undertakes great things which bloom to the benefit of the republic. This care is found not only with men: female hearts also have such sparks, through which they are stimulated to seek glory and to struggle for advantage. As this has been demonstrated in all times, so has it also yet newly by our faculty, since in celebratory distribution of rewards, the noble Frau Christiana Mariana von Ziegler, *née* Romanus, of Leipzig, has not refused to accept the conferred poetic laurel wreath, as a reward for her virtue and skill.[83]

Ziegler's coronation as poet laureate resulted in numerous accolades, many of which were collected by Johann Friedrich Lamprecht, a member of the Deutschen Gesellschaft, in his 1734 *Sammlung der Schriften und Gedichte welche auf die Poetische Krönung Der Hochwohlgebohrnen Frauen, Frauen Christianen Marianen von Ziegler gebohrnen Romanus, verfertiget worden.* In addition to the citations quoted above (in Latin and German), this collection contains an extensive foreword by Lamprecht and 38 poems and one essay in honor of Ziegler.

The celebratory tone of the volume was set by Lamprecht's foreword, as he lauded Ziegler's accomplishments, character, and family; described her literary endeavors; cited examples of honors she had received; recounted the details of her coronation as poet laureate; presented her as an example for women to follow; and defended her against her critics. Throughout the foreword, Lamprecht particularly praised Ziegler for her accomplishments as a woman in the field of poetry, thus continuing many of the themes of women's learning found in Ziegler's own writings.

Lamprecht's treatment of gender, however, is complex. On the one hand, he stated: "How praiseworthy this testimony, that in Germany excellence will be recognized and rewarded without respect to gender."[84] But while praising Ziegler, Lamprecht simultaneously denigrated German women as a category, characterizing them as being preoccupied with trivialities and pleasure rather than learning. Lamprecht stated about Ziegler, "It was too slight for her to stop with the worthless trivialities by which so many of her gender still constantly amuse themselves,"[85] and, in relation to her membership in the Deutschen Gesellschaft:

---

83 "Honos alit artes: neque fieri potest, quin fructuosa in primis reipublicæ sit dispensatio honorum, qui ornant doctrinam, & commendant. Incendit illa animos generosos ad laudis æmulationem, ut intendant nervos, atque ardua conentur, olim civitati profutura. Neque iam viros seorsum hæc occupat cura: femineum quoque pectus igniculos alit, atque, veniens in laudis societatem, de palma contendit. Quod cum alias, tum nuper, probavit se Ordini nostro, cum in distributione præmiorum solenni, Femina Generosissima, CHRISTIANA MARIANA DE ZIEGLER, GENTE ROMANA oriunda, patria Lipsiensis, oblatam virtuti suæ meritisque Laurum Poeticam accipere non dedignaretur." In Lamprecht, ed., *Sammlung ... auf die Poetische Krönung Der ... Ziegler*, 10.

84 "Wie ruhmwürdig bleibet dieses Zeugniß, daß auch in Dutschland Vorzüge ohne Ansehen des Geschlechts erkannt und belohnet werden!" Lamprecht, "Vorrede" to *Sammlung ... auf die Poetische Krönung Der ... Ziegler*, xiv.

85 "Es war Ihr zu wenig bey den nichtswürdigen Kleinigkeiten, womit sich noch so viele von ihrem Geschlechte beständig unterhalten, stehen zu bleiben." Lamprecht, "Vorrede" to *Sammlung ... auf die Poetische Krönung Der ... Ziegler*, iii–iv.

It was easy to draw a lady into the society of critical men, who in all of her enterprises demonstrated so much masculinity. It was easy to set her apart from that number of her sex, who either seek their entire pleasure in the judgement of their neighbors or yet amuse themselves at least with such worthless entertainments that reveal often their evil and always their weaknesses.[86]

However, while characterizing women thus, Lamprecht did not argue against women's learning. He rather promoted it, stating that women did not lack talent or ability but rather desire and training. Like Gottsched before him, Lamprecht presented Ziegler as a model for all women and called on others to follow her example:

The entire fair sex is obliged to Frau von Ziegler; yet not only for the glory which she has likewise acquired for them, but also for the undisturbed fervor with which she has blazed the trail for them to the temple of virtue and has demonstrated for them the path in which to follow. A woman who has once begun the course of virtue is generally often more steadfast in her resolution than men are … . How awakened now will not the noble courage of so many German women be, since they are encouraged by such an exceptional predecessor?[87]

The poems which comprise the bulk of Lamprecht's volume share, and expand upon, many of the themes in Lamprecht's foreword. These texts, in German, Latin, French, Italian, and Dutch, include both official poems composed for Ziegler's coronation and additional ones sent by friends and admirers to honor her accomplishment. Most are general poems in praise of Ziegler, many of them dominated by references to mythological figures associated with poetry (for example, Apollo, the Muses, and Minerva) and several attesting to the divine inspiration of Ziegler's poetry. The poems further laud Ziegler for her erudition, literary skill, goodness, and virtue, as well as for the glory she brings to Germany and Saxony. The nature of these poems is well represented in the following stanza by Christiana Rosina Spitzin of Augsburg:

---

86 "Es war billig, eine Dame in die Gesellschaft vernünftiger Männer zu ziehen, welche in allen Ihren Unternehmungen, so viel männliches merken ließ. Es war billig, Sie von derjenigen Anzahl ihres Geschlechtes zu unterscheiden, welche entweder ihr ganzes Vergnügen in frecher Beurtheilung ihres Nächsten suchet; oder sich doch wenigstens an solchen nichtswürdigen Unterhaltungen belustiget, die oft ihre Bosheit, allezeit aber ihre Schwäche verrathen." Lamprecht, "Vorrede" to *Sammlung … auf die Poetische Krönung Der … Ziegler*, viii.

87 "Das ganze schöne Geschlechte ist der Frau von Ziegler verpflichtet; doch nicht allein für die Ehre, welche Sie ihnen zugleich erworben, sondern auch für den ungestörten Eifer, mit welchem Sie Ihnen die Bahn zum Tugend=Tempel gebrochen, und Ihnen den Weg zur Nachfolge gezeigt hat. Eine Schöne, die einmal den Lauf der tugend angefangen, ist gemeiniglich standhafter in ihrer Entschliessung, als oft Männer sind … . Wie aufgeweckt wird nun nicht der edle Muth so vieler deutschen Schönen werden, da Sie eine so ausnehmende Vorgängerin ermuntert?" Lamprecht, "Vorrede" to *Sammlung … auf die Poetische Krönung Der … Ziegler*, xvi.

Sie griff nach Kiel und Blatt mit unermüdtem Fleiß:	She grips the quill and page with untiring diligence:
Ihr edler Geist ist selbst vom Himmel ausgeheitert:	Her noble spirit has itself been illumined from heaven:
Sie bleibet Sachsens Ruh, und Deutschlands hoher Preis.	She remains Saxony's glory and Germany's high prize,
Weil sich ihr Geist und Glanz in aller welt erweitert.	Since her spirit and splendor have extended into all the world.
Deswegen hat man sie mit allem Recht gekrönet,	Therefore, one has with every right crowned her,
Weil ihre Grosmuth sich was kluges angewöhnet.	Since her generosity has taken to something wise.[88]

As in Lamprecht's foreword, issues of gender are prevalent throughout the poems. Many of the authors praised Ziegler for exceeding the normal limitations of her gender, honoring her for her "masculine understanding" and for equaling and even exceeding men's writings.[89] In his essay "Pretende dimonstrare, che le femine sono piu habili per la poesia che gli uomini" ("To demonstrate that women are more naturally disposed to poetry than men"), Augusto di Klüx echoed many of the thoughts found in Ziegler's own writings. He stated that reason, will, and the senses were given by God and nature to all humans, regardless of gender; that women naturally spoke better than men and therefore had a better foundation for poetry; and that women's more delicate spirit and more passionate nature was more inclined to poetic expression.[90]

But, like Lamprecht, many of the authors lamented women's general disdain for learning and thus presented women in a negative light. Christina Rosina Spitzin stated that women were for the most part inclined to seek vanity and finery: "Jewelry is loved by them; books are hated."[91] And the anonymous L. F. J. testified of Ziegler:

Die Zeit, da sich die Weiber schminken,	The time when women make themselves up,
Und in den offnen Fenstern winken,	And wave through the open windows,
Hast du mit Lesen zugebracht.	You have spent with reading.
Die Kunst den Nächsten zu verlästern,	The art of abandoning your neighbors,
Die ganze Klugheit dummer Schwestern,	The whole wisdom of stupid sisters,
Hat deinen Geist noch nie gerührt.	Has never touched your spirit.
Die Eitelkeit bethörter Sinnen,	The vanity of foolish ideas,
Durch Stolz den Vorzug zu gewinnen,	To win the privilege through pride,
Hat andre wohl, dich nie verführt.	Has tempted others, but never you.[92]

---

88 Spitzin, "Das weibliche Geschlecht ist mehrentheils geneigt," in Lamprecht, ed., *Sammlung ... auf die Poetische Krönung Der ... Ziegler*, 41.

89 See, for example, Anna Helena Volkmann, "Berühmte Zieglerin! Vollkommnes Tugendbild," in Lamprecht, ed., *Sammlung ... auf die Poetische Krönung Der ... Ziegler*, 37–40.

90 In Lamprecht, ed., *Sammlung ... auf die Poetische Krönung Der ... Ziegler*, 55–60.

91 "Dem Schmuck ist ihnen lieb; die Bücher sind verhaßt." In Lamprecht, ed., *Sammlung ... auf die Poetische Krönung Der ... Ziegler*, 40.

92 In Lamprecht, ed., *Sammlung ... auf die Poetische Krönung Der ... Ziegler*, 85.

In addition to praising Ziegler for exceeding others of her gender, the authors also promoted Ziegler as an example of learning and virtue and hoped that she would inspire other women as well. Johann Joachim Schwabe called on women to better themselves by learning from Ziegler's example, and also invoked the Muses to inspire female poets:

Ja, Musen, auf! vermehrt den Fleiß,	Arise, Muses! increase the diligence,
Vermehrt den Witz, bey denen die euch gleichen;	Increase the wit, by which they become like you;
Befördert euren eignen Preis	Promote your suitable prize
Und laßt ein schönes Volk nicht mehr im finstern schleiche.	And allow a fair people no more to creep around in darkness.
Es hat ja Kraft und Fähigkeit	It truly has strength and talent:
Bringt solches nur auch zur Vollkommenheit	Only bring such also to perfection
Und laßt uns manche Frucht von dessen Geiste lesen.	And allow us to read many a fruit from these spirits.[93]

Ziegler was further seen as liberating women from pursuing only household occupations. Schwabe stated that even if women had merely been born to cook, it could not continue to be so after Ziegler's accomplishments:

Die Frauen wären nur zum Küchendienst gebohren.	"Women were only born for cooking service."
In Zukunft kan noch mehr geschehn;	In the future this can no longer be;
Wenn andre scharf auf dieses Beyspiel sehn.	When others clearly see this example.[94]

And Jacob Stählin censured those who would attack Ziegler, stating that their criticism resulted from her exceeding the prescribed limits of her gender: "If you knew merely cooking, bed, and needle, there would be no rebuke."[95] An anonymous contributor (A. W. v. S.) argued that Ziegler's coronation had determined conclusively that women were worthy of academic distinction:

Endlich wird der Wahn doch fallen:	Finally the delusion will now fall:
Daß der Wissenschaften Ruhm,	That the academic glory
Als der Männer Eigenthum,	As the property of men
Diesen nur allein gebühre.	Is due to them alone.
Und nicht auch die Schönen ziere.	And does not also adorn the fair ones.
Edle Zieglerin! dein Werth,	Noble Ziegler! your merit,
Dessen Lob schon längst erklungen,	Whose praise has already long been heard,
Hat den Satz durch sich erklärt,	Has cleared up this matter,
Und dieß Vorurtheil bezwungen.	And conquered this prejudice.[96]

---

93   In Lamprecht, ed., *Sammlung ... auf die Poetische Krönung Der ... Ziegler*, 77.

94   In Lamprecht, ed., *Sammlung ... auf die Poetische Krönung Der ... Ziegler*, 71.

95   "Kenntest du bloß Küche, Bett und Nadel; / Wäre kein Tadel." In Lamprecht, ed., *Sammlung ... auf die Poetische Krönung Der ... Ziegler*, 80.

96   In Lamprecht, ed., *Sammlung ... auf die Poetische Krönung Der ... Ziegler*, 46.

In praising Ziegler as a female poet, many of the authors in Lamprecht's volume, including Lamprecht himself, aimed to shield Ziegler from criticism. Lamprecht concluded his foreword by addressing would-be critics. He censured those who would attack Ziegler for her newly-achieved glory and stated that Ziegler had every right to the praise she had received.[97] Christoph Dietrich von Böhlau's "Fliehe nur, beschämter Neid" likewise addressed Ziegler's critics, stating that praise should be on the basis of merit, not gender:

Schnöde Thorheit! Selbstbetrug!	Disdainful foolishness! Self-deception!
Toller Schluß! Verworfner Glaube!	Mad conclusion! Confused belief!
Raast die Weisheit in der Haube?	Does wisdom race in the hood?
Macht der Hut die Tummheit klug?	Does the cap make stupidity intelligent?
Wann ein Mann nach bangem Schwitzen	When a man after anxious sweat
Nichts als Misgeburthen bringt,	Brings nothing other than miscarriages,
Und ein Weib bey Rahm und Spitzen	And a woman with cream and lace
Lieblicher als Naso singt,	Sings lovelier than Naso,
Welches Haupt von diesen zweyen,	Which head of these two,
Sollte wohl der Kranz erfreuen?	Should well enjoy the crown?
O verschanzt doch nicht durch Hohn,	O entrenched, yet not through derision,
Um in diesen schönen Kindern	In order in these lovely children
Trieb und Feuer zu verhindern,	To hinder the impulse and fire
Den bestiegnen Helikon!	Of the ascending Helicon!
Glaubt, durch Gift und bittres Scherzen	Believe, that through venom and bitter jokes
Wird das Feuer nicht verstopft,	The fire will not be stopped,
Das in kluger Frauen Herzen,	That beats in intelligent women's hearts—
Oefters mehr als männlich, klopft.	Often more than in masculine ones.
Glut und Absicht grosser Geister	Ardor and intent of great spirits
Wird der Hindernisse Meister.	Will be master of the obstacles.[98]

Ziegler and Her Critics

Despite these efforts to stave off criticism, Ziegler was subjected to a series of attacks after her coronation as poet laureate. In 1734, two anonymous texts circulated, parodies of her coronation which went as far as accusing her of seducing university students. While four Leipzig students were charged for this slander, they claimed that the texts came from Halle. The students appealed to Dresden and were cleared of responsibility. Ironically, the Dresden court instead stated that because of the evil results stemming from reactions to Ziegler's coronation, the Universities of Wittenberg and Leipzig should not grant such high honors without conferring with Dresden first.[99]

---

97 Lamprecht, "Vorrede" to *Sammlung ... auf die Poetische Krönung Der ... Ziegler*, xvi–xix.

98 In Lamprecht, ed., *Sammlung ... auf die Poetische Krönung Der ... Ziegler*, 51–52.

99 Goodman, *Amazons and Apprentices*, 169–71. See also Philipp Spitta, "Sperontes' 'Singende Muse an der Pleiße': Zur Geschichte des deutschen Hausgesanges im achtzehnten

Another anonymous criticism of Ziegler was the song "Ihr Schönen, höret an," published in Sperontes's *Singende Muse an der Pleisse* in Leipzig in 1736 but likely circulated as a broadside before this. The text of "Ihr Schönen, höret an," a satire on women who aspired to learning, appeared in the volume's appendix labeled as coming from the poetry of Johann Christian Günther. The text, however, does not appear in Günther's works, and Philipp Spitta speculates that Sperontes himself (Leipzig resident Johann Sigismund Scholze) was its author.[100]

"Ihr Schönen, höret an" mocks women who aspire to learning by envisioning a university at which women enroll. The first stanza reflects well the nature of the satire:

Ihr Schönen höret an,	Pay attention, you fair ones,
Erwählet das *Studiren*,	Choose the academic life,
Kommt her, ich will euch führen,	Come here: I will lead you
Zu der Gelehrten Bahn,	To the path of the learned:
Ihr Schönen höret an,	Pay attention, you fair ones.
Ihr *Universitäten*,	You universities,
Ihr werdet zwar erröten,	You will truly blush
Wenn *Doris* disputiert,	When *Doris* disputes
Und *Amor* praesidiert,	And *Amor* presides.
Wenn art'ge *Professores*,	When well-mannered professors,
Charmante Auditores,	And charming auditors,
Verdunkeln euren Schein,	Darken your reputation,
Gebt euch geduldig drein.	Behave patiently in this respect.[101]

The song continues its harsh treatment of women: not only does the second stanza disparage the morals of learned women, but the third also states that the primary topics at this university are gallantry and love. The poem culminates with an imagined day at such a university followed by concluding thoughts after graduation:

Theilt hübsch die Stunden ein,	Judiciously divide the hours:
Um neun Uhr seid beflissen,	At 9:00 diligently study
Wie art'ge Kinder müssen,	How well-behaved children must be
Galant und häuslich seyn,	*Galant* and domestic:
Theilt hübsch die Stunden ein.	Judiciously divide the hours.
Um zehn Uhr lernt mit Blicken,	At 10:00 learn with glances
Ein freies Hertz bestricken,	How to captivate an unattached heart,
Um ein Uhr *musiziert*,	At 1:00 make music,
Um zwey *poetisiert*,	At 2:00 write poetry,
Um drey Uhr lernt in Briefen,	At 3:00 learn to engross
Ein wenig euch vertiefen,	Yourselves a bit in letters,
Denn höret von der Eh',	Then hear about marriage,
Hernach so trinkt *Coffée*.	Afterwards, drink coffee.

Jahrhundert," in *Musikgeschichtliche Aufsätze* (Berlin, 1894; reprint, Hildesheim, 1976), 248–58.

100 Spitta, "Sperontes' 'Singende Muse an der Pleiße'," 248.
101 Qtd. in Spitta, "Sperontes' 'Singende Muse an der Pleiße'," 248–49.

Kontiniuiert drei Jahr,	Continue three years,
Denn könnt ihr *promovieren*	Then you can graduate
Und andere *dozieren*,	And teach others,
O schöne Musen-Schar,	Oh fair crowd of Muses:
Kontiniuiert drei Jahr.	Continue three years.
Ich sterbe vor Vergnügen,	I will die for pleasure
Wenn ihr an statt der Wiegen,	When, rather than cradles,
Euch den *Katheder* wählt,	You choose the lectern,
Statt Kinder Bücher zählt,	Instead of counting children, books;
Ich küßt euch Rock und Hände,	I kiss your skirt and hands,
Wenn man euch *Doctor* nännte,	When one calls you "Doctor,"
Drum, Schönste, fangt doch an,	Then, fair ones, you should begin
Kommt zur Gelehrten Bahn.	To tread the path of the learned.[102]

"Ihr Schönen, höret an" was a more subtle attack than the earlier parody on Ziegler's coronation, and it did not mention Ziegler by name. However, given Ziegler's defense of women's rights to education, her recent association with the University of Wittenberg through her coronation as poet laureate, and the volume's publication in Leipzig, it seems likely that the song was aimed at her. The message of the song was clear: women had no place in the realm of learning.

Despite this and other attacks by critics, none of which actually discussed the quality or content of her writings, Ziegler appears to have been relatively unaffected by negative criticism or slander. She became increasingly less concerned with critical responses to her works, as evidenced by her comments in the foreword to her 1735 translation of Madeleine de Scudéry's *Scharffsinnige Unterredungen, von Dingen, Die zu einer wohlanständigen Aufführung gehöregn*. Rather than concluding with an appeal for critics to not judge her work too harshly, as she had in her three previous books, Ziegler stated instead that she was not concerned about critical response:

> The manifold unashamed attacks have given me the advantage, that I yield no step to all evil and perfidious methods; in short, my enviers and enemies are in no position to wound and anger me in the least. That wise man has likewise written the rule before me: "No one is able to insult a wise person."[103]

Ziegler's energetic and aggressive spirit was evident when she responded in kind to "Ihr Schönen, höret an" with a song of her own. "Das männliche Geschlechte, im Namen einiger Frauenzimmer besungen" may also have been distributed as a broadside, and Ziegler later published it in her 1739 *Vermischete Schriften*, a compendium of her writings from the previous decade.[104] Ziegler began the song with an introductory stanza: she stated that she would sing in praise of men, but that it would sound quite different from those songs coming from men themselves:

---

102 Qtd. in Spitta, "Sperontes' 'Singende Muse an der Pleiße'," 249–50.

103 "Die vielfältigen unverschämten Schmähungen haben mir den Vortheil gegeben, daß ich allem boshaften und niederträchtigen Verfahren keinen Schritt weiche; kurz, meine Neider und Feinde sind nicht im Stande, mich im geringsten zu kränken und aufzubringen. Jener Weise hat vor mich ebenfalls die Regel geschrieben: Ein Weiser könne niemals beleidiget werden." Ziegler, "Vorrede" to *Scharffsinnige Unterredungen* (Leipzig, 1735), xiv.

104 Ziegler, *Vermischete Schriften*, 67–71.

Du Weltgepriesenes Geschlechte,	You highly praised sex,
Du in dich selbst verliebte Schaar,	You crowd of those who love yourselves,
Prahlst allzusehr mit deinem Rechte,	Boast all too much about your right,
Das Adams erster Vorzug war.	That Adam's was the first priority.
Doch soll ich deinen Werth besingen,	Yet if I should praise the worth
Der dir auch wirklich zugehört;	That really belongs to you;
So wird mein Lied ganz anders klingen,	Then my song will sound wholly different,
Als das, womit man dich verehrt.	Than the one by which you are honored.

While Ziegler's poetry was often lighthearted in its nature, reflecting her jocular temperament, this song is quite harsh in its content. In its 14 stanzas, Ziegler attacked men for narcissism, arrogance, rage, jealousy, infidelity, neglect, lust, rudeness, drunkenness, greed, and vain ambition. In response to "Ihr Schönen, höret an," Ziegler particularly attacked men's learning. In stanza 2, she stated that men needed to borrow women's intelligence, and in stanza 11:

Die, welche sich nur selbst erheben,	Those who only exalt themselves,
Die gerne groß und vornehm sind,	Who would gladly be great and noble,
Nach allen Ehrenämtern streben,	Striving after all honorary positions,
Da doch den Kopf nichts füllt als Wind:	But whose heads are filled with nothing but wind:
Die keine Wissenschaften kennen,	Who know not science,
Und dringen sich in Würden ein,	And force titles on themselves,
Die kann man wohl mit Namen nennen,	They one can well call by name,
Daß sie der Thorheit Kinder seyn.	As the children of foolishness.

After this criticism of men's supposed learning, Ziegler asserted the equality of women with men in stanza 12. She concluded by arguing for an opposite state of affairs from the one society enforced. Instead of silencing women, men should instead silence themselves:

Der Mann muß seine Frau ernähren,	The man must support his wife,
Die Kinder, und das Hausgesind.	The children, and the household.
Er dient der Welt mit weisen Lehren,	He serves the world with wise teachings,
So, wie sie vorgeschrieben sind.	Just as they are dictated.
Das Weib darf seinen Witz nicht zeigen:	The wife may not display her wit:
Die Vorsicht hat es ausgedacht,	Caution has devised it,
Es soll in der Gemeine schweigen,	She should be silent in company,
Sonst würdet ihr oft ausgelacht.	Otherwise you would be often laughed at.
Ihr klugen Männer schweigt nur stille:	You clever men, just be silent:
Entdecket unsre Fehler nicht.	Do not discover our failures.
Denn es ist selbst nicht unser Wille,	Since it is not our will,
Daß euch die Schwachheit wiederspricht.	That weakness speaks against you.
Trag eines nur des andern Mängel,	Only bear one another's faults,
So habt ihr schon genug gethan,	Then you have already done enough,
Denn Menschen sind fürwahr nicht Engel,	For humans are truly not angels,
An denen man nichts tadeln kann.	About whom one can criticize nothing.

Far from shrinking back in the face of negative criticism, Ziegler asserted her rights to literary expression, defended all women's rights to learning and publication, and attacked men instead for their shortcomings. The culmination of Ziegler's defense of women's rights, including the reprint of her ode "Das männliche Geschlecht," came with her final original publication, the *Vermischete Schriften* of 1739.

Vermischete Schriften in gebundener und ungebundener Rede (1739)

Although apparently prepared for publication in 1737, Ziegler's *Vermischete Schriften in gebundener und ungebundener Rede* appeared in Göttingen in 1739.[105] The *Vermischete Schriften* was a compendium of Ziegler's poetry and prose written throughout the 1730s, and it included many pieces published in various venues throughout the decade. The most substantial of Ziegler's four published volumes, it contains 118 poems, 34 prose selections, and three translations. The *Vermischete Schriften* also displays Ziegler's ongoing focus on themes which had been central to her earlier writings, including the proper use of the German language in speech and writing, the importance of pure conversation and correct behavior in polite society, and the rights of women to education and literary enterprise.

As in her 1735 Scudéry translation, Ziegler was increasingly disinterested in critical response to her works. Her 1739 foreword is of a rather different nature from those in her earlier publications, very brief in comparison and containing none of the appeals to critics which characterized her other volumes. Rather than arguing in favor of a woman's right of authorship, Ziegler simply stated her right to publish because of her status as an observer of the world's events. She wrote on the basis of common human experience rather than of gender and thus dismissed any criticism of female authors as irrelevant: all humans have equal right to literary enterprise.[106] And if Ziegler had sought to mollify her critics in 1729 by publishing primarily sacred poetry, considered more appropriate for a woman, such an intention was wholly lacking in 1739. The *Vermischete Schriften* treats only secular themes.

Furthermore, among the many topics found in the *Vermischete Schriften*, that of women's rights was still prominent. Ziegler included a number of significant texts on this theme from the previous decade, including her two speeches presented before the Deutschen Gesellschaft, "Antrittsrede in der Deutschen Gesellschaft zu Leipzig, abgelesen" (381–89) and "Abhandlung, ob es dem Frauenzimmer erlaubet sey, sich nach Wissenschaften zu bestreben" (394–99), which defended women's literary enterprise and learning. And, if anything, Ziegler increased her vehemence on behalf of women. As we have seen, her ode "Das männliche Geschlechte, im Namen einiger Frauenzimmer besungen" (67–71) criticized men for their own failings and thus called on them to cease from maligning women. Ziegler's cantata "Die Männer

---

105 Johann David Köhler in 1737 refered to the *Vermischete Schriften* as being currently "unter der Presse" and cited three selections from this publication. "Gedächtnüs-Müntze, auf die Poetische Krönung der vortrefflichen Frauen Christianen Marianen von Ziegler/gebohrnen Romanus, in Leipzig," *Historischer Münz-Belustigung* 9 (1737): 140.

106 Ziegler, "Vorrede" to *Vermischete Schriften*, vii–viii.

sagen uns wohl immer" (319–20) further attacked men's faults, citing their infidelity, deception, bragging, flattery, seduction, and hypocrisy.

Aria.

Die Männer sagen uns wohl immer,	The men say to us quite constantly
Nichts sey so schlimm als Frauenzimmer;	That nothing is as bad as a woman;
Allein sie kennen sich noch nicht.	But they do not yet know themselves.
Ihr Trotzen, Pralen, Trügen, Heucheln	Their defiances, braggings, deceptions, hypocrisies
Verführen, und mit Worten schmeicheln,	Seduce and flatter with words,
Führt oft die klügste hinters Licht.	Leading often the most sensible away from the light.
Ihr wollt in allem zwar	You truly wish in all things
Gesetzt und hoch vernünftig seyn;	To be sedate and highly sensible;
Allein	However
Erweg ich euren Wankelmuth,	I consider your fickleness,
Was der aus Uebereilung thut,	What you do out of haste,
So müst ihr euch gar oft bequemen	Thus you must often deign
Euch vor euch selbst zu schämen.	To be ashamed of yourselves.
Ihr Näscher denkt nur nach:	Your nibbling only thinks about:
Was könnt ihr nicht ersinnen,	What could you not contemplate
Des Frauenzimmers Gunst	Of women's favor
Leicht zu gewinnen?	Easily to gain?

Aria.

Bald liebt ihr eure Schäfer Magd	Quickly you love your shepherd maid
Wenn euch der Liebeskützel plagt;	When the love pangs torment you;
Bald sehnt ihr euch nach andern Frauen.	Quickly you long after other women.
Der Henker hat das Ding erdacht,	The executioner has thought of the thing,
Daß ihr den Mädchens Nasen macht;	To make you an attraction to the maidens;
Kein Frauenzimmer sollt euch trauen.	No woman shall mourn over you.
Man fraget, das ist wahr,	One asks whether this is true,
Und noch dazu ganz offenbar:	And yet it seems to be entirely evident:
Ist noch ein weiser Mann in eurem Orden?	Is there yet a wise man in your order?
Weil unser Frauenvolk so oft betrogen worden.	Since we women are so often deceived.
Ja, wo sie künftighin so zärtlich sind.	Yes, where they are in the future so tender.
So ist das weibliche Geschlechte,	Thus is the female sex—
Und das mit gröstem Fug und Rechte,	And that most rightly so—
Von herzens Grunde blind.	Blind to the motives of the heart.

Aria.

Plagen, Sorgen, und Verdruß	Troubles, cares, and annoyances
Hat man bey euch im Ueberfluß.	One has with you in abundance.
Ihr könnt euch zwar wie Engel stellen;	You could set yourselves up as angels;
Allein ihr reines Wesen fehlt,	But your pure disposition fails:

So bald ihr uns das Herze stehlt,	As quickly as you steal our heart,
Sucht ihr uns auch zugleich zu fällen.	You seek even at the same time to cut us down.

Despite all the attacks she had suffered throughout the 1730s, Ziegler had the last word in her debate with the critics by publishing this final, substantial volume with no concessions to their opinions. The *Vermischete Schriften*, in addition to representing the culmination of her literary work in the previous decade, marked a triumph for Ziegler through her continued involvement in public discourse despite the critics who sought to silence her.

Remarriage and Later Life (1741–60)

Despite such a noteworthy publication in 1739 and the fact that she lived for two more decades, Ziegler's *Vermischete Schriften* was her last volume of orginal work. Her only publication in the final years of her life was her translation from the French of Abte Trublet's *Gedanken über verschiedene Sachen, welche zur Gelehrsamkeit und Sittenlehre gehören* (Griefswald and Leipzig, 1744), the completion of an earlier project (it had been announced as forthcoming in Leipzig in 1738).

While Ziegler stated in her foreword that a number of circumstances had deterred her from completing the volume earlier, she did imply that one of these was her recent marriage. After living as an aristocratic widow in Leipzig for the previous two decades, Ziegler instead became the wife of a professor in Frankfurt an der Oder. On 19 September 1741, Ziegler married Wolf Balthasar Adolf von Steinwehr (1704–71), a fellow member of the Deutschen Gesellschaft who had been serving as professor at the newly established University of Göttingen. Upon their marriage, the couple moved to Frankfurt an der Oder, where Steinwehr had been appointed Royal Prussian Court Counselor, professor of history and natural law, and university librarian. While no longer publishing her own work (with the exception of the Trublet translation), it is likely that Ziegler assisted Steinwehr in a number of French translations which he published in the 1740s and 1750s, including *Der Frau Marquisin von Chastellet Naturlehre an ihren Sohn* (1743); several volumes of essays on physics, chemistry, and botany published by the Royal Academy of Sciences in Paris; and an excerpt from Rousseau's *La nouvelle Heloise* (1762).[107] In addition, it is likely that Ziegler was involved with Steinwehr's establishment of a Deutsche Gesellschaft in Frankfurt an der Oder, founded on 20 December 1743 and apparently continuing until 1760, the year of Ziegler's death. While no documentation of Ziegler's involvement in the society exists, what we know of her participation in Leipzig's Deutschen Gesellschaft makes it difficult to imagine her not being actively involved in a similar society founded by her husband in Frankfurt.[108]

It appears odd to us today that Ziegler should spend her final years in literary silence, or at least anonymity, particularly after her monumental *Vermischete*

---

107 Goodman, *Amazons and Apprentices*, 268.

108 Ralf-Rüdiger Targiel, "Zum 300. Geburtstag von Wolf Balthasar Adolph von Steinwehr," *Uni on* 44 (2004): 23.

Schriften. Given the lack of evidence or explanation from Ziegler herself, we can only speculate as to the reasons for this. Perhaps, as Katherine Goodman suggests throughout her *Amazons and Apprentices*, the weight of harsh criticism did come to bear upon Ziegler. While such an explanation would certainly be understandable, we see no evidence of this in Ziegler's writings, and her treatment of her critics in the *Vermischete Schriften* seems to argue against it.

In the end, Ziegler seems to have been more discouraged by the lack of progress she saw in women's writing than she was by criticism from men. In the foreword to her Trublet translation, Ziegler did not address her male critics but rather her female counterparts. While Ziegler had bemoaned women's proclivity for vain pursuits in some of her earlier writings, she here went further in criticizing women who would write without having the proper education and lamenting that women did not work diligently in improving their education. She merely hoped that by reading good books, such as this one, women would improve their learning and their writing. While Ziegler did not fault women for the fact that they were not educated in their youth, her discouragement, even disillusionment, with the state of women's writing and education is evident:

> Few [women] desire to write something, and perhaps it is good that it is few. One who wishes to write must keep his thoughts aligned with one another; one who wishes to deal with it often thinks about it and does not allow himself to be disrupted by sensual amusements. Few of our sex could get used to such work and patience … . They laugh when anyone would doubt that they could not also, like others, involve themselves in book writing. But at the same time, they forget that it is necessary to have learned the fundamentals of spelling in order to write syllables and words. I think with grief about how lamentably the quills of many of our women would be led.[109]

Ziegler hoped this volume would encourage women to pursue learning in adulthood. And while thus addressing women, Ziegler at least concluded with men and women on equal footing. She censured both men and women who did not speak German properly and stated her hope that both sexes would pursue the reading of good books in order to improve their speaking and writing, as well as their profundity of thought. In Ziegler's estimation, men and women were equally in need of such improvements as Trublet set forth in this volume.[110]

---

109 "Wenige darunter wollen etwas schreiben, und vielleicht ist es gut, daß es wenige wollen. Wer schreiben will, muß seine Gedanken wohl bey einander behalten; dasjenige, wovon es handeln will, ofte überdenken, und sich durch keine sinnliche Ergötzlichkeiten stören lassen. Wenige unsers Geschlechts können sich zu solcher Arbeit und Geduld gewöhnen … . Sie lachen, wenn jemand zweifeln wollte, sie könnten nicht auch, gleich andern, sich mit Bücherschreiben einlassen. Sie vergessen aber dabey, daß das Buchstabieren aus dem Grunde gelernet zu haben, auch nur zum Sylben= und Wörter schreiben nothwendig ist. Daran gedenke ich mit Kummer, wie kläglich die Federn vieler unsers Frauenzimmer geführt werden." Ziegler, "Vorrede" to *Gedanken über verschiedene Sachen*, ii–iv.

110 Ziegler, "Vorrede" to *Gedanken über verschiedene Sachen*, iv–vi.

Conclusion

Whether granted the highest honor of poet laureate or harshly derided by her critics, Ziegler remained in the public eye as a significant female poet for over a decade. In her writings, Ziegler repeatedly called for women to be granted the right of a public voice, and she was herself a fulfillment of that call. But with Ziegler's essential departure from the public forum after her 1739 *Vermischete Schriften*, women's literature in Germany lost its chief advocate. Although Luise Gottsched (*née* Kulmus, 1713–62), Germany's most erudite woman, continued to labor until her death in 1762, she discouraged other women from venturing into the field of literature and published most of her own works either anonymously or under the name of her husband, Johann Christoph Gottsched (they had married in 1735). Despite her husband's urgings, Luise Gottsched did not approve of Ziegler's public role as a female poet and rejected such a role for herself. She thought it presumptuous that Ziegler published under her own name, did not approve of Ziegler being a member of the Deutschen Gesellschaft, refused to become a member of the society herself, and disapproved of Ziegler's coronation as poet laureate. Despite their proximity in Leipzig and the importance of each for women's literature, Luise Gottsched and Ziegler were fundamentally at odds in their conception of women's learning and writing.

The course of German women's literature during this time could have been very different had it not been for the untimely death of Ziegler's most ardent follower, Sidonia Hedwig Zäunemann (1714–40). Like Ziegler, Zäunemann strongly defended women's rights to learning and literary enterprise and, even more than Ziegler, purposely invaded the world of men. Zäunemann spurned marriage, pursued philosophy and science, wrote about heroism and the soldier's life, and rejected men's claims to be sole arbiters on literature and art.[111] She published two substantial literary works, her *Poetische Rosen in Knospen* of 1738 and *Die von denen Faunen gepeitschte Laster* of 1739, a verse satire of contemporary German society which ridiculed the subordination of women in general and women artists in particular.[112]

It is clear from her writings that Zäunemann knew and admired Ziegler's work. Zäunemann's assertions of women's intellectual abilities and her defenses of women's poetry clearly rely on Ziegler's ideas, and Zäunemann cited Ziegler as an inspiration in her poem "Ihr Vorbild hat mein Blut erhitzt."[113] Like Ziegler, Zäunemann embraced her role as a woman in the public realm, publishing her works under her own name and, like Ziegler, being crowned as poet laureate, an honor which she received from the University of Göttingen in 1738. However, Zäunemann's promising future was cut short by her unfortunate death by drowning at the age of 27.

With Zäunemann's death, Ziegler's retirement, and Luise Gottsched's rejection of a public role, no well-known public figure in Germany remained to defend female

---

111 John L. Flood, "Sidonia Hedwig Zäunemann," in *Encyclopedia of German Literature*, ed. Matthias Konzett, Vol. 2 (Chicago, 2000), 1026–27 and Jutta Tragnitz, "Sidonia Hedwig Zäunemann," in *The Feminist Encyclopedia of German Literature*, 581–82. See also E. Einert, "Eine vergessene Dichterin," in *Aus den Papieren eines Rathauses*, 183–96 (Arnstadt, 1892).

112 Sidonia Hedwig Zäunemann, *Poetische Rosen in Knospen* (Erfurt, 1738) and *Die von denen Faunen gepeitschte Laster* (Frankfurt and Leipzig, 1739).

113 Zäunemann, *Poetische Rosen in Knospen*, 635.

authorship and learning and to give an example of an erudite woman. While German literature of the mid-eighteenth century was filled with literary images of women (often in the form of an abstract, unattainable ideal), female writers themselves were conspicuously absent. It was not until the final decades of the century, with such poets as Anna Louisa Karsch (1722–91) and Sophie von La Roche (1731–1807), that female authors once again gained prominence and Ziegler's efforts for the promotion of women's rights to learning and literature began to bear greater fruit.

Chapter 2

Anonymous Voice: Mariane von Ziegler's Sacred Cantata Texts

With only few exceptions, the life of women in early eighteenth-century Germany was one of silence. Society allowed women little opportunity for public expression, as public life remained the exclusive domain of men. And the church was no exception to this state of affairs. Drawing upon the teachings of Martin Luther, the eighteenth-century German church allowed women no speaking role in the worship service. While Luther himself held women in higher esteem than his followers generally did, he still did not allow them to speak in church. In his 1532 letter "Von den Schleichern und Winkelpredigern" ("Infiltrating and Clandestine Preachers"), Luther presented several examples of women prophesying in the Old Testament, including Deborah, Huldah, Sarah, and Hannah. However, he went on to state:

> But in the New Testament the Holy Spirit, speaking through St. Paul, ordained that women should be silent in the churches and assemblies, and said that this is the Lord's commandment. Yet he knew that previously Joel had proclaimed that God would pour out his Spirit also on handmaidens. Furthermore, the four daughters of Philip prophesied. But in the congregations or churches where there is a ministry women are to be silent and not preach. Otherwise they may pray, sing, praise, and say "Amen," and read at home, teach each other, exhort, comfort, and interpret the scriptures as best they can.[1]

In Leipzig, however, one of the most orthodox of Lutheran cities, Mariane von Ziegler overcame this stricture in a unique way. Ziegler "spoke" in the Leipzig churches in 1725 through her liturgical cantata texts set to music by town cantor, Johann Sebastian Bach. While Ziegler herself was not speaking verbally, her own poetic expositions of the Gospel texts were proclaimed in music on the nine Sundays and feast days from Jubilate to Trinity Sunday of 1725 (listed in Table 2.1; see Appendix B for complete texts and translations of the nine cantatas). Furthermore, Ziegler's words were available in print for members of the congregation: the importance of the cantata and its text in Leipzig had led to the practice of printing text booklets for the sake of the congregation's attention to the text. In describing this practice in 1717, Christoph Ernst Sicul stated:

---

1 Martin Luther, "Ein Brief D. Mart. Luthers Von den Schleichern und Winkelpredigern, 1532," in *D. Martin Luthers Wercke*, Vol. 30, 510–27 (Weimar, 1910). English translation as "Infiltrating and Clandestine Preachers, 1532," in *Luther's Works*, American Edition, vol. 40, trans. and ed. Conrad Bergendoff, 379–94 (Philadelphia, 1958), 390–91.

Figure 2.1   Title page to Christiane Mariane von Ziegler, *Versuch in gebundener Schreib-Art* (1728). Herzog August Bibliothek Wolfenbüttel (Lo 8318).

So that this polyphonic music, especially on high festivals, may be heard with the greater devotion, it has become custom for some time for the honorable cantor to have the texts of the music printed beforehand ... under the title *Kirchen-Music*, so that everyone can provide himself with these and read along.[2]

Given the mandates against women's public involvement in the worship service, it is truly remarkable that Ziegler was allowed such proclamation in Leipzig's services both in song and in print.

Table 2.1   J. S. Bach's cantatas to texts by Mariane von Ziegler

Date (1725)	Liturgical occasion	Gospel	BWV	Title
22 April	Jubilate	John 16:16–23	103	*Ihr werdet weinen und heulen*
29 April	Kantate	John 16:5–15	108	*Es ist euch gut, daß ich hingehe*
6 May	Rogate	John 16:23–30	87	*Bisher habt ihr nichts gebeten*
10 May	Ascension	Mark 16:14–20	128	*Auf Christi Himmelfahrt allein*
13 May	Exaudi	John 15:26–16:4	183	*Sie werden euch in den Bann tun*
20 May	Pentecost Sunday	John 14:23–31	74	*Wer mich liebet, der wird mein Wort halten*
21 May	Pentecost Monday	John 3:16–21	68	*Also hat Gott die Welt geliebt*
22 May	Pentecost Tuesday	John 10:1–11	175	*Er rufet seinen Schafen mit Namen*
27 May	Trinity Sunday	John 3:1–15	176	*Es ist ein trotzig und verzagt Ding*

After exploring Ziegler's unique position as a female cantata librettist for the Lutheran church in the early eighteenth century, I will examine in this chapter Ziegler's distinctive approach to the liturgical cantata as a genre. Drawing upon examples from Ziegler's cantata texts set by Bach, I describe Ziegler's treatment of the assigned Gospel text, the theological nature of her libretti, the poetic qualities of

---

2   Christoph Ernst Sicul, *Neo annali Lipsiensium Continuatio II: Oder des mit 1715ten Jahre Neuangegangenen Leipziger Jahrbuchs Dritte Probe* (Leipzig, 1717), 570; qtd. in Günther Stiller, *Johann Sebastian Bach and Liturgical Life in Leipzig*, trans. Herbert J. A. Bouman, Daniel F. Poellot, and Hilton C. Oswald, ed. Robin A. Leaver (St. Louis, 1984), 121–22.

See also Martin Petzoldt, *Texthefte zur Kirchenmusik aus Bachs Leipziger Zeit* (Stuttgart, 2000) for an introduction to the text booklets and for facsimiles of the extant booklets from Bach's tenure in Leipzig.

her texts, and her focus on themes of speech and silence. I then note an important shift in Ziegler's relationship with the liturgical cantata: from anonymous author of texts performed locally in Leipzig's churches to a publicly known female author who included sacred cantata libretti in her published collections of poetry. The chapter concludes with a consideration of the significance of Ziegler's nine sacred cantata texts set by Bach for her later poetic endeavors.

Mariane von Ziegler as Cantata Librettist

Few details are known about the collaboration between Mariane von Ziegler and Johann Sebastian Bach, although both were prominent members of Leipzig society. The composer was nearing the end of his second year as Leipzig's town cantor, completing a two-year period characterized by intense compositional focus on the sacred cantata. But while a member of an important Leipzig family, Ziegler was not publicly recognized as a poet—she would not publish her first book of poetry for another three years. Ziegler was, in fact, far from a typical cantata librettist for the eighteenth-century Lutheran church. As a woman, she did not have access to a university education and held no official position in church, court, or town. Her standing was instead defined by her high family status: as a young, aristocratic widow living with her mother in one of Leipzig's most splendid houses, Ziegler had both the time and the opportunity to pursue her poetic endeavors. Still, her education, as well as her daily life, centered around the home. Her study of poetry took place privately with tutors, and her knowledge of theology was obtained through her own reading and through church attendance.

These characteristics are particularly revealing in contrast with Bach's other known sacred cantata librettists (listed in Table 2.2). While pursuing a number of different careers, Salomo Franck, Christian Friedrich Henrici (Picander), Johann Oswald Knauer, Georg Christian Lehms, and Erdmann Neumeister each gained a university education and were employed either in a church or administrative position. Their lives centered around the public sphere, and for each the writing of poetry was subsidiary to their other career-related ventures.

Ziegler clearly recognized her unique standing as a woman writing for the church and made every effort to construct cantata texts fitting for the Lutheran liturgy. She paid careful attention to the theological content and liturgical appropriateness of each cantata, while fashioning poetic texts with vibrancy and depth of expression. In so doing, Ziegler confirmed the appropriateness of her own poetic voice proclaimed through music in the church. Through her singular approach to the cantata text, she thus sought to silence those potential critics who might deem her unworthy, as a woman, to write liturgical cantatas for Leipzig's services.

Table 2.2   Other known librettists for J. S. Bach's sacred cantatas

Name	Dates	# of Bach cantatas	University education	Employment type
Salomo Franck	1659–1725	18	Jena	Court
Christian Friedrich Henrici (Picander)	1700–64	9	Wittenberg and Leipzig	Town
Johann Oswald Knauer	unknown	3	unknown	Church
Georg Christian Lehms	1684–1717	10	Leipzig	Court
Erdmann Neumeister	1671–1756	5	Leipzig	Church

Treatment of the Gospel Text

The nature and placement of the sacred cantata in Leipzig's Sunday and feast day liturgy required its close connection with the Gospel reading specified for the day. The rubrics for the order of service in the *Leipziger Kirchen-Staat* of 1710 show that the two assigned readings, of the Epistle and the Gospel, continued to be central to the Lutheran liturgy, with the sermon then offering an exposition of the Gospel text. Immediately following the chanting of the Gospel text but preceding the sermon was performed a piece of concerted music or a chorale "in keeping with the nature of the Gospel."[3]

But while it was expected that a cantata text would be appropriate for, and even grow out of, the assigned Gospel reading, the extent to which Ziegler depended on the Gospel is significant. While other librettists tended to employ the Gospel text as a starting point for their own theological reflections, Ziegler made every effort to align her poetry with the biblical text and rarely introduced any theological themes that were not explicit in the Gospel for the day.

Ziegler's cantata for Pentecost Sunday, *Wer mich liebe, der wird mein Wort halten* (BWV 74), provides a typical example of how Ziegler crafted her text on the basis of the assigned Gospel reading, John 14:23–31 (see Appendix B for text and translation of the cantata). The text of the Gospel reads:

[23] Jesus antwortete und sprach zu ihm: Wer mich liebt, der wird mein Wort halten; und mein Vater wird ihn lieben, und wir werden zu ihm kommen und Wohnung bei ihm machen. [24] Wer mich aber nicht liebt, der hält meine Worte nicht. Und das Wort, das ihr hört, ist nicht mein, sondern des Vaters, der mich gesandt hat. [25] Solches habe ich zu euch geredet, solange ich bei euch gewesen bin. [26] Aber der Tröster, der Heilige Geist, welchen mein Vater senden wird in meinem Namen, der wird euch alles lehren und euch erinnern alles des, das ich euch gesagt habe. [27] Den Frieden lasse ich euch, meinen Frieden gebe

---

3   "Ferner wird entweder *musiciret* oder ein Lied nach Beschaffenheit des Evangelii, …" *Leipziger Kirchen-Staat* (Leipzig, 1710), 6.

ich euch. Nicht gebe ich euch, wie die Welt gibt. Euer Herz erschrecke nicht und fürchte sich nicht. [28] Ihr habt gehört, daß ich euch gesagt habe: Ich gehe hin und komme wieder zu euch. Hättet ihr mich lieb, so würdet ihr euch freuen, daß ich gesagt habe: "Ich gehe zum Vater"; denn der Vater ist größer als ich. [29] Und nun ich es euch gesagt habe, ehe denn es geschieht, auf daß, wenn es nun geschehen wird, ihr glaubet. [30] Ich werde nicht mehr viel mit euch reden; denn es kommt der Fürst dieser Welt, und hat nichts an mir. [31] Aber auf daß die Welt erkenne, daß ich den Vater liebe und ich also tue, wie mir der Vater geboten hat: stehet auf und lasset uns von hinnen gehen. (*Luther-Bibel*, 1545)

[[23] Jesus answered him, "If anyone loves me, he will keep my word, and my Father will love him, and we will come to him and make our home with him. [24] Whoever does not love me does not keep my words. And the word that you hear is not mine but the Father's who sent me. [25] These things I have spoken to you while I am still with you. [26] But the Helper, the Holy Spirit, whom the Father will send in my name, he will teach you all things and bring to your remembrance all that I have said to you. [27] Peace I leave with you; my peace I give to you. Not as the world gives do I give to you. Let not your hearts be troubled, neither let them be afraid. [28] You heard me say to you, 'I am going away, and I will come to you.' If you loved me, you would have rejoiced, because I am going to the Father, for the Father is greater than I. [29] And now I have told you before it takes place, so that when it does take place you may believe. [30] I will no longer talk much with you, for the ruler of this world is coming. He has no claim on me, [31] but I do as the Father has commanded me, so that the world may know that I love the Father. Rise, let us go from here." (*English Standard Version*)]

Biblical Quotation

Ziegler's particular attention to the assigned Gospel reading can first of all be seen in her frequent use of biblical quotation. In fact, three of BWV 74's eight movements are Bible verses (movements 1, 4, and 6), two of them drawn from the Gospel text: movement 1 quotes John 14:23 and movement 4 quotes John 14:28. A comparison with Bach's other cantatas reveals that Ziegler employed biblical quotation with more frequency than any other of Bach's librettists, a characteristic of her texts observed both by Philipp Spitta and Albert Schweitzer.[4] As demonstrated in Table 2.3, 13 of the 55 movements in Ziegler's nine cantatas set by Bach are Bible verses, 11 of them from the Gospel for the day. Biblical quotation thus accounts for 24 per cent of the total movements in the Ziegler/Bach cantatas. The comparison with Bach's cantatas to texts by other librettists is striking: of 1,067 texted movements, 77 are Bible verses, only 7 per cent of the total. Furthermore, Ziegler included at least one Bible verse in eight of her nine cantatas, as opposed to 60 out of the 169 cantatas by Bach's other librettists.

A comparison with two other published cantata Jahrgänge of the period, those by Johann Oswald Knauer (1720) and Picander (1729), further emphasizes Ziegler's proclivity for biblical quotation. While Knauer employed biblical quotation consistently, beginning each part of his double cycle with a Bible verse, Ziegler still included Bible verses more frequently. And Picander's infrequent use of biblical

---

4   See Philipp Spitta, *Johann Sebastian Bach*, vol. 3 (New York, 1951; original German version, 1879–80), 70, and Albert Schweitzer, *J. S. Bach*, vol. 2 (New York, 1966; first English edition, 1911), 331.

Table 2.3   Bible verse quotation in sacred cantatas

	Ziegler (1725)	**Bach's other librettists**[a]	**Knauer (1720)**[b]	**Picander (1729)**[c]
Bible verse movements[d]	13	77	145	9
Total number of texted movements	55	1,067	837	383
Percentage	24	7	17	2
Cantatas containing at least one Bible verse movement	8	60	72	9
Total number of cantatas	9	169	72	70
Percentage	89	36	100	13

[a] Includes Bach's extant sacred cantatas for the regular Sundays and feast days of the church year (excluding cantatas composed for weddings, funerals, and installations of the Leipzig town council), except for the nine to texts by Ziegler.

[b] Johann Oswald Knauer, *Gott=geheiligtes Singen und Spielen des Friedensteinischen Zions, nach allen und jeden Sonn= und Fest=Tags=Evangelien, vor und nach der Predigt / angestellet Vom Advent 1720. bis dahin 1721* (Gotha, 1720).

[c] Picander [Christian Friedrich Henrici], "Cantaten auf die Sonn= und Fest=Tage durch das gantze Jahr, Leipzig 1729," In *Picanders Ernst=Schertzhaffte und Satÿrische Gedichte*, vol. 3 (Leipzig, 1732).

[d] The number of Bible verse movements includes only those movements for which the biblical quotation represents at least half of the movement's text.

quotation shows that it was not requisite. Ziegler's frequent inclusion of Bible verses thus constitutes a defining feature of her cantata libretti.

Ziegler expressed her belief in the importance of Bible verses and their liturgical place in her sacred cantatas in the foreword to her *Versuch in gebundener Schreib-Art, anderer und letzter Theil* of 1729. In introducing the 64 liturgical cantata texts in this volume (which, when combined with her nine texts set by Bach and published in 1728, formed a complete yearly cycle), Ziegler encouraged potential composers to treat her texts flexibly should they choose to set them to music. Recognizing that the texts as published were too long for a normal service cantata (most are 10–12 movements), Ziegler suggested that a composer could choose only certain movements, could perform half of the cantata before the sermon and half after, or could even split the texts into two yearly cycles. However, Ziegler insisted that composers set the quoted Bible verses for their proper liturgical occasion.[5]

Poetic Borrowings from the Gospel Text

But Ziegler's dependence on the Gospel reading went even further than quotation, as her poetic texts often provided responses to, and reiterated key themes of, the quoted Bible verses. As a result, Ziegler's newly-written poetic texts (arias and recitatives) were closely integrated with the movements she quoted (Bible verses and chorale verses) and grew organically out of the Gospel reading.

BWV 74 once again provides a typical example of Ziegler's approach. The connections between the quoted and newly-composed movements are evident from early in the cantata, as Ziegler's first poetic text, her movement 2 aria "Komm, komm, mein Herze steht dir offen," recites every key word from the opening movement's Bible verse: "lieben" (love), "Wort" (word), "Vater" (Father), "kommen" (come), and "Wohnung" (dwelling). Table 2.4 illustrates the close connection between the two movements:

Table 2.4   Text, BWV 74, movements 1–2 (shared words in italics in German text)

Text	Translation
Movement 74/1	**Movement 74/1**
Wer mich *liebet*, der wird mein *Wort* halten, und mein *Vater* wird ihn *lieben*, und wir werden zu ihm *kommen* und *Wohnung* bei ihm machen.	Whoever loves me will keep my word, and my Father will love him, and we will come to him and make our abode with him.
Movement 74/2	**Movement 74/2**
Komm, komm, mein Herze steht dir offen,	Come, come, my heart stands open to you,
Ach, laß es deine *Wohnung* sein!	Ah, let it be your dwelling!
Ich *liebe* dich, so muß ich hoffen:	I love you, so I must hope:
Dein *Wort* trifft itzo bei mir ein;	Your word will now be fulfilled in me;
Denn wer dich sucht, fürcht', *liebt* und ehret,	For whoever seeks, fears, loves, and honors you,
Dem ist der *Vater* zugetan.	To him the Father is devoted.
Ich zweifle nicht, ich bin erhöret,	I doubt not, I have been heard,
Daß ich mich dein getrösten kann.	So I can comfort myself in you.

And the cantata continues with similar connections: Ziegler's third-movement recitative focuses on the key ideas "Wohnung" (dwelling) and "Herz" (heart) from the opening two movements. It also serves as a transition to the next pair of movements by introducing the theme of Jesus going away ("von mir zu gehn") which is then the focus of the movement 4 Gospel text and movement 5 aria. Ziegler's final

---

5   Christiane Mariane von Ziegler, "Vorbericht" to *Versuch in gebundener Schreib-Art, anderer und letzter Theil* (Leipzig, 1729), v–vi.

aria (movement 7) not only incorporates key words from the movement 6 Bible verse ("nichts" [nothing] and "Jesu" [Jesus]), but also essentially restates the same meaning as the second half of the concluding chorale (the second verse of Paul Gerhardt's *Gott Vater, sende deinen Geist*):

74/7, lines 1–5	Nichts kann mich erretten	Nothing can save me
	Von höllischen Ketten	From hell's chains
	Als Jesu, dein Blut.	But, Jesus, your blood.
	Dein Leiden, dein Sterben	Your passion, your dying
	Macht mich ja zum Erben:	Makes me indeed an heir:
74/8, lines 4–6	Hier gilt gar nichts als Lieb und Gnad,	Nothing at all is effective here but love and grace,
	Die Christus verdienet hat	Which Christ has earned for us
	Mit Büßen und Versühnen.	With his atonement and reconciliation.

Ziegler thus adhered closely to the Gospel for the day by focusing on key verses in biblical quotation which then served as the basis for her own poetic texts. While she did make reference to some key words from other verses of the Gospel (for example, the references to "glauben" [believe] and "Satan" in BWV 74/5 are drawn from John 14:29–30), Ziegler focused primarily on those verses that were quoted in the cantata and did not feel obligated to treat the Gospel text in its entirety.

That Ziegler continued to be concerned with grounding her sacred cantatas in the biblical text is once again clear from her introduction to her later cantata texts in the *Versuch in gebundener Schreib-Art, anderer und letzter Theil*. Ziegler stated that she had considered inserting notes in the cantatas to indicate the sources of her thoughts in the arias and recitatives.[6] While she decided not to include such notes, Ziegler's mention of them would have indicated to readers that her theological ideas did not originate with herself but rather grew out of the biblical text.

Conclusion: Ziegler and the Gospel Text

Ziegler's approach to the Gospel text, both in quotation and as the basis of her recitatives and arias, thus represents a defining feature of her approach to the liturgical cantata as a genre. While other librettists certainly quoted verses and drew ideas and key words from the assigned Gospel readings, their newly-composed poetic texts (recitatives and arias) generally did not adhere as closely to the Gospel as did Ziegler's. Consider, for example, two of Bach's other cantatas for Pentecost Sunday: BWV 172, composed in 1714 to a text likely by Salomo Franck, and BWV 59, composed in 1723 or earlier to a text by Erdmann Neumeister. While both quote the same Gospel verse that Ziegler does, each treats the main themes of the verse more freely in the surrounding movements and does not depend on the quoted text to the same extent as Ziegler (see Tables 2.5 and 2.6).

---

6   Ziegler, "Vorbericht" to *Versuch in gebundener Schreib-Art, anderer und letzter Theil*, v–vi.

Table 2.5   Text, BWV 172, movements 1–3 (shared words in italics in German text)

Text	Translation
Movement 172/1	**Movement 172/1**
Erschallet, ihr Lieder, erklinget, ihr Saiten!	Resound, you songs; ring out, you strings!
O seligste Zeiten!	O most blessed of times!
Gott will sich die Seelen zu Tempeln bereiten.	God would prepare our souls as temples for himself.
Movement 172/2	**Movement 172/2**
Wer mich liebet, der wird mein Wort halten, und mein Vater wird ihn lieben, und wir werden zu ihm *kommen* und Wohnung bei ihm machen.	Whoever loves me will keep my word, and my Father will love him, and we will come to him and make our abode with him.
Movement 172/3	**Movement 172/3**
Heiligste Dreieinigkeit,	Most holy Trinity,
Großer Gott der Ehren,	Great God of glory,
Komm doch, in der Gnadenzeit	Come, in this time of grace,
Bei uns einzukehren,	And lodge with us;
Komm doch in die Herzenshütten,	Come into the tabernacles of our hearts,
Sind sie gleich gering und klein,	Though they be modest and small,
Komm und laß dich doch erbitten,	Come and let your self be entreated,
Komm und kehre bei uns ein!	Come and lodge with us!

Table 2.6   Text, BWV 59, movements 1–2 (shared words in italics in German text)

Text	Translation
Movement 59/1	**Movement 59/1**
Wer mich *liebet*, der wird mein Wort halten, und mein *Vater* wird ihn *lieben*, und wir werden zu ihm kommen und *Wohnung* bei ihm machen.	Whoever loves me will keep my word, and my Father will love him, and we will come to him and make our abode with him.
Movement 59/2	**Movement 59/2**
O, was sind das für Ehren,	Oh, what are those honors
Worzu uns Jesus setzt?	To which Jesus leads us?
Der uns so würdig schätzt,	He who reckons us so worthy
Daß er verheißt,	That he promises,
Samt *Vater* und dem Heilgen Geist	Together with the Father and the Holy Spirit,
In unsre Herzen einzukehren.	To lodge in our hearts.
O, was sind das für Ehren?	Oh, what are those honors?
Der Mensch ist Staub,	Mankind is dust,
Der Eitelkeit ihr Raub,	The prey of vanity, *continued*

Text	Translation
Der Müh und Arbeit Trauerspiel	The tragic drama of toil and trouble,
Und alles Elends Zweck und Ziel.	And the object and goal of all misery.
Wie nun? Der Allerhöchste spricht,	How then? The Most High says,
Er will in unsern Seelen	He desires our souls
Die *Wohnung* sich erwählen.	To elect as his dwelling.
Ach, was tut Gottes *Liebe* nicht?	Ah, what does God's love not do?
Ach, daß doch, wie er wollte,	Ah, that indeed, as he wished,
Ihn auch ein jeder *lieben* sollte.	Everyone would love him.

In BWV 172, Franck opened the cantata with a poetic text followed by a Bible verse quotation. But while drawing upon the general theme of John 14:23, BWV 172/1 does not share any key words with the Gospel text. The ensuing poetic text, BWV 172/3, focuses on a single key word from the Gospel, "kommen" ("come") (see Table 2.5). And although Neumeister quoted more key words from the Gospel in BWV 59/2 ("Vater," "Wohnung," "Liebe"), he departed even further than Franck in his theological reflections upon the text. Like Ziegler, Neumeister opened the cantata with the quotation of John 14:23, but he followed this with a recitative reflecting upon the nature of mankind and the love of God, themes which do not appear explicitly in the Gospel reading (see Table 2.6).

Ziegler's careful treatment of the assigned Gospel text for each cantata's liturgical occasion is also distinctive in relation to another type of poetry, the sacred devotional writing more typical of a female author in early eighteenth-century Germany. One example of this kind of poetry is Sophie Regina Gräf's *Liebes-Opffer* of 1715, which contains her poetic reflections on the Gospel texts of the church year. While they take their inspiration from the assigned Gospel readings, these poems are designed for personal, devotional use rather than for a corporate liturgy. The volume's subtitle explains: "Poetic applications of the Sunday and feast day Gospels written for her own edification and the joy of her soul." The nature of Gräf's approach and its difference from Ziegler's is evident in the first and last stanzas of Gräf's poem for Pentecost Sunday:

1

Du edles Feuer süsser Liebe,	You noble fire of sweet love,
Komm, komm, beseele Sinn und Geist;	Come, come, quicken sense and spirit;
Laß meiner Seelen heisse Triebe	Let my soul's ardent impulse
Nur geh'n auff das, was himmlisch heiß't.	Only rise to that which is heavenly.
Du allerheil'gster Freuden=Schein,	You all-holy manifestation of joy,
Komm, flösse dich dem Hertzen ein.	Come, fill my heart.

5

Drum komm mein Trost! drum komm mein Leben!	Therefore come, my comfort! Therefore come, my life!
Komm süsser Quell! Komm edler Schatz!	Come, sweet spring! Come, noble treasure!
Dir, dir hab' ich mich gantz ergeben,	To you, to you have I given my whole self,

Komm, nimm in meiner Seelen Platz;	Come, take a seat in my soul;
Beherrsche Geist, Hertz, Muth, und Sinn,	Rule spirit, heart, courage, and sense,
Daß ich nicht mein, nur deine bin.	That I am not mine, but yours alone.[7]

In this text, Gräf remained faithful to the main theme of the Gospel, the coming of the Holy Spirit, but sought personal application rather than proclamation. As demonstrated in Chapter 1, Gräf's poetry was more representative than Ziegler's of the type of poetry commonly expected of German women at the time. Ziegler, with her sacred cantatas for the public liturgy and her poetic proclamation of the Gospel text, once again surpassed the bounds of what was considered appropriate for a woman.

Theological Content

While we cannot know Ziegler's reasons for approaching the cantata with such careful attention to the Gospel text, it is interesting to reflect on some possible motivations. First of all, Ziegler may have found such an approach to be eminently practical. Since these texts came very early in Ziegler's poetic career (before any of her published poetry), it may have helped her writing to focus on key words provided by the Gospel itself. Furthermore, given Ziegler's lack of formal theological training, training not available to women in early eighteenth-century Germany, she may have seen this approach as a way to ensure the theological and liturgical appropriateness of her cantata texts. Such a close adherence to the Gospel text could further have helped Ziegler avoid any potential criticisms of her as a woman providing texts for the public liturgy: should anyone have questioned Ziegler's right to provide such texts, she could have quickly pointed to their grounding in the Gospel for the day. She could have argued that the ideas in the cantatas did not originate with herself, but that they were rather a proclamation of the Gospel itself, often in its own words.

Ziegler's dependence on the Gospel in constructing her cantatas had the added benefit of ensuring that her texts aligned closely with the writings of prominent Lutheran theologians, including those of Martin Luther himself. For example, a comparison of Ziegler's cantata for Pentecost Sunday (BWV 74) with Luther's *Haus-Postille*, with Johann Olearius's commentary on John 14 in his *Biblische Erklärung* of 1681, and with the four prayers for Pentecost in the *Leipziger Kirchen-Staat* of 1710 demonstrates a similarity of content, and sometimes expression, between Ziegler and these authors. This does not mean, however, that Ziegler used any of these writings as sources for her own work (although they would have all likely been readily available to her in Leipzig), but rather that she shared with them an approach to biblical interpretation founded in the Gospel text.

Such connections are clearly exhibited between Ziegler's text for BWV 74 and Luther's third sermon for Pentecost Sunday 1532, that on the Gospel reading for the

---

7   [Gräf, Sophia Regine], *Eines andächtigen Frauenzimmers S. R. G. Ihrem JESU im Glauben dargebrachte Liebes-Opffer, d. i. Poetische Applicationes derer Sonn- und Fest-täglichen Evangelien zu Ihrer eigenen Erbauung und Vergnügung Ihrer Seelen abgefasset, Und Ohne Dero Wissen zum Druck befördert von N. N.* (Leipzig, 1715), 39–40.

day, John 14:23–31.[8] Ziegler, like Luther, centers her text around the opening verse of the Gospel: "If anyone loves me, he will keep my word, and my Father will love him, and we will come to him and make our home with him" (John 14:23). After beginning her text by quoting this verse, Ziegler's first aria (BWV 74/2) expounds upon the main themes of dwelling in God, of love, and of God's word:

Komm, komm, mein Herze steht dir offen,	Come, come, my heart stands open to you,
Ach, laß es deine Wohnung sein!	Ah, let it be your dwelling!
Ich liebe dich, so muß ich hoffen	I love you, so I must hope:
Dein Wort trifft itzo bei mir ein;	Your word will now be fulfilled in me;

Luther's sermon also focuses on these themes, and in summarizing them near the end of the sermon, he states: "We will abide with God's Word and allow no threat whatever to divert us from it, from our love for Christ, our Lord, because that is the only way by which we understand that God holds us dear and draws nigh to us to make his abode with us."[9] Furthermore, Ziegler concludes this aria with the idea of the believer's comfort as a result of God's indwelling: "Daß ich mich dein getrösten kann" ("So I can comfort myself in you"). This link between dwelling and comfort is also evident in Luther's sermon, where he states, "This is surely a most excellent comfort, so that no Christian need ever wonder … how he will ascend into heaven, for it will be so. God Father, Son, and Holy Spirit desires to be with him and make their abode with him."[10]

While similar connections between Ziegler's text and Luther's sermon are evident in Ziegler's movement 3 recitative and movement 5 aria, they are even more striking in Ziegler's final aria, BWV 74/7:

Nichts kann mich erretten	Nothing can save me
Von höllischen Ketten	From hell's chains
Als, Jesu, dein Blut.	But, Jesus, your blood.
Dein Leiden, dein Sterben	Your passion, your dying
Macht mich ja zum Erben	Makes me indeed an heir:
Ich lache der Wut.	I laugh at the fury.

While such themes of individual salvation are not explicit in the Gospel reading, they are prominent in Luther's sermon, where he draws them from the idea of the believer dwelling in God which is central to the Gospel. Luther relates Jesus' blood, passion, and death (lines 3–4 of Ziegler's text) directly to the opening verse of the Gospel when he states: "Christ's words are indeed very plain, 'If a man love me, he will

---

8   Luther's sermon (originally printed in his *Haus-Postille*) appears in English translation in *The Complete Sermons of Martin Luther*, vol. 6, ed. Eugene F. A. Klug, trans. Klug et al (Grand Rapids, 2000), 177–84.

Luther's *Haus-Postille* was commonly available in early eighteenth-century Germany. Bach's own library, for example, included two copies. Robin A. Leaver, *Bachs Theologische Bibliothek / Bach's Theological Library*, Beiträge zur theologischen Bachforschung 1 (Neuhausen-Stuttgart, 1983), 66–68, 126–29.

9   Luther, *Complete Sermons*, vol. 6, 183.

10   Luther, *Complete Sermons*, vol. 6, 180.

keep my words,' my words about my death and resurrection," and "But a Christian's heart will right now be the dwelling place wherein God wants to live, if only we will firmly apprehend Christ, because we know that it was for us that he suffered and died." Furthermore, on the main theme of the aria, the believer's being saved from hell and gaining eternal salvation, Luther states: "Christ certainly does not lie when he here affirms: When you have come to love me and cleave to my Word, it is your highest joy and delight to know that I have rescued you from the devil's power, so that sin can no longer harm you, or death swallow you, and everlasting life and salvation are made sure, as my Word promises." And Ziegler's concluding thought, that of the believer laughing at hell's fury, is also found in Luther's sermon: "When faith is there we will come safely through; and if the world storms and protests, the believer responds: Storm if you will not laugh; it makes no difference to me, for Christ and his Word mean more to me than your vehemence."[11]

Whether or not Ziegler read Luther's sermon (or any other source outside of the biblical text itself) in preparation for writing her cantata, it is clear that she approached her liturgical poetry with the same concern as Luther for the assigned Gospel reading for the day. The close connections between Ziegler's texts and the writings of prominent Lutheran theologians confirms that the Gospel reading was central to Ziegler's conception of the sacred cantata. By focusing on the words of the Gospel both in quoted movements and in her newly-composed poetry, Ziegler insured the theological and liturgical appropriateness of her texts.

Poetic Qualities

But when modern commentators have described Ziegler's cantatas, it is not her theological orthodoxy grounded in the Gospel text on which they have focused (although Spitta and Schweitzer both noted her frequent use of biblical quotation), but rather their depth of feeling and their vibrancy of expression. Indeed, Ziegler's astute theological content was consistently combined with a depth of poetic expression. Albert Schweitzer even made a point of observing that Ziegler's poetry was superior to that of Bach's better-known librettist, Picander.[12] Philipp Spitta described Ziegler's texts thus: "The feeling of the text is deeper and purer than the average of those in the earlier cantatas in the madrigal style, and it often rises to real devotional strength."[13] Fred Hamel, writing in 1950, stated that Ziegler's cantata texts are "distinguished not only through fertility of ideas, control of speech, genuineness of emotion, and warmth of expression, but just as much through a religious tone of profound simplicity."[14]

---

11   Luther, *Complete Sermons*, vol. 6, 179–81.
12   Schweitzer, *J. S. Bach*, 331.
13   Spitta, *Johann Sebastian Bach*, vol. 3, 70.
14   "… sich nicht nur durch Gedankenreichtum, Sprachbeherrsehung, Echtheit der Empfindung und Wärme des Ausdrucks, sondern ebenso durch einen religiösen Klang von tiefer Schlichtheit auszeichnen." Qtd. in Friedrich Zander, "Die Dichter der Kantatentexte Johann Sebastian Bachs," *Bach-Jahrbuch* 54 (1968), 25.

Although still in an early stage of development, Ziegler's poetic skill is evident in her cantata texts set by Bach, texts which possess a vibrancy of expression rarely found to such a degree in cantatas by Bach's other librettists. BWV 74 contains a number of such memorable phrases. For example:

BWV 74/3, line 5	Das laß ich nimmermehr, ach nimmermehr geschehen!
BWV 74/5, lines 1–2	Kommt, eilet, stimmet Sait und Lieder In muntern und erfreuten Ton.
BWV 74/7, complete	Nichts kann mich erretten Von höllischen Ketten Als, Jesu, dein Blut. Dein Leiden, dein Sterben Macht mich ja zum Erben: Ich lache der Wut.

Examples from other Ziegler cantatas further demonstrate the richness of her poetic language:

BWV 103/5, lines 5–8	Mein Jesus läßt sich wieder sehen, O Freude, der nichts gleichen kann! Wie wohl ist mir dadurch geschehen, Nimm, nimm mein Herz zum Opfer an.
BWV 87/6, complete	Ich will leiden, ich will schweigen, Jesus wird mir Hülf erzeigen, Denn er tröst mich nach dem Schmerz. Weicht, ihr Sorgen, Trauer, Klagen, Denn warum sollt ich verzagen? Fasse dich betrübtes Herz!
BWV 68/2, complete	Mein gläubiges Herze, Frohlocke, sing, scherze, Dein Jesus is da! Weg Jammer, weg Klagen, Ich will euch nur sagen: Mein Jesus ist nah.
BWV 175/2, complete	Komm, leite mich, Es sehnet sich Mein Geist auf grüner Weide! Mein Herze schmacht', Ächzt Tag und Nacht, Mein Hirte, meine Freude.
BWV 175/5, lines 3–5	O! Törin, merke doch, wenn Jesus mit dir spricht, Daß es zu deinem Heil geschicht.

BWV 176/5, lines 1–3   Ermuntert euch, furchtsam und schüchterne Sinne,
                                 Erholet euch, höret, was Jesus verspricht:
                                 Daß ich durch den Glauben den Himmel gewinne.

Ziegler's sacred cantatas of 1725 thus exhibit the richness and variety of poetic structures and the facility of language that would come to characterize her later poetry. As Steven Huff wrote in 1992:

> Another important and distinguishing feature of much of the poetry in the *Versuch in gebundener Schreib-Art* is the sense of spontaneity, the lightness and freedom from stylistic prescription it conveys … . Surprisingly, this exuberance manifests itself even in the sacred cantata texts, despite their generic, liturgically requisite adherence to established Lutheran tradition.[15]

Themes of Speech and Silence

Ziegler, then, approached the genre of the liturgical cantata with particular attention to its theological, liturgical, and poetic characteristics. She sought to provide texts that were both appropriate for their context within the Lutheran liturgy in Leipzig and of high poetic quality. In doing so, and particularly in grounding her cantatas in their assigned Gospel readings, Ziegler ensured that the biblical text, both in literal quotation and poetic summary, was the focus of her own texts, while still maintaining her concern for vibrant poetic expression.

But despite such theological and poetic concern in her cantatas, Ziegler did not neglect a theme that would prove to be of central importance throughout her poetic career, that of women's rights to involvement in public discourse. Of course, the very fact that Ziegler, as a woman, was providing texts to be proclaimed in Leipzig's churches contributed to her defense of such rights. But Ziegler went further and subtly argued in her sacred cantata texts for women's equal right of self-expression. While the liturgical and theological nature of the cantata prohibited any overt defenses of women's rights, Ziegler's focus on the voice in her cantatas defended her belief that voice was a shared characteristic of all humans, whether male or female, and that all should likewise share the right to employ that voice. Eleven of Ziegler's 55 movements refer specifically either to some kind of verbal proclamation, speech, or to the lack thereof, silence (see Table 2.7).[16]

Themes of speech and silence thus appear in 20 per cent of Ziegler's movements and in eight of her nine cantatas (see Table 2.8). While the percentage of total movements addressing themes of voice is not vastly greater than in cantatas by Bach's other librettists (187 of 1,067 total movements, or 17.5 per cent), the consistency

---

15   Steven R. Huff, "Christiane Mariane von Ziegler's *Versuch in gebundener Schreib-Art* (Volume I, 1728)," in *"Der Buchstab tödt—der Geist macht lebendig": Festschrift zum 60. Geburtstage von Hans-Gert Roloff von Freunden, Schülern und Kollegen*, vol. 2, ed. James Hardin and Jörg Jungmayr, 977–88 (Bern, 1992), 983.

16   Each of these movements contains a reference which clearly indicates verbal expression. I have not included other more general references to concepts such as "praise" or "prayer," which could imply verbal expression but do not necessarily do so.

Table 2.7   Speech and silence in Ziegler's cantata texts set by Bach

BWV	Text type	Type of reference	Description
108/4	Bible verse	Speech	Vox Christi text describing Holy Spirit speaking
87/3	Aria	Speech	Quotation of believer's voice, prayer that God will speak clearly
87/6	Aria	Silence	Believer vows to remain silent in suffering
128/3	Aria + Recitative	Speech + silence	Proclamation of Jesus' Ascension + believer's call to self to be silent before God's omnipotence
128/4	Aria	Silence	Believer declares silence before God's omnipotence
183/5	Chorale	Speech	Reference to Holy Spirit praying in song
74/5	Aria	Speech	Proclamation in song because of Jesus' promised return
68/2	Aria	Speech	Proclamation in song because Jesus is present
175/4	Aria	Speech	Reference to voice of the true shepherd
175/5	Recitative	Speech	Reference to Jesus speaking
176/6	Chorale	Speech	Proclamation in song in heaven

Table 2.8   Themes of speech and silence in sacred cantatas

	Ziegler (1725)	Bach's other librettists[a]	Ziegler (1729)[b]
Movements with themes of speech or silence	11	187	148
Total number of texted movements	55	1,067	584
Percentage	20	17.5	25
Cantatas containing at least one reference to speech or silence	8	107	62
Total number of cantatas	9	169	64
Percentage	89%	63%	97%

[a] Includes Bach's extant sacred cantatas for the regular Sundays and feast days of the church year (excluding cantatas composed for weddings, funerals, and installations of the Leipzig town council), except for the nine to texts by Ziegler.
[b] Ziegler, *Versuch in gebundener Schreib-Art, anderer und letzter Theil*, 5–256.

of their treatment is. Ziegler included themes of speech or silence in 89 per cent of her cantatas, while such themes appear in only 63 per cent of cantatas by Bach's other librettists. That Ziegler continued her focus on the voice in her sacred cantatas is exhibited through her 64 sacred cantata texts published in 1729, in which such references are even more frequent: they appear in 25 per cent of the total movements spanning 62 of the 64 cantatas.

As demonstrated in Chapter 1, Ziegler maintained a concern for voice, and particularly women's voice, throughout her poetic career. She insisted that women should be granted the opportunity to be involved in public discourse, especially through the publication of their literary works. While the idea of speech for Ziegler was at times limited to that of artful conversation (in the French salon tradition), it more often served as a metaphor for proclamation and self-expression.

Ziegler clearly recognized the common societal structure by which men were the public voice and women silent. In her 1730 speech to the Deutschen Gesellschaft upon being appointed its first female member, Ziegler asked the assembly, "Do you not remember the sacred prohibition which states that the woman is to be silent in a congregation?"[17] But Ziegler challenged such a structure by asserting the equality of women and men in creation, as well as by emphasizing the five senses as shared by women and men. In her *Moralische und vermischte Send-Schreiben* of 1731, Ziegler stated: "[Women] likewise bring five senses into the world as [men] do; understanding and reason are distributed by nature among the sexes, and memory is also granted by her as part of our dowry."[18]

Throughout her writings, Ziegler particularly argued that since men and women shared the faculty of speech, they should likewise share the right to communicate, whether publicly or privately. In the final two stanzas of her "Das männliche Geschlechte, im Namen einiger Frauenzimmer besungen," Ziegler challenged women's enforced silence and insisted that men should rather be silent:

Der Mann muß seine Frau ernähren,	The man must support his wife,
Die Kinder, und das Hausgesind.	The children, and the household.
Er dient der Welt mit weisen Lehren,	He serves the world with wise teachings,
So, wie sie vorgeschrieben sind.	Just as they are dictated.
Das Weib darf seinen Witz nicht zeigen:	The wife may not display her wit:
Die Vorsicht hat es ausgedacht,	Caution has devised it,
Es soll in der Gemeine schweigen,	She should be silent in company,
Sonst würdet ihr oft ausgelacht.	Otherwise you would be often laughed at.
Ihr klugen Männer schweigt nur stille:	You clever men, just be silent:
Entdecket unsre Fehler nicht.	Do not discover our failures.

---

17   "Erinnern sie sich nicht dabey eines geheiligten Verbothes, welches das Weib in einer Gemeine schweigen heisset?" Christiane Mariane von Ziegler, "Antrittsrede der Hoch=Wohlgebohrnen Frauen Christianen Marianen von Ziegler, geb. Romanus, aus Leipzig," in *Der Deutschen Gesellschaft in Leipzig Gesammlete Reden und Gedichte, Welche bey dem Eintritte und Abschiede ihrer Mitglieder pflegen abgelesen zu werden*, ed. Johann Christoph Gottsched, 287–95 (Leipzig, 1732), 292.

18   "Wir bringen ja eben sowohl fünff Sinnen mit auf die Welt, wie jenes [Geschlecht], Verstand und Vernunfft werden unter beyderley Geschlechten von der Natur ausgetheilet, und das Gedächtnis wird uns zur Mitgifft von Ihr mit angerechnet." Christiane Mariane von Ziegler, *Moralische und vermischte Send-Schreiben, An einige Ihrer vertrauten und guten Freunde gestellt* (Leipzig, 1731), 8.

Denn es ist selbst nicht unser Wille,	Since it is not our will,
Daß euch die Schwachheit wiederspricht.	That weakness speaks against you.
Trag eines nur des andern Mängel,	Only bear one another's faults,
So habt ihr schon genug gethan,	Then you have already done enough,
Denn Menschen sind fürwahr nicht Engel,	For humans are truly not angels,
An denen man nichts tadeln kann.	About whom one can criticize nothing.[19]

For Ziegler, speech represented the right of self-expression, to which all persons, male or female, should have equal access. Silence for Ziegler was an appropriate response in some situations, but not something that should be the result of an imposed limitation on self-expression.

Ziegler's frequent reference to speech and silence in her sacred cantatas demonstrates that her concern for the shared right of self-expression permeated every area of her literary enterprise. Her treatment of such themes further emphasized her belief that the voice was a unifying and equalizing element for all persons. In her nine cantata texts set by Bach, Ziegler referred to speech and silence in a variety of ways and in a variety of movement types (both quoted texts—Bible verses and chorales—and newly-composed poetry—recitatives and arias).

Ziegler's references to speech and silence may be considered in two groups of movement types on the basis of the one who is speaking. One category of texts is those referring to the voices of God, Jesus, or the Holy Spirit (in BWV 108/4, 87/3, 183/5, 175/4, and 175/5). For Ziegler, such references served as positive examples to the believer of speech, proclamation, or expression. The following two examples, the first a Bible verse and the second a chorale verse, particularly highlight the voice of the Holy Spirit as one Christians should emulate:

BWV 108/4	Wenn aber jener, der Geist der Wahrheit, kommen wird, der wird euch in alle Wahrheit leiten. Denn er wird nicht von ihm selber reden sondern was er hören wird, das wird er reden; und was zukünftig ist, wird er verkündigen.	But when he, the Spirit of truth, will come, he will lead you into all truth. For he will not speak of himself, but rather what he will hear, that will he speak; and what is in the future, he will proclaim.
BWV 183/5	Du bist ein Geist, der lehret, Wie man recht beten soll; Dein Beten wird erhöret, Dein Singen klinget wohl. Es steigt zum Himmel an, Es steigt und läßt nicht abe, Bis der geholfen habe, Der allein helfen kann	You are a Spirit who teaches How one should truly pray; Your praying is heard, Your singing resounds well. It rises to heaven, It rises and does not cease Until he has helped, Who alone can help.

Ziegler clearly did not advocate proclamation or self-expression merely for their own sake; they were rather to be used in service to God and in keeping with examples of God's speech.

---

19   Christiane Mariane von Ziegler, *Vermischete Schriften in gebundener und ungebundener Rede* (Göttingen, 1739), 70–71.

A second category of Ziegler's texts treating speech and silence is those referring to the voice of the Christian believer (BWV 87/3, 87/6, 128/4, 74/5, 68/2, and 176/6). In these movements Ziegler promoted many different kinds of speech, proclamation, and expression, providing positive examples of how the believer should use speech as in the first four lines of BWV 74/5:

BWV 74/5	Kommt, eilet, stimmet Sait und Lieder	Come, hasten, tune strings and songs
	In muntern und erfreuten Ton.	In lively and glad sound.
	Geht er gleich weg, so kömmt er wieder,	Though he goes away, he will come again,
	Der hochgelobte Gottessohn.	The highly exalted son of God.

Ziegler also exhibited proper contexts for silence, with the believer remaining silent in the face of suffering (BWV 87/6) and also in light of God's omnipotence (BWV 128/3 and 128/4) as seen in the following examples:

BWV 87/6, lines 1–3	Ich will leiden, ich will schweigen,	I would suffer, I would keep silent,
	Jesus wird mir Hülf erzeigen,	Jesus will reveal his help to me,
	Denn er tröst mich nach dem Schmerz.	For he comforts me after my suffering.

BWV 128/4, lines 1–3	Sein Allmacht zu ergründen,	To fathom his omnipotence
	Wird sich kein Mensche finden,	Will no human be able,
	Mein Mund verstummt und schweigt.	My mouth falls dumb and becomes silent.

Ziegler thus emphasized that for every believer, male or female, both speech and silence have their proper place: in certain circumstances, the believer is to speak or proclaim, in others to be silent.

Conclusion

In crafting sacred cantata texts with close dependence on the Gospel reading, with vibrant poetic language, and with special attention to themes of speech and silence, Ziegler thus established an individual voice as cantata librettist. Interestingly, she was not best known in such a capacity. After this early collaboration with Bach, Ziegler went on to become one of the most prominent female poets in German-speaking lands. She published four volumes of her poetry and prose, in addition to several translations, and in 1733 was crowned Germany's first female poet laureate.

In light of these later achievements, Ziegler's nine cantatas set by Bach seem rather insignificant. Ziegler was not recognized as librettist when the pieces were first performed in Leipzig's churches (neither librettist nor composer were named in the text booklets), and the nine cantatas were first performed over the span of hardly more than a month. Ziegler wrote the texts three years prior to her first major publication (the first to bear her name), the *Versuch in gebundener Schreib-Art* of 1728, at a time when she was still learning the poetic art. And when the texts were at last published in her 1728 *Versuch*, they appeared in revised versions and were interspersed with other sacred poetry with no reference to their origin or to their musical settings.

The nine cantatas, however, were not unimportant for Ziegler's literary career. They represented Ziegler's first public, albeit anonymous, poetic venture. Furthermore, they required of her both theological and liturgical astuteness, as well as poetic skill, all under the pressure of providing the texts in time for their musical setting and performance. The nine cantatas also contributed to Ziegler's later ventures into the public realm under her own name. The texts were not only published in her 1728 *Versuch in gebundener Schreib-Art*, but also directly led to the additional 64 texts (completing a year-long liturgical cycle) which Ziegler published a year later in her *Versuch in gebundener Schreib-Art, anderer und letzter Theil*. Through her collaboration with Bach, Ziegler began her development as sacred cantata librettist and also became the only woman known to have provided texts for the Lutheran liturgy in the eighteenth century. Ziegler thus fulfilled a fundamental theme of her writings, stated thus near the end of her poetic career: "Even so it will be allowed for me, and for the least of my gender, to speak."[20]

---

20 "Itzo wird es mir erlaubet seyn, für mich und die wenigen meines Geschlechtes zu reden." Ziegler, *Vermischete Schriften*, 396.

Chapter 3

Divine Voice: The Significance of the Vox Christi for Ziegler and for Bach

The Theological and Musical Significance of the Vox Christi

As detailed in the previous chapter, one of the defining features of Mariane von Ziegler's sacred cantata texts is their focus on Bible verses, as Ziegler incorporated biblical quotation into her cantatas more frequently than any other of Bach's librettists. In Ziegler's nine cantatas set by Bach, the texts of 13 of the 55 movements are Bible verses, with at least one Bible verse appearing in eight of the nine cantatas. But Ziegler's treatment of biblical quotation is noteworthy not only in its frequency, but also for a particular type of Bible verse on which she focused: 11 of the 13 Bible verses record the divine voice, that is, the words of God or Jesus in biblical quotation, a text type commonly known as the Vox Christi.[1]

The number of Vox Christi movements in the Ziegler cantatas is, in fact, remarkable when compared with texts by Bach's other librettists. Bach set the Vox Christi in his cantatas a total of 41 times, so the 11 movements in the Ziegler cantatas represent 26 per cent of his total Vox Christi movements. The number is even more striking in light of the total number of cantatas under consideration: 11 Vox Christi movements in nine cantatas by Ziegler, and 30 Vox Christi movements in 169 cantatas by Bach's other librettists (see Table 3.1). Ziegler's cantatas thus represent the highest concentration of Vox Christi movements within Bach's output.

Table 3.1   Vox Christi in sacred cantatas

	Ziegler (1725)	Bach's other librettists[a]	Ziegler (1729)[b]
Vox Christi movements	11	30	69
Total number of cantatas	9	169	64

[a] Includes Bach's extant sacred cantatas for the regular Sundays and feast days of the church year (excluding cantatas composed for weddings, funerals, and installations of the Leipzig town council), except for the nine to texts by Ziegler.
[b] Christiane Mariane von Ziegler, *Versuch in gebundener Schreib-Art, anderer und letzter Theil* (Leipzig, 1729), 5–256.

---

1   Throughout this chapter, I will treat Vox Dei (words of God in biblical quotation) and Vox Christi (words of Jesus in biblical quotation) as a single group. While there are different theological implications depending on whether God or Jesus is the speaker, Vox Dei and Vox Christi movements are essentially treated as a single text type in Ziegler's cantata libretti.

On the one hand, Ziegler's frequent inclusion of the Vox Christi grew naturally out of her close adherence to the assigned Gospel readings for her cantatas' liturgical occasions in the post-Easter season. The Sundays and feast days from Quasimodogeniti (the First Sunday after Easter; Ziegler's first cantata, BWV 103, was written for Jubilate, the Third Sunday after Easter) to Trinity Sunday (the day of Ziegler's final cantata, BWV 176) form a distinct section within the church year, one in which the Gospel readings are drawn primarily from the gospel of John and all have a special focus on Jesus' words.[2] The Gospel texts during this period are not stories about Jesus' life on earth (as in many of the readings from Christmas to Easter) or records of Jesus speaking in parables or performing miracles (as in the readings for the Sundays after Trinity), but are accounts of Jesus addressing his disciples in order to give them instruction. Hence, the majority of verses in these Gospel readings are Vox Christi texts: of the 81 total verses in the Gospel readings from Jubilate to Trinity Sunday, 61 verses record the words of Jesus. Since Ziegler frequently quoted these Gospel readings in her cantata texts, it was, therefore, natural that she would often incorporate the Vox Christi.

However, the nature of the Gospel readings themselves is not sufficient to explain Ziegler's proclivity for Vox Christi texts. In Bach's other cantatas composed for the same liturgical occasions as the Ziegler cantatas (from Jubilate to Trinity Sunday), the librettists included a total of seven Vox Christi movements in 16 cantatas as opposed to Ziegler's 11 Vox Christi movements in nine cantatas. The importance of the Vox Christi for Ziegler is further evidenced by the 69 Vox Christi movements in her 64 sacred cantatas published in 1729 (see Table 3.1). By including such a high number of Vox Christi texts, Ziegler chose to identify with an important theological tradition within Lutheranism, one which originated with Martin Luther himself and highlighted the theological significance of the words of Jesus in biblical quotation.

The theological and liturgical significance of the Vox Christi in the Lutheran tradition traced its roots to Luther's revision of the mass in the 1520s. Robin A. Leaver has demonstrated that the centrality of the Vox Christi for Luther was particularly evident in relation to the Verba Testamenti, the Words of Institution which Jesus spoke at the Last Supper and which formed the foundation of the Eucharistic portion of the mass (taken from I Corinthians 11:23–25).[3] While in the Roman Catholic mass the Verba Testamenti were spoken aloud only in part, with the majority being whispered by the celebrating priest, Luther dictated that the entire text should be proclaimed aloud in the vernacular.[4] The following two statements summarize Luther's understanding of the importance of the Verba Testamenti proclamation and demonstrate his special concern for Jesus' spoken words in this context:

> In the first place, let us pay no heed to ... those foolish people [who] have invented and persuaded the whole world to believe ... that the words of consecration have been

---

2   The only exception being Ascension (Himmelfahrt), for which the Gospel reading is Mark 16:14–20. The only Ziegler/Bach cantata not to contain a Vox Christi or Vox Dei text is the one written for Ascension, BWV 128.

3   Robin A. Leaver, "Theological Consistency, Liturgical Integrity, and Musical Hermeneutics in Luther's Liturgical Reforms," *Lutheran Quarterly* 9 (1995): 117–38.

4   Leaver, "Theological Consistency," 123–24.

kept secret and their use and knowledge entrusted to no one but the priests ... . These words, after all, should fittingly have been common knowledge to all people, because faith, consolation, and salvation of all people is contained in them.

The whole power of the mass consists of the words of Christ, in which he testifies that forgiveness of sins is bestowed on all those who believe that his body is given and his blood poured out for them. This is why nothing is more important for those who go to hear the mass than to ponder these words diligently and in full faith. Unless they do this, all else they do is vain.[5]

Luther also prescribed that the Words of Institution be set apart musically, thereby further highlighting their special nature. Luther established the musical presentation of the Verba Testamenti in both his *Formula missae* of 1523 and his *Deutsche Messe* of 1526, dictating that these words be chanted to the same tone as the Gospel. The words of Jesus in both the Gospel and the Verba Testamenti were also to be emphasized by being sung to a pitch a third lower than the narration sung by the evangelist. In his *Deutsche Messe*, Luther presented a system in which the words of the evangelist, quotations of other people, and the voice of Christ (labeled "Vox Christi") were each given their own punctuation formulae and reciting tones. Such a representation of various speakers by different pitches, which had been characteristic of the chanting of the passion narratives during Holy Week, thus became a weekly experience. The congregation would quickly come to perceive the Vox Christi in both the Gospel and the Verba Testamenti through its lower pitch, with such a musical device emphasizing the importance of the voice of Jesus and ensuring that it was specially recognized by the hearers.[6]

That this practice of chanting both the Gospel and the Words of Institution was still in practice in Leipzig during Ziegler's and Bach's time is indicated by the rubrics in the 1711 *Leipziger Kirchen-Staat*, which state, "After the chorale, the priest sings the Gospel before the altar," and, "At this time the office of Holy Communion is celebrated before the altar with the singing of the Our Father and the Words of Institution."[7] Martin Geck has further emphasized the special treatment of, and preference for, the Vox Christi in the Leipzig liturgy:

In Leipzig Bach approached the theme of the Vox Christi in a wholly new manner: he no longer had to deal with librettists who composed in the environment of the court and granted no absolute priority to the words of the Bible or the special words of Jesus. Rather, in a city officially committed to Lutheran Orthodoxy, the setting of biblical text and chorale traditionally occupied the highest position.[8]

---

5   Qtd. in Leaver, "Theological Consistency," 121–22.

6   Leaver, "Theological Consistency," 126–27. See also Martin Luther, "Deutsche Messe und Ordnung Gottesdiensts, 1526," in *D. Martin Luthers Wercke*, vol. 19, 44–113 (Weimar, 1897), 90–91.

7   "Nach dem Liede singet der Priester vor dem Altar das Evangelium." "Allsdenn wird vor dem Altar das Ammt der Heiligen Communion celebriret / mit Absingung des Vater Unsers / und der Worte der Einsetzung." *Leipziger Kirchen-Staat* (Leipzig, 1710), 6, 10.

8   "In Leipzig stellt sich Bach das Thema *vox Christi* ganz neu: Er hat es nicht länger mit Librettisten zu tun, die in höfischem Milieu dichten und dem Bibel- oder speziell

By including such a high number of Vox Christi texts in her nine cantatas, Ziegler provided another context in the liturgy, in addition to the Gospel and the Words of Institution, in which the words of Jesus would be highlighted musically. By embracing the Vox Christi tradition and thus giving priority to the words of Jesus in biblical quotation, Ziegler placed herself clearly within Leipzig's theological tradition of Lutheran orthodoxy.

Bach's Compositional Response to Ziegler's Vox Christi Texts

But Ziegler's focus on the Vox Christi in her cantatas had a further effect, as well, in that it provided an impetus for Bach's striking musical treatment of these unique texts. Expanding upon Luther's instructions for the chanting of the Vox Christi, it was incumbent upon Lutheran composers to set apart the Vox Christi musically. In dramatic works, such as passions and oratorios, this was conventionally done by setting the words of Jesus for solo bass voice in recitative or arioso style. Due to the dramatic nature of these works, Jesus was thus represented in a realistic speech-like presentation in combination with narrative (the voice of the Evangelist) and dialogue (with Pilate, Peter, etc.).[9]

However, composers often treated the Vox Christi differently in non-dramatic works, such as the motet or the sacred cantata, in which the words of Jesus were not part of a narrative context. In tracing the history of the Vox Christi tradition in seventeenth-century Germany, Martin Geck has observed Heinrich Schütz's rejection of the "realistic" single voice for the Vox Christi in his non-dramatic compositions. Schütz tended rather to emphasize the special nature of the Vox Christi by setting it as a multi-voice movement, as in his "Ich bin die Auferstehung und das Leben" for two tenors and bass (*Kleine Geistliche Konzerte*, part II, 1639) and "Ich bin ein rechter Weinstock, mein Vater ein Weingärtner" for six-part choir (*Geistliche Chormusik*, 1648). Schütz's students Matthias Weckmann and Christoph Bernhard, as well as Dieterich Buxtehude in the following generation, returned to the solo setting of the Vox Christi but not to a realistic dialogue style. As opposed to the simple recitative/arioso convention in dramatic works, the solo settings of the Vox Christi by these composers were musically elaborate, employing text repetition and melismatic passages.[10]

In considering the Vox Christi in light of settings by earlier Lutheran composers, Bach thus had a number of options at his disposal, from realistic recitative settings to more elaborate solo or multi-voice movements. In his passions, Bach continued in the dramatic tradition of setting the Vox Christi for solo bass voice in recitative. But in his sacred cantatas, he embraced the tradition of non-dramatic Vox Christi movements by setting the Vox Christi as simple recitative, in an arioso or aria style,

---

Jesuswort keinen absoluten Vorrang einräumen. In einer offiziell der lutherischen Orthodoxie verpflichteten Stadt steht vielmehr die Vertonung von Bibeltext und Choral traditionell an oberster Stelle." Martin Geck, "Die *vox-Christi*-Sätze in Bachs Kantaten," in *Bach und die Stile*, ed. Martin Geck, 79–101 (Dortmund, 1999), 79.

9   Geck, "Die *vox-Christi*-Sätze in Bachs Kantaten," 79.

10   Geck, "Die *vox-Christi*-Sätze in Bachs Kantaten," 79–84.

or as chorus. Bach thus identified with the Vox Christi tradition both through specific musical devices, such as the bass voice, and through his characterization of the Vox Christi as a special text type that should be musically distinctive.

Prior to his Ziegler cantatas, Bach had set the Vox Christi 24 times in his sacred cantatas in Weimar and Leipzig. In these 24 movements, Bach generally set the text either as a solo movement for bass in a recitative or arioso style (in the liturgical passion tradition) or as a fairly straightforward chorus (in the motet tradition). But Bach's settings of the Vox Christi in the Ziegler cantatas (listed in Table 3.2) represent a distinctive approach to this text type, both in the high number of Vox Christi movements in a brief period of time and in Bach's particular musical treatment of them.

Table 3.2   Vox Christi and Vox Dei movements in Bach's Ziegler cantatas

BWV	Liturgical occasion	Source	Movement type
103/1	Jubilate	John 16:20	Chorus + Recitative (bass)
108/1	Kantate	John 16:7	Aria (bass)
108/4	Kantate	John 16:13	Chorus
87/1	Rogate	John 16:24	Aria (bass)
87/5	Rogate	John 16:33	Aria (bass)
183/1	Exaudi	John 16:2	Recitative (bass)
74/1	Pentecost Sunday	John 14:23	Chorus
74/4	Pentecost Sunday	John 14:28	Aria (bass)
68/5	Pentecost Monday	John 3:18	Chorus
175/1	Pentecost Tuesday	John 10:3	Recitative (tenor)
176/1	Trinity Sunday	Jeremiah 17:9	Chorus

The following discussion of these movements is organized by genre, addressing Bach's settings of the Vox Christi as recitative, aria, and chorus in the Ziegler cantatas. It considers the relation of these movements to the composer's earlier Vox Christi settings, as well as Bach's exploration of new ways of setting this text type.

Vox Christi as Recitative

Bach's two recitative settings of the Vox Christi in the Ziegler cantatas, BWV 183/1 and 175/1, are unique within his output, and particularly striking in light of his earlier Vox Christi recitatives. Bach had set the Vox Christi as recitative five times previously in his sacred cantatas, four of these in Weimar. Rather than employing a more elaborate Vox Christi style such as Schütz and Buxtehude in their non-dramatic works, Bach in his Weimar cantatas set the Vox Christi in the dramatic passion tradition of bass recitative. Of these four movements, only BWV 61/4 is accompanied recitative, with pizzicato strings to represent knocking as the bass sings the text "Behold, I stand at the door and knock" ("Siehe, ich stehe vor der Tür und klopfe an," Revelation 3:20). The remaining three movements (BWV 18/2, 182/3, and 172/2) are simple recitatives in which the bass voice declaims the text supported by basso continuo and concludes with a brief arioso section emphasizing a particular word or phrase through text repetition and a slightly more elaborate musical style. Bach's only other Vox Christi recitative composed prior to the Ziegler cantatas is BWV 7/5, in which the Vox Christi text is combined with poetic text. The style, however, is similar to his Weimar settings: scored for bass voice with strings and continuo, the movement begins with recitative to poetic text and concludes with a Vox Christi text in arioso style.

When Bach returned to recitative settings of the Vox Christi in his Ziegler cantatas (BWV 183/1 and 175/1), it was with a very different musical style from the simple recitatives of his Weimar cantatas or his *Johannes-Passion*, the second version of which had been performed just over three weeks before Bach's first cantata to a Ziegler text. Furthermore, Bach did not draw upon the Vox Christi practices that earlier Lutheran composers had employed in their non-dramatic works.

Bach's treatment of Vox Christi recitative in the Ziegler cantatas differed from earlier settings first of all because of the placement of the movements within the cantata, with both of the recitatives appearing as first movements. Only six other of Bach's cantatas open with a recitative (BWV 134, 155, 158, 173, 184, and 199), all of them to poetic texts rather than biblical quotation. The setting of a first-movement Vox Christi as recitative in BWV 183 and 175 thus represented a significant compositional choice for Bach, as he eschewed large-scale opening choruses in favor of short recitatives (of five and four measures respectively).

BWV 183/1 and 175/1 further differed from Bach's earlier Vox Christi recitatives in their scorings. While Bach employed the conventional bass voice in BWV 183/1, he instead set the Vox Christi for tenor in BWV 175/1. Furthermore, both recitatives are accompanied by woodwinds and continuo rather than continuo alone (as in BWV 18/2, 182/3, and 172/2) or strings with continuo (as in BWV 61/4 and 7/5). The first movement of BWV 183 is striking in its use of four oboes (two oboes d'amore and two oboes da caccia) with continuo, a unique scoring within Bach's cantata output. The oboes do not play figural music, but simply realize the accompanying chords in long notes. The first movement of BWV 175 is also notable for its instrumentation, as three recorders play a figural sixteenth-note accompaniment throughout. Bach had accompanied a recitative with three recorders only once previously during his first two years in Leipzig, in the soprano recitative BWV 122/3 to a poetic text.

A consideration of Bach's later settings of the Vox Christi as recitative further highlights the unique nature of his Ziegler movements. Bach set the Vox Christi as recitative only twice in his later cantatas, in BWV 28/3 and 32/2. Both of these movements are in a recitative style reminiscent of his Weimar settings in the liturgical passion tradition, simple settings for bass voice concluding with an arioso section.

Vox Christi as Aria

Like Weckmann, Bernhard, and Buxtehude before him, Bach often set the Vox Christi for solo voice not in simple recitative but in an arioso or aria style. In fact, Bach most often set the Vox Christi in such a style in his Leipzig cantatas: seven of Bach's Leipzig Vox Christi movements prior to the Ziegler cantatas are for bass arioso or aria, as are four movements in the Ziegler cantatas. In both groups of cantatas, there is a marked difference in compositional style between middle-movement and first-movement Vox Christi arias, with the middle movements tending to be simpler and the first movements more elaborate.

Middle Movements   Bach set the Vox Christi as a middle-movement aria twice in his Ziegler cantatas, in BWV 87/5 and 74/4. These movements are related to Bach's earlier settings of the Vox Christi as middle-movement aria (BWV 153/3, 154/5, and 81/4), all of which are in an arioso style and are relatively short in length (58, 22, and 21 measures respectively). These earlier settings are fairly simple, accompanied only by continuo and generally without independent instrumental sections of significant length. In these movements, Bach essentially appropriated the arioso style with which he had concluded each of his Weimar Vox Christi recitatives, adopting this style for the entire movement. An example of this movement type is BWV 81/4, "Ihr Kleingläubigen, warum seid ihr so furchtsam?" (Example 3.1).

Example 3.1   BWV 81/4, mm. 1–3

While retaining certain features of these earlier settings, particularly the bass voice and basso continuo accompaniment, the middle-movement Vox Christi arias in the Ziegler cantatas incorporate elements of a more virtuosic aria type rather than the simpler arioso style. BWV 87/5 and 74/4 are longer than their predecessors (75 and 77 measures), with independent instrumental sections employing ritornello procedures. They are also more virtuosic both in their vocal and instrumental writing, as is evident from the first vocal statement in BWV 87/5 (Example 3.2).

The style of these movements, while distinct from Bach's earlier Vox Christi continuo ariosi, is closely related to Bach's Jahrgang I continuo arias with poetic texts (for example, BWV 76/10 and 89/3). In BWV 87/5 and 74/4, Bach drew on his earlier compositional procedures, applying them to Vox Christi texts for the first time in the Ziegler cantatas. So while Bach's style of composition was not new in the middle-movement Vox Christi arias of the Ziegler cantatas, the context for such a style was.

First Movements   Bach set the Vox Christi as first-movement aria four times prior to his two settings in the Ziegler cantatas, BWV 108/1 and 87/1. Like their middle-movement counterparts, Bach's first-movement Vox Christi arias share a number of similarities in compositional style. Reflecting their prominent position within each cantata, these movements tend to be on a larger scale with a more virtuosic treatment of voice and instruments. Bach's first-movement Vox Christi arias prior to the Ziegler cantatas (BWV 89/1, 166/1, 86/1, and 85/1) are significantly longer than the middle-movement ariosi and are all scored for bass voice with oboes and strings in addition to continuo. The first-movement settings also include distinct instrumental opening, interlude, and closing sections employing ritornello procedures. A typical example of this type is BWV 166/1, "Wo gehest du hin" (Example 3.3).

Bach's two first-movement arias in the Ziegler cantatas, BWV 108/1 and 87/1, share a number of general features with these earlier Leipzig settings. They are scored for bass voice with oboes, strings, and continuo, with virtuosic treatment of voice and instruments. However, Bach once again approached the Vox Christi in new ways in his Ziegler settings. Rather than following more conventional procedures of form and of the relationship between voice and instruments as he had in his earlier settings, Bach manipulated traditional formal procedures in the instrumental parts to unify each movement and provide a structure for a distinctly independent vocal line.

In BWV 108/1, Bach combined a tripartite sectional form in which each new line of text is given new thematic material (as in a motet) with ritornello procedures. While the instrumental parts are based throughout on the opening ritornello, each of the three sections of text is based upon a different vocal melody, only the first of which shares the musical material of the ritornello. The result is a fascinating combination of compositional procedures, in which Bach employed repeated material in the instrumental parts to unify the musically varied vocal sections. Example 3.4 presents the opening measures of the instrumental ritornello, followed by the initial measures of each vocal section.

In BWV 87/1, Bach once again experimented with thematic treatment and with independence between voice and instruments, now employing imitative rather than ritornello procedures to unify the through-composed vocal line. BWV 87/1 demonstrates similarities to the opening movement of BWV 86, performed on the same Sunday of the previous year. BWV 86/1 is also a Vox Christi aria for solo bass, here accompanied by strings and basso continuo. After the instrumental exposition of the main theme in imitation, BWV 86/1 contains three vocal sections, each based on the main theme from the instrumental exposition and each presenting the entire Vox Christi text.

BWV 87/1 begins in a similar, though more complex, fashion. Rather than treating a single theme imitatively as he had in BWV 86/1, Bach here began in the style of a double fugue with one theme (x) presented by Ob II/V II and imitated 2 ½ measures later by Ob I/V I at the fifth above and a second theme (y) presented by Ob da cacc/Va and imitated two quarter notes later by the continuo at the octave below (see Example 3.5a). A third theme (z) appears initially as an extension of y in measure 3, but is then imitated in all four voices throughout the remainder of the instrumental exposition. As in BWV 86/1, the voice begins by stating the first theme (x) from the instrumental exposition. However, from this point on, the movement is markedly different from its predecessor. The first difference grows out of the multiple themes of the exposition, all three of which are combined in the first vocal statement (Example 3.5b) as opposed to the single theme presented in imitation in BWV 86/1. But a more significant difference is Bach's treatment of the vocal line.

Example 3.2   BWV 87/5, mm. 9–18

Example 3.3   BWV 166/1, mm. 12–21

Example 3.4   BWV 108/1

a. mm. 1–3, instrumental ritornello

b. initial vocal statements in each section

After the initial statement on theme *x*, the bass voice sings new musical material for the remainder of the movement while the loosely imitative instrumental lines are based on the initial three themes throughout.

In his Vox Christi arias of the Ziegler cantatas, Bach thus expanded significantly upon the Vox Christi tradition, employing the convention of solo bass voice but treating it in new ways to further highlight the significance of this text type. The same is true of his Vox Christi choruses, as Bach drew upon the tradition of multi-voice settings of biblical text.

Vox Christi as Chorus

In his five movements in the Ziegler cantatas Bach approached the Vox Christi chorus in two different ways. In the two middle-movement choruses, Bach appropriated the

Example 3.5   BWV 87/1

a. initial statements of three main themes, mm. 1–4

motet style more strictly than he had in the Vox Christi choruses of Jahrgang I, while in the three first-movement choruses he largely eschewed the motet style in favor of new compositional ideas. The following section discusses first Bach's middle-movement Vox Christi choruses in light of the motet tradition and his Jahrgang I settings and then his highly individualized treatment of the Vox Christi in his three first-movement choruses.

BWV 108/4 and 68/5: The Motet Tradition   Bach's two non-first-movement Vox Christi choruses in the Ziegler cantatas are closely related to the German motet tradition. Both BWV 108/4 and 68/5 fit Daniel Melamed's description of a movement in motet style: a choral movement without independent instrumental parts (basso continuo excepted) in alla breve with imitative texture.[11] Example 3.6 demonstrates such a style in the opening measures of BWV 108/4.

BWV 108/4 and 68/5 are clearly related to Bach's five Vox Christi choruses in his first Leipzig Jahrgang (BWV 24/3, 77/1, 65/1, 144/1, and 37/1), each of which is fairly short and inclines toward an older musical style. Four of these movements incorporate motet-like sections, with features such as imitative texture, continuous

---

11   Daniel R. Melamed, *J. S. Bach and the German Motet* (Cambridge, 1995), 111–15.

Example 3.5   BWV 87/1

b. initial vocal statement, mm. 12–16

voice parts, and instruments doubling the voices (BWV 24/3, mm. 38–104; BWV 77/1, mm. 22–77; BWV 65/1, mm. 19–47; and BWV 144/1 in its entirety). The fifth, BWV 37/1, while not specifically motet-like, is described by Melamed as "old-fashioned" in its style.[12]

But Bach's treatment of the motet style in BWV 108/4 and 68/5 is altered from that of the Vox Christi choruses of Jahrgang I. In the earlier cantatas, Bach generally employed motet-like characteristics within a larger form, but in the Ziegler cantatas he applied motet style more rigorously throughout each movement. BWV 108/4 and 68/5 are comparable in approach only to 144/1 in employing motet style for an entire Vox Christi movement. These movements are thus more closely related to a number of Bach's non-Vox Christi movements that employ a motet-like style throughout (for

---

12   Melamed, *J. S. Bach and the German Motet*, 111.

Example 3.6   BWV 108/4, mm. 1–5

example, BWV 64/1 and 179/1 to Bible verse texts and BWV 2/1 and 38/1 to chorale texts) than they are to his Jahrgang I Vox Christi choruses.

But Bach's innovative approach to the Vox Christi chorus is more striking in his three first-movement Vox Christi choruses of the Ziegler cantatas, BWV 103/1, 74/1, and 176/1. Rather than recalling an old-fashioned or motet-like style as he had previously, Bach experimented in these choruses with a variety of compositional procedures, including the treatment of instrumentation such as he was exploring in his Vox Christi recitatives and the treatment of formal and thematic elements such as he was exploring in his first-movement Vox Christi arias. But while the recitatives and the arias discussed shared certain similarities of approach, the three choruses are each distinct in their compositional style. These large-scale choruses provided Bach with a particular opportunity to explore creative treatment of the Vox Christi and further highlight the special nature of this text type.

BWV 103/1: Chorus and Solo Voice Combined   The opening chorus of Bach's first Ziegler cantata, BWV 103, is one of the most engaging in Bach's cantata output. In addition to its distinctive instrumental sound featuring a virtuoso flauto piccolo obbligato, this movement juxtaposes two different genres, as Bach interrupts the large-scale chorus with a bass solo in accompanied recitative/arioso style before returning to the chorus to conclude the movement (Table 3.3).

Table 3.3   Movement structure, BWV 103/1

mm.	Voices	Style	Text
1–100	SATB	Chorus	Dictum: Ihr werdet weinen und heulen, aber die Welt wird sich freuen.
101–08	B	Recitative	Dictum: Ihr aber werdet traurig sein,
109–55	SATB	Chorus	Dictum: Doch eure Traurigkeit soll in Freude verkehret werden.

Bach had combined chorus with recitative several times previously in his first two Leipzig Jahrgänge (in BWV 138/1, 138/2, 95/1, 190/2, 73/1, 178/5, 3/2, and 92/7). However, the contrasting musical styles in these earlier movements all serve to highlight distinct textual types, with chorale text sung by chorus and poetic text set as solo recitative as in BWV 92/7 (Table 3.4). BWV 103/1 is the only movement in Bach's first two Leipzig Jahrgänge to include the recitative setting of a dictum in the middle of a dictum chorus.

Bach's decision to combine movement types in a Vox Christi setting had precedent in three of his earlier Leipzig settings, although each was realized in a strikingly different fashion. Bach's creative treatment of the Vox Christi, in fact, began in the first movement of BWV 22, composed for Bach's audition in Leipzig on 7 February 1723. In this movement for tenor and bass aria followed by chorus, Bach directly appropriated the passion tradition into the cantata by dividing the text between tenor solo (in a manner similar to the role of evangelist), bass arioso to Vox Christi text, and narrative chorus (in the fashion of a turba chorus). Of similar nature to BWV 22/1 is the pair of movements BWV 44/1 and 44/2, which likewise progress from aria to chorus, although here entirely to Vox Christi text. Bach then combined movement types in a very different way in BWV 67/6, in which bass aria on Vox Christi text ("Friede sei mit euch") alternates with a trio for soprano, alto, and tenor on poetic text.

But Bach's inclusion of bass recitative with a chorus in BWV 103/1 was only his most obvious experiment with form in this movement. The composer further manipulated overtly conventional musical themes, those portraying sorrow and joy, to create the movement's large-scale form as a reflection of the final phrase of the text: "Yet your sorrow shall be transformed into joy." The text of the entire movement reads:

Table 3.4   Movement structure, BWV 92/7

mm.	Voices	Style	Text
1–5	SATB	Chorale	Chorale: Ei nun, mein Gott, so fall ich dir getrost in deine Hände.
5–8	B	Recitative	Recitative: So spricht der Gott gelass'ne Geist, wenn er des Heilands Brudersinn und Gottes Treue gläubig preist.
9–13	SATB	Chorale	Chorale: Nimm mich, und mache es mit mir bis an mein letztes Ende.
13–17	T	Recitative	Recitative: Ich weiß gewiß, daß ich ohnfehlbar selig bin, wenn meine Not und mein Bekümmernis von dir so wird geendigt werden:
18–23	SATB	Chorale	Chorale: Wie du wohl weißt, daß meinem Geist dadurch sein Nutz entstehe,
23–26	A	Recitative	Recitative: daß schon auf dieser Erden, dem Satan zum Verdruß, dein Himmelreich sich in mir zeigen muß
26–31	SATB	Chorale	Chorale: und deine Ehr je mehr und mehr sich in ihr selbst erhöhe.
31–36	S	Recitative	Recitative: So kann mein Herz nach deinem Willen sich, o mein Jesu, selig stillen, und ich kann bei gedämpften Saiten dem Friedensfürst ein neues Lied bereiten.

Ihr werdet weinen und heulen, aber die Welt wird sich freuen. Ihr aber werdet traurig sein. Doch eure traurigkeit soll in Freude verkehret werden.	You will weep and wail, but the world will rejoice. You, however, will be sorrowful. Yet your sorrow will be transformed into joy.

Initially striking is the fact that the first vocal statement presents a theme in stark contrast to that of the instrumental introduction (Example 3.7). This is opposed to Bach's normal process, in which a movement is based throughout on the musical material stated at the outset and the first vocal statement echoes the music of the instrumental opening. In BWV 103/1, the music from the instrumental introduction does not reappear until the second vocal statement, thus allowing Bach to contrast the disciples' sorrow ("Ihr werdet weinen und heulen") with the world's joy ("aber die Welt wird sich freuen").

In the final section of the movement (mm. 109–55), Bach represented the text's transformation from sorrow to joy by employing a type of thematic transformation. The composer here presented a parallel musical structure to measures 55–91 but with the themes in an altered form as a result of a new line of text, an octave displacement in the middle of the line, and a new tonal center. These alterations are evident in the parallel statements of the first theme, as seen in Example 3.8 (the two tenor entries are shown here for comparison).

Example 3.7   BWV 103/1

a. mm. 1–3

b. mm. 35–39, voice parts only

Instead of creating a strict da-capo form by bringing back the earlier music as it was or following motet-like procedures by introducing new music for the final section of text, Bach transformed the earlier themes, at once reflecting the textual progression through the changes in the themes and unifying the movement through their similarities. This musical juxtaposition of the themes of sorrow and joy is further realized in BWV 103 as a whole, as the second movement recitative with its emphasis on "Schmerzen" ("sorrows") and the ensuing F♯ minor aria contrast

Example 3.8   BWV 103/1

a. mm. 27–31, tenor

b. mm. 113–17, tenor

with the fourth movement recitative with its emphasis on "Freude" ("joy") and the ensuing celebratory tenor aria in D major with trumpet obbligato.

BWV 74: Parody and the Sacred Concerto Style   In the opening chorus of BWV 74, Bach again experimented with thematic ideas (here the working out of a single motive throughout a sectional form) and also with the combination and juxtaposition of three different instrument groups. This movement is in a somewhat different category from the other Vox Christi and Vox Dei first movements under discussion since it is a parody of an earlier work, the first movement of the Pentecost cantata BWV 59. Bach retained the same music and text from BWV 59/1 for the first movement of BWV 74, but expanded the vocal forces from tenor/bass duet to full chorus and added a third trumpet and three oboes to the instrumental parts. The resultant movement is reminiscent of the seventeenth-century sacred concerto, a large-scale sectional setting of a biblical text for multiple voices and instrumental ensemble.

Not only did Bach include the entire movement text in each of the five sections of the composition, but he also stated all the musical material for the movement in the first vocal episode (mm. 8–15). Each of the vocal sections is then heralded by the movement's opening motto, which serves as a unifying factor as it appears 33 times throughout the movement in either voices or instruments. Example 3.9 shows the motto in its first instrumental and vocal entries. In addition to employing various voice combinations and textures to present the same musical material anew each time, Bach further varied his treatment of this material through the juxtaposition and interplay of the three distinct instrument groups: trumpets and timpani, oboes, and strings (Example 3.10). Bach therefore took a movement that was singular already in its form and motivic treatment and made it even more striking by expanding both its vocal and instrumental forces.

BWV 176/1: An Elaboration of Motet Style   The opening chorus of BWV 176, Bach's final Ziegler cantata, is innovative in its manipulation of, and elaboration upon, a traditional motet style. In its basic conception, the movement contains

Example 3.9   BWV 74/1

a. m. 1, strings and continuo

b. m. 8, voices

motet-like features, presenting the text in imitation with each voice doubled by instruments and containing no solely instrumental sections. However, Bach altered the traditional motet form in a number of ways. First, he presented the entire text in one statement rather than dividing the movement into sections each based on a new line of text and a new melodic motive. He did use a sectional form, with measures 1–20 being paralleled by measures 20–40, but treated the same text and melodic material in both sections. Bach's manipulation of the motet genre is further demonstrated through the movement's fast rhythmic and harmonic motion, in contrast to more conventional long notes. Finally, Bach added independent, though not thematic, string parts which further obscure the motet-like nature of the movement. While Bach composed several other imitative choral movements

Example 3.10   BWV 74/1, mm. 35–37, instrumental parts (excluding continuo)

with independent instrumental parts, BWV 176/1 is the only one in which these instrumental parts are not based on the same themes as the vocal lines.[13]

Example 3.11 illustrates these points, showing how the movement both conforms to and expands upon the conventional motet-like practices (the example begins with the end of the first vocal statement in the bass and includes the entire second statement, by the tenor).

Conclusion: Vox Christi and First-Movement Form

In summary, while four of the Vox Christi movements in the Ziegler cantatas are fairly conventional and closely related to Bach's earlier settings (BWV 108/4, 87/5, 74/4, and 68/5), seven are musically distinct and innovative, encompassing a much broader range of movement types, styles, and scorings, and are not modeled on earlier practices to such an extent (BWV 103/1, 108/1, 87/1, 183/1, 74/1, 175/1, and 176/1).

---

13   Bach's other imitative settings of biblical texts with independent instrumental parts are BWV 17/1, 40/1 (middle section), 45/1 (second section), 47/1, and 148/1. See Melamed, *J. S. Bach and the German Motet*, 132.

Example 3.11   BWV 176/1, mm. 4–7

Interestingly, the more conventional settings all appear as middle or final movements within a cantata, while the more innovative ones are all first movements.

Bach's first-movement Vox Christi texts in the Ziegler cantatas demonstrate his desire to pursue innovative compositional techniques distinct from his earlier settings. Bach's experimentation with new modes of composition was due in some measure to the sudden end of the chorale cantata format which he had pursued for most of the previous liturgical year. From 11 June 1724 (First Sunday after Trinity) to 25 March 1725 (Annunciation of Mary), Bach composed 40 chorale cantatas, writing a new chorale cantata for every liturgical occasion during this time.[14] This period represents Bach's most systematic approach to cantata composition. But after pursuing a single type of cantata to such an extent, Bach seems to have welcomed the more varied compositional possibilities afforded by Ziegler's texts.

In particular, Martin Geck has observed Bach's compositional interactions with the high number of Vox Christi texts in the post-Easter season of 1725, as the composer explored alternatives to the large-scale opening chorus.[15] Each of the 40 chorale cantatas opens with a large-scale movement in which the first verse of the chorale text is set for chorus and orchestra with the chorale melody as cantus firmus. In contrast, Bach employed a number of different styles and genres in the opening movements of the Ziegler cantatas. While two cantatas begin with chorale-based choruses similar in style to those in the chorale cantatas (BWV 128 and 68), the remaining seven open with Vox Christi texts in a variety of musical settings: two as recitative (BWV 183 and 175), two as aria (BWV 108 and 87), and three as chorus (BWV 103, 74, and 176). By employing Vox Christi texts to open seven of her nine cantatas, Ziegler thus provided Bach with the opportunity to pursue more diverse compositional procedures in his first movements.

These Vox Christi texts inspired Bach's creativity on one level because of their variety. As opposed to the rather standardized chorale verses with their strophic forms, their regular poetic patterns of syllables, lines, and rhymes, and their associated chorale melodies, the biblical texts were all prose and of varied length with no particular melodic associations. But more important for Bach than the text structure was the theological and musical tradition of the Vox Christi. This tradition provided models for setting the Vox Christi as recitative, aria, or chorus while also dictating that the musical treatment of the Vox Christi be distinctive, highlighting the theological import of the text.

The divine voice, the words of Jesus in biblical quotation, thus inspired Ziegler as cantata librettist and Bach as cantata composer, as each embraced the particular theological and musical traditions of the Vox Christi. Furthermore, the Vox Christi movements in these cantatas demonstrate how a certain textual feature of Ziegler's libretti led directly to Bach's special compositional treatment of them. The next chapter explores further the distinctive compositional features of the Ziegler/Bach cantatas, with particular attention to the relationship between Bach's musical choices and Ziegler's texts.

---

14   On Bach's chorale cantatas, see Friedhelm Krummacher, *Bachs Zyklus der Choralkantaten: Aufgaben und Lösungen* (Göttingen, 1995).

15   Geck, "Die *vox-Christi*-Sätze in Bachs Kantaten," 90.

Chapter 4

The Composer's Voice:
Bach's Compositional Procedures
in the Ziegler Cantatas

In addition to their particular textual features, J. S. Bach's nine cantatas to texts by Mariane von Ziegler have long been recognized for their special musical nature. Albert Schweitzer described the cantatas thus: "As we read through the scores we fancy we can realize the delight with which Bach set to work on these new texts."[1] But beyond Bach's treatment of the Vox Christi in the cantatas, these musical features are more difficult to describe or even, at times, to identify. Like Schweitzer, we can more often sense Bach's fresh compositional impetus in response to Ziegler's texts than we can analyze it.

Bach's singular treatment of the Vox Christi in the Ziegler cantatas certainly illustrates one way in which Ziegler's texts allowed Bach a new compositional freedom and inspiration. As detailed in the previous chapter, Ziegler's frequent inclusion of this special text type led to Bach's varied and unique settings of it as recitative, aria, and chorus. That these movements appear in eight of the nine cantatas contributes to our sense of Bach's compositional energy throughout the Ziegler cantatas.

But while we perhaps experience them less directly than the Vox Christi movements, further aspects of Bach's compositional approach in the Ziegler cantatas do contribute to our understanding of their special compositional nature. In this chapter, I will argue that particular features of Ziegler's texts, combined with Bach's departure from the chorale cantata format, inspired the composer to a particularly fertile period of musical creativity in the post-Easter season of 1725. In particular, the chapter explores Bach's distinctive approaches to aspects of structure and scoring within these nine cantatas. It first of all addresses issues of structure: order of movements within each cantata, aria forms, and recitatives combined with other movement types. It then proceeds to examine issues of scoring, addressing Bach's variety of aria scorings, his recitatives with woodwind accompaniment, and his particular attention to three instruments which appear relatively rarely in the Leipzig cantatas: flauto piccolo, violoncello piccolo, and oboe da caccia. In surveying Bach's treatment of each of these aspects of composition in the Ziegler cantatas, I will pay particular attention to aspects of Ziegler's texts which encouraged Bach's special musical treatment of them.

---

1   Albert Schweitzer, *J. S. Bach*, trans. Ernest Newman, Vol. 2 (New York, 1966; first English edition, 1911), 331.

Structure: Order of Movements

The first point of interest regarding structure in the Ziegler/Bach cantatas is that of their movement ordering. As illustrated in Table 4.1, only two of the nine cantatas (BWV 103 and 176) share the same order of movements.

Table 4.1   Order of movements in Bach's Ziegler cantatas

BWV	Movement	Text types	Music types
103	1	Bible verse	Chorus + Recitative/Arioso
	2	Recitative	Recitative
	3	Aria	Aria
	4	Recitative	Recitative
	5	Aria	Aria
	6	Chorale	Chorale
108	1	Bible verse	Aria
	2	Aria	Aria
	3	Recitative	Recitative
	4	Bible verse	Chorus
	5	Aria	Aria
	6	Chorale	Chorale
87	1	Bible verse	Aria
	2	Recitative	Recitative
	3	Aria	Aria
	4	Recitative	Recitative
	5	Bible verse	Aria
	6	Aria	Aria
	7	Chorale	Chorale
128	1	Chorale	Chorus
	2	Recitative	Recitative
	3	Aria	Aria + Recitative
		Recitative	
	4	Aria	Aria
	5	Chorale	Chorale
183	1	Bible verse	Recitative
	2	Aria	Aria
	3	Recitative	Recitative
	4	Aria	Aria
	5	Chorale	Chorale

Cantata	Movement	Text types	Music types
74	1	Bible verse	Chorus
	2	Aria	Aria
	3	Recitative	Recitative
	4	Bible verse	Aria
	5	Aria	Aria
	6	Bible verse	Recitative
	7	Aria	Aria
	8	Chorale	Chorale
68	1	Chorale	Chorus
	2	Aria	Aria
	3	Recitative	Recitative
	4	Aria	Aria
	5	Bible verse	Chorus
175	1	Bible verse	Recitative
	2	Aria	Aria
	3	Recitative	Recitative
	4	Aria	Aria
	5	Bible verse Recitative	Recitative
	6	Aria	Aria
	7	Chorale	Chorale
176	1	Bible verse	Chorus
	2	Recitative	Recitative
	3	Aria	Aria
	4	Recitative	Recitative
	5	Aria	Aria
	6	Chorale	Chorale

Such a variety is particularly noteworthy in light of Bach's more systematic approach to movement ordering in the chorale cantatas, which generally consist of a large-scale opening chorale chorus, a series of alternating recitatives and arias, and a closing simple four-part chorale. A typical example is the second cantata in the Jahrgang, BWV 2:

1 Chorale-based chorus
2 Recitative
3 Aria
4 Recitative
5 Aria
6 Chorale

While Bach did achieve variety within this structure by occasionally combining movement types (most often chorale with aria or recitative[2]), the order of movements in the chorale cantatas was fairly standardized because of the particular textual patterns their librettist tended to follow.

Indeed, when considering the issue of the number and order of movements in a cantata, we naturally think of these as being determined by the librettist rather than the composer. However, the order of movements in the Ziegler/Bach cantatas can be seen as a collaboration between librettist and composer, perhaps more so than many of Bach's other cantatas. While Bach followed the basic ordering Ziegler had prescribed, certain features of Ziegler's texts also allowed him a degree of compositional freedom to determine movement types.

The most significant aspect of Ziegler's texts which encouraged a variety of movement orderings was her high number of Bible verses, which granted the composer the choice of movement type. While recitative or aria texts necessarily dictated the musical styles and conventions of recitative or aria, no such specific style was associated with Bible verses. Bach commonly set Bible verses as choruses, in aria or arioso style, or in recitative style. So the fact that 13 of Ziegler's 55 movements were Bible verses allowed Bach the choice of genre in these movements, a choice of which he took full advantage. In the Ziegler cantatas, Bach set five Bible verses as chorus (one of these, BWV 103/1, with a recitative/arioso B section), four as aria, and four as recitative.

Bach's enthusiasm for such varied settings in the Ziegler cantatas was a result of not only the high number of Bible verses Ziegler included but also of the absence of Bible verses in the chorale cantatas of the previous year. While chorale verses could also provide some flexibility of genre choice (they could commonly be set either as a large-scale concerted movement for SATB and instrumental accompaniment, for solo voice in arioso fashion, or in a simple, homophonic four-part setting with instruments doubling the voices), Bach generally did not take such freedom with his Jahrgang II chorale settings. He rather associated particular types of settings with the movement ordering established by the librettist: in the chorale cantatas, Bach tended to set first-movement chorale verses as large-scale concerted choruses, middle-movement chorales for solo voice, and last-movement chorales in simple four-part style. Furthermore, a chorale verse dictated a particular strict poetic form, as well as a specific chorale melody, and therefore did not provide the same flexibility as a prose Bible verse with no set melodic association.

Further contributing to the varied order of movements in the Ziegler cantatas is the fact that Ziegler included Bible verses not only as first movements, which was common, but also as middle or even last movements. Of Ziegler's 13 Bible verses, seven are first movements and six are middle or last movements. Bach once again took advantage of the flexibility this afforded. Rather than setting all the first movements as large-scale choruses, as he had in the chorale cantatas, Bach set three of the first-movement Bible verses in the Ziegler cantatas as chorus, two as aria, and three as

---

2   For a list of movements in which chorales are combined with either aria or recitative in the chorale cantatas, see Friedhelm Krummacher, *Bachs Zyklus der Choralkantaten: Aufgaben und Lösungen* (Göttingen, 1995), 160–63.

recitative. While Bach had opened 12 of his newly-composed Jahrgang I cantatas with arias, the Ziegler cantatas contain Bach's only first-movement recitatives in his first two Leipzig Jahrgänge. Furthermore, Ziegler's inclusion of Bible verses as middle or last movements resulted in some singular structures, most notably BWV 108, which opens with a dictum for bass aria and contains a dictum chorus as the fourth movement; BWV 74, with its three Bible verses set as chorus (movement 1), bass aria (movement 4), and bass recitative (movement 6); and BWV 68, which ends with a dictum chorus rather than a simple chorale verse.

While we can thus observe Bach's concern for structure on the scale of the cantata as a whole, his treatment of form in individual movements can interest us even more. The following two sections address a number of fascinating movements, first arias and then recitatives, which exhibit Bach's particular attention to movement structure in the Ziegler cantatas.

Structure: Aria Forms

In considering aria forms in the Ziegler cantatas, it is BWV 128/3 that most immediately attracts our attention. In the midst of what we suspect will be a fairly conventional bass aria, Bach suddenly shifts to recitative. And once we are settled into this mode, we are surprised by the return of the aria ritornello to conclude the movement. But this large-scale inclusion of a recitative in the midst of an aria is only Bach's most obvious manipulation of form in these cantatas. And his subtler treatments are of particular interest in light of his approach to aria form in the Jahrgang II chorale cantatas (see Appendix C).

In the early chorale cantatas, Bach focused on a variety of non-repeating aria forms (including binary, tripartite, parallel, and refrain), those types which he had been exploring at the end of his first Jahrgang (see Table 4.2).[3] But following this initial period, the majority of the remaining arias are in da-capo forms. After a marked rise in da-capo arias during the period of the Thirteenth to the Twentieth Sunday after Trinity, Bach composed da-capo arias almost exclusively for the remainder of the Jahrgang II chorale cantatas: 36 of the 40 arias in these 20 cantatas are in da-capo form (90%).

Table 4.2   Aria forms in the chorale cantatas of Jahrgang II

	Da-capo forms	**Non-repeating forms**
Trinity 1–11	10	22
Trinity 13–20	13	6
Trinity 21–Annunciation	36	4

---

3   See Stephen A. Crist, "Aria Forms in the Vocal Works of J. S. Bach, 1714–1724" (Ph.D. diss.: Brandeis University, 1988).

But having thus focused on the da-capo aria for a time, Bach seems to have welcomed the formal possibilities inherent in Ziegler's aria texts, both in their freshness and vitality and in their structure and content. Bach's choices of aria forms in the Ziegler cantatas demonstrate his careful attention to each aria text and its formal and theological implications, resulting in his exploration of a wide array of formal constructions. As opposed to the 90 per cent of arias in da-capo forms in the second half of the Jahrgang II chorale cantatas, only half of the arias in the Ziegler cantatas are in da-capo forms (see Table 4.3).

Table 4.3   Arias in Bach's Ziegler cantatas

BWV	Incipit	Scoring	Form
103/3	Kein Artzt ist außer dir zu finden	A; Fl picc; Bc	Binary
103/5	Erholet euch, betrübte Sinnen	T; Tr; Ob d'am I/II/V I; V II, Va; Bc	Tripartite
108/2	Mich kann kein Zweifel stören	T; V; Bc	Binary
108/5	Was mein Herz von dir begehrt	A; V I, II, Va; Bc	Binary
87/3	Vergib, o Vater, unsre Schuld	A; Ob da cacc I, II	Strict da-capo
87/6	Ich will leiden, ich will schweigen	T; V I, II, Va; Bc	Binary
128/3	Auf, auf, mit hellem Schall	B; Tr; V I, II, Va; Bc	Binary
128/4	Sein Allmacht zu ergründen	AT; Ob d'am; Bc	Strict da-capo
183/2	Ich fürchte nicht des Todes Schrecken	T; Vc picc; Bc	Strict da-capo
183/4	Höchster Tröster, Heilger Geist	S; Ob da cacc I/II; V I, II, Va; Bc	Strict da-capo
74/2	Komm, komm, mein Herze steht dir offen	S; Ob da cacc; Bc	Binary
74/5	Kommt, eilet, stimmet Sait und Lieder	T; V I, II, Va; Bc	Free da-capo
74/7	Nichts kann mich erretten	A; Ob I, II, da cacc; V solo, V I, II, Va; Bc	Strict da-capo
68/2	Mein gläubiges Herze	S; Vc picc; Bc (+Ob I, V I in coda)	Free da-capo
68/4	Du bist geboren mir zugute	B; Ob I, II, Taille; Bc	Free da-capo
175/2	Komm, leite mich	A; Rec. I, II, III; Bc	Free da-capo
175/4	Es dünket mich, ich seh dich kommen	T; Vc picc; Bc	Binary
175/6	Öffnet euch, ihr beiden Ohren	B; Tr I, II; Bc	Strict da-capo
176/3	Dein sonst hell beliebter Schein	S; V I, II, Va; Bc	Binary

| 176/5 | Ermuntert euch, furchtsam und schüchterne Sinne | A; Ob I/II/da cacc; Bc | Tripartite |

Bach was first of all inspired to give greater attention to formal construction by the variety of Ziegler's text structures. In the majority of these arias, Bach followed his general practices of setting short aria texts (six lines or fewer) in da-capo forms and longer texts (more than six lines) in non-repeating forms. While almost all of the aria texts in the second half of the chorale cantatas were five or six lines in length, thereby encouraging da-capo settings, Ziegler's arias are almost equally divided between short and long texts and therefore encouraged Bach's use of a higher percentage of non-repeating forms.

But while such structures may have influenced Bach's formal decisions, they were not his chief determinant, as evidenced by the fact that Bach set several of Ziegler's longer texts in da-capo forms and several shorter ones in non-repeating forms. For Bach, then, the style and content of Ziegler's texts were greater determinants of form than were the elements of text structure. Bach was first of all inspired by the vibrancy of Ziegler's texts, with their striking poetic nature inspiring his creative musical treatment of them. While the arias of the late chorale cantatas tended to be generally devotional and neutral in affect, Ziegler's texts are full of inspiring phrases such as these examples from BWV 74:

Kommt, eilet, stimmet Sait und Lieder
In muntern und erfreuten Ton. (movement 5)

Nichts kann mich erretten
Von höllischen Ketten
Als, Jesu, dein Blut.
Dein Leiden, dein Sterben
Macht mich ja zum Erben:
Ich lache der Wut. (movement 7)

In addition to their vibrant poetic nature, a number of Ziegler's specific textual devices influenced Bach's treatment of aria form. One interesting technique Ziegler employed was that of a change in thought over the course of an aria text, with many of the arias demonstrating a forward progression from the opening sentence to the rest of the text. Since the speaker (generally the Christian believer) has undergone a change during the movement, it would be odd to repeat the first sentence at the end by employing a da-capo form. An example of this type of movement is BWV 103/3:

Kein Arzt ist außer dir zu finden,	No physician is to be found other than you,
Ich suche durch ganz Gilead;	Though I search all through Gilead;
Wer heilt die Wunden meiner Sünden,	Who will heal the wounds of my sins,
Weil man hier keinen Balsam hat?	Since there is no balm here?
Verbirgst du dich, so muß ich sterben.	If you hide yourself, then I must die.
Erbarme dich, ach höre doch!	Have mercy, ah, hear me, please!

Du suchest ja nicht mein Verderben,	Surely you do not seek my ruin,
Wohlan, so hofft mein Herze noch.	Well! Then my heart still has hope.

While the first half of the text conveys a lack of hope and a search for healing, the second includes a petition followed by a confident statement of hope: "Wohlan, so hofft mein Herze noch." Bach set this text in binary form, since such a declaration could not be followed by a return to the hopeless, searching text of the opening. Ziegler's use of texts which imply progression or change in the speaker thus contributed to Bach's greater focus on non-repeating forms.

Another quality of Ziegler's texts that contributed to Bach's consideration of aria form was her creation of a tight cohesion and flow of thought over the course of a cantata. More so than the chorale cantatas, Ziegler's aria texts exhibit close textual and theological connections with their surrounding movements. In choosing his aria forms, Bach clearly recognized this quality of Ziegler's texts and constructed his arias to highlight the theological themes and connections inherent between movements. An example of this is BWV 108/2 in relation to its surrounding movements:

108/1	Es ist euch gut, daß ich hingehe; denn so ich nicht hingehe, kömmt der Tröster nicht zu euch. So ich aber gehe, will ich ihn zu euch senden.	It is good for you that I depart; for if I do not depart, then the Comforter will not come to you. But if I go, then I will send him to you.
108/2	Mich kann kein Zweifel stören, Auf dein Wort, Herr, zu hören. Ich glaube, gehst du fort, So kann ich mich getrösten, Daß ich zu den Erlösten Komm an gewünschten Port.	No doubt can deter me From hearkening to your word, Lord. I believe that if you go away, Then I can comfort myself That I with the redeemed Will arrive at the desired port.
108/3	Dein Geist wird mich also regieren, Daß ich auf rechter Bahne geh; Durch deinen Hingang kommt er ja zu mir, Ich frage sorgensvoll: Ach, ist er nicht schon hier?	Your Spirit will so rule me, That I will go on the right path; Through your departure, he indeed comes to me, I ask anxiously: Ah, is he not yet here?

Rather than setting BWV 108/2 in da-capo form, as its six lines of text and general opening statement would seem to encourage, Bach achieved more continuity between movements by not repeating the opening text and setting the aria rather in binary form. The cantata's opening movement is a Vox Christi text, recording the words of Jesus from the Gospel reading. The aria responds to this by focusing on the believer's response to Jesus' words: "Mich kann kein Zweifel stören, / Auf dein Wort, Herr, zu hören." Lines 3–6 of the aria then relate directly to the ensuing recitative. The aria text speaks of arriving at the desired port, while the recitative begins by stating how this will be accomplished: "Dein Geist wird mich also regieren, / Daß ich auf rechter Bahne geh." In choosing his aria forms, Bach therefore considered not only the structure and meaning of the aria text itself but also its relation to surrounding movements.

Bach had another aspect to consider in setting Ziegler's aria texts, that of parody in the three cantatas composed for Pentecost. Given the intensive compositional demands of the feast, with its three cantatas over three consecutive days, Bach chose to compose four arias as parodies of earlier movements (BWV 74/2, 68/2, 68/4, and 175/4). However, these are not simple cases of musical transfer. In fact, only one of the four movements retained its original form and number of measures. A comparison of the new movements with their models demonstrates that Ziegler's new aria texts were more important than the old movement forms in determining Bach's formal structure. Alfred Dürr has observed the uniqueness of Bach's parody technique in the Ziegler cantatas, explaining that the new texts were not structured after the model of the old as was common; that is, Ziegler did not write the texts with the music to be parodied in mind.[4] Bach, therefore, substantively altered the musical form of three of the four arias to accommodate the new text structures.

Bach's most extensive reworking of his earlier model was in BWV 68/2, a parody of the aria BWV 208/13 and the instrumental movement BWV 1040.[5] The forms of the two arias are not related, as the one-part BWV 208/13 was transferred to the free da-capo BWV 68/2. Furthermore, while Bach incorporated the ritornello of the earlier version virtually unchanged, he fashioned a completely new vocal melody to reflect the sentiment of the new words as well as the text's change from trochaic to dactylic meter. Example 4.1 provides a comparison of the movement texts and the opening melodies of each.

Another significant change between the two arias was the replacement of the simple closing statement of the ritornello in BWV 208/13 with an almost identical version of the instrumental movement BWV 1040 at the end of BWV 68/2. While employing earlier musical material, Bach created an entirely new form, one unique among his arias, by appending an instrumental coda of 27 measures to the aria's initial 52 measures. The introduction of such an extended instrumental section, in which oboe and violin join the violoncello piccolo and continuo, grew out of the jubilant nature of the aria text: one can almost imagine the "gläubiges Herze" itself dancing in celebration (Example 4.2).

This movement presents an instance where Ziegler's striking and vibrant poetic language inspired Bach to the heights of his compositional creativity. But Bach's special compositional treatment in the Ziegler cantatas was not limited to such arias, as a number of his recitatives demonstrate.

---

4   Alfred Dürr, *The Cantatas of J. S. Bach*, rev. & trans. Richard D. P. Jones (Oxford, 2005), 35.

5   BWV 208 is a secular cantata written to a libretto by Salomo Franck for the birthday of Duke Christian of Sachsen-Weißenfels, probably in February 1713 when Bach was paid for a series of concerts in that city. Dürr, *The Cantatas of J. S. Bach*, 797, 802.

BWV 1040 appears at the end of the original score for BWV 208, following the "Fine" marking at the end of the cantata. While its place in BWV 208 is not clear, it must be understood in relation to BWV 208/13 because of their thematic connection, with BWV 1040 being based upon the ritornello for BWV 208/13. See Alfred Dürr, *Kritischer Bericht* to *Johann Sebastian Bach: Neue Ausgabe Sämtlicher Werke* I/35 (Kassel, 1964), 46–47.

Example 4.1   BWV 208/13 and 68/2

a. BWV 208/13, mm. 1–6

208/13	Weil die wollenreichen Herden	As long as the wool-rich flocks
	Durch dies weitgepriesne Feld	Through this widely-praised land
	Lustig ausgetrieben werden,	Are merrily herded,
	Lebe dieser Sachsenheld!	So long may this Saxon hero live!

Structure: Recitatives Combined with Other Movement Types

In keeping with late-Baroque convention, most of Bach's recitatives in his cantatas are simple settings for solo voice and continuo which fulfill their role of clearly communicating the text while effecting a modulation between the surrounding movements. Most of the recitatives in the Ziegler cantatas are no exception: nine of the 17 movements are in such a simple style. While there are some noteworthy moments in these nine movements (for example, the contrasted settings of the words "Schmerzen" in BWV 103/2 and "Freude" in BWV 103/4 which highlight the theological message of both the cantata's opening movement and the cantata as a whole), they generally follow Bach's conventional approach to simple recitative composition.

However, several of Bach's recitatives in the Ziegler cantatas are of compositional interest in their departures from such convention. Particularly noteworthy are the two movements in which Bach combined recitative with other text or movement types: dictum and recitative in BWV 175/5, and aria and recitative in BWV 128/3. In each example, the texts were originally designed by Ziegler as two separate movements, but Bach combined them into a single movement to emphasize their textual relationships to each other and also to their surrounding movements.

BWV 175/5

Set for alto and bass voices, BWV 175/5 is unique in its musical setting among the cantatas of Bach's first two Leipzig Jahrgänge. While the decision to have two

Example 4.1   BWV 208/13 and 68/2

b. BWV 68/2, mm. 1–6

68/2	Mein gläubiges Herze,	My believing heart,
	Frohlocke, sing, scherze,	Rejoice, sing, jest,
	Dein Jesus is da!	Your Jesus is here!
	Weg Jammer, weg Klagen,	Away misery, away lamentation,
	Ich will euch nur sagen:	I would simply say to you:
	Mein Jesus ist nah.	My Jesus is near.

voice parts sing in a recitative is itself rare, Bach's other such movements are all duets where the two voices either alternate in dialogue (BWV 60/2 and 60/4), sing homophonically (BWV 62/5), or do a combination of both (BWV 126/3). BWV 175/5 is the only recitative in two distinct sections, one for each voice part. The movement is all the more striking for its combination of Bible verse and poetic recitative text, with the dictum stated first by alto in simple recitative and the bass responding with the poetic text in accompanied recitative.

Ziegler's libretto for BWV 175 provided a clear impetus for Bach's singular setting through its close textual connections between movements. Bach clearly recognized the textual interrelationships between movements and highlighted, and even intensified, them musically. BWV 175/5 appears in the middle of three movements dealing with the senses of speech and hearing in a variety of contexts. While not employing Vox Christi text, these movements do focus on the words of Jesus and on the believer's response to them, themes which appear often in Ziegler's texts. BWV 175/4 is an aria referring to the voice of Jesus as the true shepherd, in which the believer states: "Ich kenne deine holde Stimme" ("I recognize your gracious voice"). In contrast to the believer's positive response to Jesus' voice in

Example 4.2   BWV 68/2, mm. 53–56

BWV 175/4, BWV 175/5 opens by stating "Sie vernahmen aber nicht, was es war, das er [Jesus] zu ihnen gesaget hatte" ("But they did not understand what it was that he had said to them"), a quotation from John 10:6 from the Gospel for the day. While this dictum describes the original hearers' response to Jesus' words, the ensuing poetic recitative text relates the Christian believer's response to the dictum's statement and applies it to a modern response to Jesus' words. The text begins:

Ach ja! Wir Menschen sind oftmals den Tauben zu vergleichen:	Ah, yes! We humans are often like deaf persons:
Wenn die verblendete Vernunft nicht weiß, was er gesaget hatte.	When our deluded reason does not understand what he has said.

It then goes on to highlight the importance of Jesus' words:

O! Törin, merke doch,	Oh, fool, note indeed,
wenn Jesus mit dir spricht,	when Jesus speaks with you,
Daß es zu deinem Heil geschicht.	That it concerns your salvation.

In Ziegler's published version of this cantata text (which appeared three years after Bach's setting of it), the dictum and recitative texts appear as separate movements, and it is likely that this was how Ziegler intended the movements for Bach's setting.[6] The composer, however, recognized the close relationship between the two texts and highlighted it dramatically by combining them in a single movement. Bach employed the recitative as a flexible genre which served to state a Gospel dictum, to present a commentary on that dictum, and to introduce the ensuing aria. He divided BWV 175/5 into three sections which build musically to the final textual statement that when Jesus speaks it is in regard to salvation.

Bach first employed a secco recitative style for the opening dictum text, setting the full biblical quotation for alto and continuo (Example 4.3). With the beginning of the poetic recitative text, Bach clearly distinguished a new voice and text type through the sudden shift to the bass voice and the addition of strings in accompanied recitative (Example 4.4). While continuing the same text type of poetic recitative, Bach highlighted the final portion of the movement's text with its reference to Jesus speaking. He increased the musical activity further in this final arioso-like section, with figural sixteenth-notes in the strings and eighth-note motion in the continuo replacing the sustained chords of the previous section (Example 4.5). Furthermore,

Example 4.3   BWV 175/5, mm. 1–3

Example 4.4   BWV 175/5, mm. 3–5

---

6   Christiane Mariane von Ziegler, *Versuch in gebundener Schreib-Art* (Leipzig, 1728), 267.

Example 4.5   BWV 175/5, mm. 7–11

in keeping with this arioso style, Bach employed text repetition for the first time in the movement, as the last two lines of the text are presented twice in their entirety.

The final arioso section not only emphasizes Ziegler's textual reference to Jesus' words, but also serves as a musical preparation for the following aria, BWV 175/6. The text of this aria elaborates upon the theme of Jesus speaking through its opening command to hear Jesus' words:

Öffnet euch, ihr beiden Ohren,	Open both your ears,
Jesus hat euch zugeschworen,	Jesus has sworn to you,
Daß er Teufel, Tod erlegt.	That he slays devil, death.

Musically, the aria serves as a continuation of the previous movement through its use of similar musical materials: bass voice, D major tonality, and sixteenth-note motion (Example 4.6).

Example 4.6   BWV 175/6, mm. 9–13

Furthermore, BWV 175/6 represents the final portion of a continuum of musical activity established in the previous recitative: from secco recitative (BWV 175/5, mm. 1–3) to accompanied recitative (BWV 175/5, mm. 3–7) to arioso (BWV 175/5, mm. 7–14) to aria (BWV 175/6). Bach, therefore, created a unique recitative structure in BWV 175/5 to emphasize the textual link between the Gospel dictum and Ziegler's poetic recitative and also to closely relate these texts not only to each other but also to the ensuing aria. His recognition of the unique nature of Ziegler's text thus resulted in a singular recitative setting.

BWV 128/3

In BWV 128/3, Bach again combined into a single movement texts which Ziegler had intended as two separate movements, here an aria and a recitative.[7] Bach had combined aria and recitative in a single movement only twice previously in his first two Leipzig Jahrgänge, in BWV 83/2 and 127/4. But both of these movements

---

7   Like the dictum and recitative combined in BWV 175/5, Ziegler's later publication of the libretto for BWV 128 presents the aria and recitative as two separate movements. Ziegler, *Versuch in gebundener Schreib-Art*, 255–56.

consist of brief alternating sections of aria and recitative, rather than a large-scale interruption of an aria by recitative as in BWV 128/3 (Table 4.4).

Table 4.4   Movement structure, BWV 128/3

mm.	Style	Time	Tonality
1–60	Aria	3/4	D major
61–71	Recitative	C	B minor
72–88	Aria ritornello	3/4	D major

The movement begins as a fairly conventional aria, in which the bass voice and obbligato trumpet reflect the joyous and proclamatory nature of the text (see Example 4.7):

Auf, auf, mit hellem Schall	Rise up, rise up with bright sound
Verkündigt überall:	Proclaim everywhere:
Mein Jesus sitzt zur Rechten!	My Jesus sits at the right hand [of God]!

Likewise, the B section of this binary form begins typically with the next line of text set to contrasting musical material:

Wer sucht mich anzufechten?	Who seeks to attack me?

However, Bach suddenly interrupts the aria with a recitative in B Minor and common time for bass, strings, and continuo (see Example 4.8). The textual shift is also sudden, going from the aria rejoicing that the believer will follow Jesus up to heaven to the recitative in which the believer seeks to hide from God's presence but cannot. The recitative concludes with a call for the mouth to be silent in light of God's omnipotence (Example 4.9):

So schweig, verwegner Mund,	So be silent, presumptuous mouth,
Und suche nicht dieselbe zu ergründen!	And do not seek to fathom it!

Rather than the recitative's command to be silent being answered immediately by the literal silence of the movement's end or by a musical style evoking silence, Bach concluded rather with a full statement of BWV 128/3's aria ritornello. This clear representation of proclamation immediately following the recitative's command to be silent may appear to be a musical contradiction. However, rather than contradicting the recitative's command, Bach emphasized Ziegler's point that speech and silence each have their proper place: the believer should proclaim God's greatness, but should not presume to fully understand God's omnipotence.

Furthermore, by incorporating the recitative into the third movement aria and therefore returning to the aria ritornello at the end of the movement, Bach contrasted the ideas of proclamation and silence not only within the third movement but also between the cantata's two arias. Bach directly juxtaposed the ritornellos of BWV 128/3 and 128/4 and, in so doing, highlighted musically the textual contrast between the theme of proclamation in BWV 128/3 and that of silence in BWV 128/4. To

Example 4.7   BWV 128/3, mm. 17–21

the third movement recitative's command for the believer to be silent, the fourth movement aria responds positively:

Sein Allmacht zu ergründen,	To fathom his omnipotence
Wird sich kein Mensche finden,	Will no human be able,
Mein Mund verstummt und schweigt.	My mouth falls dumb and becomes silent.

The affect of BWV 128/4 is one that Bach often employed for texts related to the believer pondering heaven and Jesus sitting at God's right hand (most notably in the "Qui sedes" of the Mass in B Minor): a minor key, 6/8 time signature, oboe d'amore, and alto or tenor voice (here alto and tenor duet). By incorporating the recitative into BWV 128/3 rather than delineating it as a separate movement, Bach thus strikingly

Example 4.8   BWV 128/3, mm. 58–62

contrasted the trumpet obbligato, D major tonality, and 3/4 time of BWV 128/3 with the oboe d'amore obbligato, B minor tonality, and 6/8 time of BWV 128/4. Bach clearly recognized Ziegler's focus on the themes of vocal expression, that is, proclamation and silence, in BWV 128 and created a unique movement structure to highlight these themes.

Scoring: Arias and Recitatives

In the issues of compositional structure above—order of movements, aria forms, recitative combined with other movement types—it is clear that particular features of Ziegler's texts contributed to Bach's compositional choices. Like his special treatment of the Vox Christi, we can recognize the influences Ziegler's textual choices had on Bach's settings of them. A further musical feature of the Ziegler/Bach cantatas, their scorings, cannot be easily tied to their textual distinctiveness, but certainly

Example 4.9   BWV 128/3, mm. 68–73

contributes to the special sound of the cantatas, to our understanding of them as a distinct compositional group, and to our sense of "the delight with which Bach set to work on these new texts."[8] After surveying some features of scoring in Bach's arias and recitatives in this section, the next section examines Bach's treatment of flauto piccolo, violoncello piccolo, and oboe da caccia in the Ziegler cantatas.

---

8   Schweitzer, *J. S. Bach*, vol. 2, 331.

Aria Scoring

One notable feature of the Ziegler cantatas is their varied scorings, particularly in the arias (see Table 4.3 for a listing of all arias in these cantatas). The distinctive sound of the first aria, BWV 103/3, with its flauto piccolo obbligato, alerts the listener to Bach's attention to instrumental color in these works. Continued study further reveals Bach's explorations of the instrumental palette in the Ziegler cantatas: for example, the three recorders in BWV 175/2; the three unison oboes in BWV 176/5; the highly virtuosic treatment of solo oboe da caccia in BWV 74/2; the three oboes with solo violin and strings in BWV 74/7; and the rare violoncello piccolo in BWV 183/2, 68/2, and 175/4.

Upon further study, we realize that with the exception of four arias with strings alone, the only aria scoring Bach repeated in the Ziegler cantatas was solo violoncello piccolo with continuo in three movements (see Table 4.5). Outside of these movements, he employed a different scoring in every aria of the Ziegler cantatas.

Table 4.5   Aria scorings in Bach's Ziegler cantatas (excluding arias accompanied by strings and continuo alone)

With strings and continuo	With continuo
Ob I, II, Ob da cacc; V solo (74/7)	Fl picc (103/3)
Ob da cacc I/II (183/4)	Rec I, II, III (175/2)
Tr (128/3)	Ob I/II/Ob da cacc (176/5)
Tr; Ob d'am I/II/V I (103/5)	Ob I, II, Taille (68/4)
	Ob d'am (128/4)
	Ob da cacc (74/2)
	Ob da cacc I, II (87/3)
	Tr I, II (175/6)
	V (108/2)
	Vc picc (183/2, 68/2, 175/4)

Such an approach was different than Bach's treatment of aria scoring in the chorale cantatas of Jahrgang II, where he tended rather to explore the treatment of a particular scoring across a variety of movements. Of the 99 arias in these cantatas, 14 are set with basic string accompaniment (V I, V II, Va; Bc) and 17 are accompanied by continuo alone. Within the remaining 68 movements, a number of scorings stand out for the frequency with which Bach employed them: violin and continuo in seven arias, flute and continuo in nine, and various combinations with oboe in 27 (solo oboe or oboe d'amore in five movements, two oboes or two oboes d'amore in 11 movements, three oboes in five movements, solo oboe or oboe d'amore with strings in six movements). In the Ziegler cantatas, therefore, Bach sought to vary the sounds of the arias rather than continue to explore such common scorings from the previous year.

Recitatives with Woodwind Accompaniment

But while we may expect such a creative treatment of scoring in arias, Bach's interest in instrumental color is notable also in the recitatives of the Ziegler cantatas. Of particular note are the four accompanied recitatives with woodwind instruments rather than the more typical strings (listed in Table 4.6).

Table 4.6   Recitatives with woodwind accompaniment in Bach's Ziegler cantatas

BWV	Voice	Instrumentation
183/1	Bass	Ob d'am I, II, Ob da cacc I, II; Bc
183/3	Alto	Ob d'am I, II, Ob da cacc I, II; V I, II, Va; Bc
74/6	Bass	Ob I, II, Ob da cacc; Bc
175/1	Tenor	Rec I, II, III; Bc

Prior to the Ziegler cantatas, Bach had set only eight solo recitative movements with woodwind accompaniment in his Leipzig cantatas (BWV 46/2, 119/4, 107/2, 94/3, 5/4, 180/4, 122/3, and 111/5). Of these eight movements, four combine recitative with chorale text or melody (BWV 107/2, 94/3, 5/4, and 122/3). In the other four movements, Bach used a particular woodwind combination to reflect the theological content of the text: parallel sixteenth-note figures in the recorders in BWV 46/2 to represent Jesus weeping over Jerusalem, trumpet flourishes for the festive nature of BWV 119/4 written for the installation of the Town Council, two recorders in BWV 180/4 to reflect the mystery of the Eucharist, and two oboes in BWV 111/5 for a text relating to death.

But Bach did not employ woodwinds either in association with chorales or with particular textual themes in the recitatives of the Ziegler cantatas. In fact, such a textual association is evident only in BWV 175/1, in which three recorders reflect the pastoral nature of the text. In the other three movements, Bach seems to have chosen woodwind accompaniments for the sake of highlighting the textual importance of each movement within its cantata. For two of the three (BWV 183/1 and 74/6), the text is a biblical quotation which is thus set apart by its unique scoring. Furthermore, in BWV 183/1 and 183/3, the shared scoring of four oboes emphasizes the textual connection inherent between the two movements, with the words of Jesus in the opening movement being answered by the believer in the third movement:

183/1	Sie werden euch in den Bann tun, es kömmt aber die Zeit, daß, wer euch tötet, wird meinen, er tue Gott einen Dienst daran.	They will excommunicate you, there is indeed coming a time when whoever kills you will think he is doing God a service thereby.
183/3	Ich bin bereit, mein Blut und armes Leben	I am prepared my blood and poor life
	Vor dich, mein Heiland, hinzugeben,	To give up for you, my Savior;

Mein ganzer Mensch soll dir gewidmet sein;	My entire person will be dedicated to you;
Ich tröste mich, dein Geist wird bei mir stehen,	I console myself that your Spirit will stand by me,
Gesetzt, es sollte mir vielleicht zuviel geschehen.	If it should ever become too much for me.

Recognizing Ziegler's related textual themes between these two movements, Bach highlighted their interrelationship not only through their shared genre of recitative but also through their common use of four oboes.

Scoring: Flauto piccolo, Violoncello piccolo, and Oboe da caccia

In addition to his variety of scorings in the arias and his attention to recitatives with woodwind accompaniment, Bach's interest in instrumental color in the Ziegler cantatas is exhibited through his attention to three instruments rarely found in his earlier cantatas: flauto piccolo, violoncello piccolo, and oboe da caccia. Once again, while nothing inherent in Ziegler's texts pointed Bach to employ such instruments, his exploration of them provides further evidence of these cantatas as a distinct period of creativity, one in which Bach concerned himself with a variety of compositional possibilities.

Flauto piccolo

The special nature of Bach's scorings is evident from the first of the Ziegler cantatas, BWV 103, whose opening chorus and first aria both feature a flauto piccolo obbligato. Bach employed flauto piccolo (soprano recorder sounding an octave higher than notated) in only five movements during his first two years in Leipzig (listed in Table 4.7), the final two of which are in BWV 103. Furthermore, it is not certain which type of instrument Bach intended for the two movements in BWV 8, whether soprano recorder as in BWV 96 and 103 or a small traverso sounding a whole tone higher.[9]

Bach's style of flauto piccolo writing is similar in all five movements, with the instrument emerging as the primary voice in each not only by virtue of its high range but also due to its virtuosic nature with rapid, often arpeggiated, figuration. Example 4.10 demonstrates Bach's general style of flauto piccolo writing as represented in BWV 103/1.

---

9   See Helmuth Osthoff and Rufus Hallmark, *Kritischer Bericht* to *Johann Sebastian Bach: Neue Ausgabe Sämtlicher Werke* I/23 (Kassel: Bärenreiter, 1984), 76–78. Bach later provided alternate versions of BWV 96/1, 103/1, and 103/3 with the flauto piccolo part given to violino piccolo in BWV 96/1 and to either violino concertato or flauto traverso in BWV 103/1 and 103/3.

Table 4.7   Flauto piccolo in Bach's sacred cantatas (Ziegler in bold)

Date	BWV	Movement	Scoring
24 Sept 1724	8/1	Chorus	SATB; Cor; Fl picc, Ob d'am I, II; V I, II, Va; Bc
24 Sept 1724	8/4	Aria	B; Fl picc; V I, II, Va; Bc
8 Oct 1724	96/1	Chorus	SATB; Cor; Fl picc, Ob I, II; V I, II, Va; Bc
22 Apr 1725	**103/1**	Chorus	SATB; Fl picc; Ob d'am I, II; V I, II, Va; Bc
22 Apr 1725	**103/3**	Aria	A; Fl picc; Bc

Example 4.10   BWV 103/1, mm. 1–13, flauto piccolo

While sharing the rapid passagework and virtuosic nature of the earlier examples, the flauto piccolo part in BWV 103/3 is of further interest as the only movement of the five in which the flauto piccolo appears as solo instrument with voice and continuo. In keeping with its role as solo obbligato instrument in this aria, the flauto piccolo writing is not only virtuosic but also beautifully melodic (Example 4.11).

Violoncello piccolo

Bach's exploration of distinctive instrumental sounds in his Ziegler cantatas is further demonstrated through his use of violoncello piccolo. As listed in Table 4.8, Bach employed violoncello piccolo in only nine movements in his Leipzig cantatas. With the exception of the later BWV 49, the movements with violoncello piccolo spanned a relatively brief time period, from 22 October 1724 to 22 May 1725. Furthermore, five of these eight movements, including those in the Ziegler cantatas, occurred in the post-Easter season of 1725.

As opposed to those with flauto piccolo, Bach's movements with violoncello piccolo are all for solo voice and small ensemble, reflecting the intimate nature of the instrument. Furthermore, Bach employed a similar style of violoncello piccolo writing throughout, featuring agile, leaping sixteenth-note motion in highly virtuosic

Example 4.11   BWV 103/3, mm. 1–12, flauto piccolo

Table 4.8   Violoncello piccolo in Bach's sacred cantatas (Ziegler in bold)

Date	BWV	Movement	Scoring
22 Oct 1724	180/3	Chorale	S; Vc picc; Bc
5 Nov 1724	115/4	Aria	S; Fl; Vc picc; Bc
1 Jan 1725	41/4	Aria	T; Vc picc; Bc
2 Apr 1725	6/3	Chorale	S; Vc picc; Bc
15 Apr 1725	85/2	Aria	A; Vc picc; Bc
13 May 1725	**183/2**	Aria	T; Vc picc; Bc
21 May 1725	**68/2**	Aria	S; Vc picc; Bc (+ Ob I, V I in Ritornello)
22 May 1725	**175/4**	Aria	T; Vc picc; Bc
3 Nov 1726	49/4	Aria	Ob d'am; Vc picc; Bc

fashion. The movements are all dance-like in their nature, and Miriam Bolduan argues that all nine are in Allemande style.[10]

---

10   Miriam F. Bolduan, "The Significance of the *Viola Pomposa* in the Bach Cantatas," *BACH: Journal of the Riemenschneider Bach Institute* 14 (1983): 12–17 (14). On Bach and the violoncello piccolo, see also Winfried Schrammek, "Viola pomposa und Violoncello piccolo bei Johann Sebastian Bach," in *Bericht über die Wissenschaftliche Konferenz zum III. Internationalen Bachfest der DDR, Leipzig, 1975*, ed. Werner Felix, Winfried Hoffmann, and Armin Schneiderheinze, 345–54 (Leipzig, 1977); Laurence Dreyfus, *Bach's Continuo Group: Players and Practices in His Vocal Works* (Cambridge, MA, 1987), 172–75; Ulrich Drüner, "Violoncello piccolo und Viola pomposa bei Johann Sebastian Bach: Zu Fragen von Identität und Spielweise dieser Instrumente," *Bach-Jahrbuch* 73 (1987): 85–112; Alfred Dürr, "Philologisches zum Problem Violoncello piccolo bei Bach," in *Festschrift Wolfgang Rehm zum 60. Geburtstag*, 45–50 (Kassel, 1989); and Mark M. Smith, "Joh. Seb. Bachs Violoncello piccolo: Neue Aspekte–offene Fragen," *Bach-Jahrbuch* 84 (1998): 63–81.

The three movements with violoncello piccolo in Bach's Ziegler cantatas represent two different affects for the instrument within this same general style. The first, represented by BWV 183/2, is in a minor key and common time, reflecting the Christian's quiet confidence even in the face of death (Example 4.12). The movement is similar in affect to Bach's preceding aria with violoncello piccolo, BWV 85/2, in which the believer expresses confidence in Jesus as the good shepherd. BWV 68/2 and 175/4, on the other hand, are joyous movements in major keys and alla breve, most closely related in affect to Bach's final movement with violoncello piccolo, BWV 49/4. Bach's style of violoncello piccolo writing for such celebratory texts is demonstrated in the opening measures of BWV 68/2 (Example 4.13).

Example 4.12   BWV 183/2, mm. 1–5, violoncello piccolo

Example 4.13   BWV 68/2, mm. 1–4, violoncello piccolo

Oboe da caccia

Of further interest regarding Bach's scoring practices in the Ziegler cantatas is his frequent use of oboe da caccia. While much more common in Bach's works than either flauto piccolo or violoncello piccolo, oboe da caccia was a relatively new instrument that had not been available to Bach before his arrival in Leipzig. After initial experimentation with oboe da caccia in his early Leipzig cantatas, Bach did not often employ it in his cantatas until the end of Jahrgang II, with special attention to it in the Ziegler cantatas. In fact, of Bach's 34 movements with oboe da caccia in his first two Leipzig Jahrgänge, 15 of them appear in the Ziegler cantatas.[11] Furthermore,

---

11   These numbers include movements with parts labeled either "oboe da caccia" or "taille." Reine Dahlqvist argues that Bach intended the same instrument for both designations, with oboe da caccia indicating more soloistic treatment and "taille" being assigned to less involved third oboe parts. Reine Dahlqvist, "Taille, Oboe da Caccia and Corno Inglese,"

Bach's treatment of oboe da caccia in his Ziegler cantatas differed from his earlier approach, particularly in the function of oboe da caccia in the choruses, the number of recitatives with oboes da caccia, and the increased number of arias with virtuosic oboe da caccia writing.

Choruses   What is striking about Bach's use of oboe da caccia in the choruses of the Ziegler cantatas is the frequency with which he included the instrument, as well as the consistency of function he assigned to it within the instrumental fabric. First of all, Bach included oboe da caccia in five of the seven choruses in the Ziegler cantatas, after having employed it in only six choruses previously in his Leipzig cantatas (see Table 4.9).

Table 4.9   Choruses with oboe da caccia in Bach's sacred cantatas, Jahrgang I and II (Ziegler in bold)

Date	BWV	Scoring
1 Aug 1723	46/1	Tr da tir; Rec I, II, Ob da cacc I, II; V I, II, Va; Bc
6 Jan 1724	65/1	Cor I, II; Rec I, II, Ob da cacc I, II; V I, II, Va; Bc
23 Apr 1724	104/1	Ob I, II, Taille; V I, II, Va; Bc
22 Oct 1724	180/1	Rec I, II, Ob, Taille; V I, II, Va; Bc
25 Mar 1725	1/1	Cor I, II; Ob da cacc I, II; V conc I, II, V I, II, Va; Bc
2 Apr 1725	6/1	Ob I, II, Ob da cacc; V I, II, Va; Bc
10 May 1725	**128/1**	Cor I, II; Ob I/V I, Ob II/V II, Ob da cacc/Va; Bc
20 May 1725	**74/1**	Tr I, II, III, Timp; Ob I, II, Ob da cacc; V I, II, Va; Bc
21 May 1725	**68/1**	Cor; Ob I/V I, Ob II/V II, Taille/Va; Bc
21 May 1725	**68/5**	Cornetto/Ob I/V I, Trb I/Ob II/V II, Trb II/Taille/Va, Trb III; Bc
27 May 1725	**176/1**	Ob I, II, Ob da cacc; V I, II, Va; Bc

Furthermore, in the choruses of the Ziegler cantatas, Bach consistently employed oboe da caccia for its timbral qualities in doubling voices rather than as an independent instrumental line. In all five movements, Bach used a single oboe da caccia as the third oboe, with the three oboes serving to double the strings or voices or both. Only in BWV 74/1 do the oboes play any independent lines (although they still double the strings at times), but this chorus is a parody of an earlier duet, BWV 59/1. Such a regular approach to the oboe da caccia contrasts Bach's earlier treatment of the instrument in the six choral movements prior to the Ziegler cantatas, in which he employed a variety of approaches. In these earlier movements, Bach included sometimes one and sometimes two oboes da caccia, with the instruments sometimes doubling voices in motet-like movements or sections and at other times playing independent parts.

Gaplin Society Journal 26 (1973): 58–71 (59–61). In the ensuing discussion, I will use the term "oboe da caccia" for both oboe da caccia and taille designations.

Recitatives   In contrast to this regular approach to oboe da caccia writing in the choruses, Bach's use of oboe da caccia in three recitatives of the Ziegler cantatas is varied (see Table 4.10).

Table 4.10   Recitatives with oboe da caccia in Bach's sacred cantatas, Jahrgang I and II (Ziegler in bold)

Date	BWV	Scoring
30 Aug 1723	119/4	B; Tr I, II, III, IV, Timp; Rec I, II, Ob da cacc I, II; Bc
13 May 1725	**183/1**	B; Ob d'am I, II, Ob da cacc I, II; Bc
13 May 1725	**183/3**	A; Ob d'am I, II, Ob da cacc I, II; V I, II, Va; Bc
20 May 1725	**74/6**	B; Ob I, II, Ob da cacc; Bc

Not only is the inclusion of oboes da caccia in recitative itself noteworthy (as the composer had done so only once before), but Bach also treated the instrument differently in each of the three movements. In BWV 183/1, two oboes d'amore and two oboes da caccia play sustained notes. In BWV 183/3, Bach once again employed two oboes d'amore and two oboes da caccia, now with strings added. In this movement, the strings play the sustained accompanimental chords which had been assigned to the oboes in BWV 183/1, while the oboes play paired figural lines contributing to a fairly elaborate instrumental texture. Bach used oboe da caccia differently again in BWV 74/6, with a single oboe da caccia appearing as the third oboe in accompaniment, first with sustained chords and then a simple eighth-note pattern.

Arias   In both the choruses and recitatives of the Ziegler cantatas then, Bach's treatment of the oboe da caccia focused on the distinctive sound it contributed to the instrumental palette, rather than on the technical capabilities of the instrument. It was in the arias, however, that Bach explored the oboe da caccia as a virtuosic instrument (see Table 4.11).

The Ziegler cantatas are notable both for their high number of arias with oboe da caccia (six movements in nine cantatas) and for their virtuosic treatment of the instrument. While three of the arias in the Ziegler cantatas employ oboe da caccia as third oboe (BWV 74/7, 68/4, and 176/5) in similar fashion to the choruses, three others treat it instead as a virtuosic obbligato instrument (BWV 87/3, 183/4, and 74/2). Example 4.14 demonstrates this latter type of movement.

Such a virtuosic treatment of the oboe da caccia is striking in light of Bach's earlier treatment of the instrument. In the arias of Jahrgang I, Bach employed one or two oboes da caccia playing simple, flowing lines, often in an imitative texture. These movements contain no virtuosic treatment of the instrument and often invoke a pastoral feel, as in this typical example from BWV 179 (see Example 4.15).

But after his Epiphany cantata, BWV 65 (composed for 6 January 1724), Bach did not set another aria with oboe da caccia for over seven months. When he did

Table 4.11   Arias with oboe da caccia in Bach's sacred cantatas, Jahrgang I and II (Ziegler in bold)

Date	BWV	**Scoring**
24 June 1723	167/3	SA; Ob da cacc; Bc
1 Aug 1723	46/5	A; Rec I, II, Ob da cacc I, II
8 Aug 1723	179/5	S; Ob da cacc I, II; Bc
15 Aug 1723	69a/3	T; Rec, Ob da cacc; Bc
30 Aug 1723	119/3	T; Ob da cacc I, II; Bc
6 Jan 1724	65/4	B; Ob da cacc I, II; Bc
6 Jan 1724	65/6	T; Cor I, II; Rec I, II, Ob da cacc I, II; V I, II, Va; Bc
13 Aug 1724	101/4	B; Ob I, II, Taille; Bc
13 Aug 1724	101/6	SA; Fl, Ob da cacc; Bc
22 Oct 1724	180/5	S; Rec I, II, Ob, Taille; V I, II, Va; Bc
25 Mar 1725	1/3	S; Ob da cacc; Bc
2 Apr 1725	6/2	A; Ob da cacc or Va; Bc
6 May 1725	**87/3**	A; Ob da cacc I, II; Bc
13 May 1725	**183/4**	S; Ob da cacc I/II; V I, II, Va; Bc
20 May 1725	**74/2**	S; Ob da cacc; Bc
20 May 1725	**74/7**	A; Ob I, II, Ob da cacc; V solo, V I, II, Va; Bc
21 May 1725	**68/4**	B; Ob I, II, Taille; Bc
27 May 1725	**176/5**	Ob I/II/Ob da cacc; Bc

resume within his Jahrgang II chorale cantatas, beginning with BWV 101 on 13 August 1724, his treatment of the instrument was markedly different. On the one hand, Bach sometimes employed the oboe da caccia in a similar fashion as in his choruses, where it served as third oboe and did not have a prominent role in the movement (for example, BWV 101/4). On the other hand, Bach also introduced in the arias of the chorale cantatas a more virtuosic treatment of the oboe da caccia (for example, BWV 1/3). Bach's writing for the oboe da caccia in the arias of the Ziegler cantatas was thus consistent with his approach to the instrument in Jahrgang II, as he sometimes employed it as a third oboe and sometimes explored its virtuosic possibilities as a solo instrument.

In considering Bach's approach to scoring in the Ziegler cantatas from such a variety of perspectives, I believe it is insightful to conclude with the consideration of a single cantata, BWV 183 (see Table 4.12).

Listening to this cantata, or, indeed, any of the Ziegler cantatas, will illustrate simply Bach's concern for exploring new instrumental sounds during this period. BWV 183 opens with a Vox Christi recitative set apart by its distinctive scoring for two oboes d'amore and two oboes da caccia, followed by an aria accompanied by the rare violoncello piccolo. After strings join the four oboes for the third movement recitative, the final aria features two virtuosic oboes da caccia playing a unison

Example 4.14   BWV 74/2, mm. 13–20, instrumental parts

Example 4.15   BWV 179/5, mm. 1–5

Table 4.12   BWV 183, scoring

BWV	Movement type	Scoring
183/1	Recitative	B; Ob d'am I, II, Ob da cacc I, II; Bc
183/2	Aria	T; Vc picc; Bc
183/3	Recitative	A; Ob d'am I, II, Ob da cacc I, II; V I, II, Va; Bc
183/4	Aria	S; Ob da cacc I/II; V I, II, Va; Bc
183/5	Chorale	S/Ob d'am I/Ob d'am II/V I; A/Ob da cacc I/V II; T/Ob da cacc II/Va; B/Bc

obbligato over strings. The cantata closes with a simple chorale accompanied by the entire instrumental ensemble. While there is much in the forms and structures of the Ziegler cantatas that can interest us, often it is such distinctive instrumental sounds which provide us with the clue to their special nature.

Conclusion

As demonstrated through this and the previous chapter, Ziegler's singular approach to the cantata libretto provided Bach with special compositional impetus that resulted in a number of singular musical settings. The nine Ziegler cantatas show Bach at the height of his compositional creativity in the genre of the sacred cantata, a genre in which he would never again compose as regularly as he did in his second Leipzig Jahrgang. That Bach continued to value his cantatas to Ziegler texts in later years is evidenced by his subsequent performances of them. Of the nine cantatas, the presence of later source material indicates that Bach certainly performed four of them at a later date (BWV 103, 108, 175, and 176).[12] Two others, BWV 128 and 68, he considered part of his chorale cantata Jahrgang by virtue of their large-scale chorale chorus first movements.[13]

But despite both their textual and musical interest, the Ziegler cantatas have received little attention in the Bach literature, often being relegated to a passing reference in the midst of a larger study. While downplaying Ziegler's significant contribution to Bach's sacred cantata output, scholars have been quick to assert that Bach (or perhaps another librettist) altered Ziegler's texts for his settings and to observe that Bach never set any of the 64 liturgical cantata texts from Ziegler's 1729 *Versuch in gebundener Schreib-Art, anderer und letzter Theil*. The next chapter takes up the history of the reception of the Ziegler cantatas in the scholarly literature and calls for a reconsideration of Ziegler's significance for Bach's sacred cantata output.

---

12   Of these, only one performance can be dated, BWV 108 on 15 April 1731. While there is no known source evidence to indicate later performances of the remaining five Ziegler cantatas, such evidence would not exist if Bach performed them unaltered.

13   Dürr, *The Cantatas of J. S. Bach*, 329.

Chapter 5

Woman's Voice Restored:
The Reception of the Ziegler Cantatas
and their Significance in Bach's Output

Despite the special nature of both the texts and the music of the Ziegler/Bach cantatas and Ziegler's role as Bach's only female librettist, representations of Ziegler in the Bach literature of the past 50 years have often been ambivalent. Ziegler has first of all suffered from neglect, receiving little detailed scholarly attention either in literary studies or in musicology. The fact that the present volume provides the first in-depth study of the Ziegler cantatas or of Ziegler herself serves to highlight this state of affairs.

In the field of German literature, while Ziegler is frequently mentioned in surveys of women's writing in eighteenth-century Germany or in dictionaries of female authors, few detailed studies of her have been undertaken. The most comprehensive treatment of Ziegler is in Katherine Goodman's *Amazons and Apprentices: Women and the German Parnassus in the Early Enlightenment*.[1] Goodman focuses throughout on Ziegler and Luise Gottsched within the context of women's involvement in the literary life of early eighteenth-century Germany. But while she does treat Ziegler's life and works in more detail than any other scholar, Goodman tends to cast Ziegler in a rather negative light (in contrast to Luise Gottsched), particularly in describing Ziegler after Luise Gottsched's arrival in Leipzig in 1735. Only two articles in the field of literary studies have presented critical considerations of Ziegler's writings: Sunka Simon's "'Als sie ihr Bildness schildern sollte:' Die sprachliche Struktur der Innen- und Aussenporträts in der Lyrik Christiana Mariana von Zieglers"[2] and Steven R. Huff's "Christiane Mariane von Ziegler's *Versuch in gebundener Schreib=Art* (Volume I, 1728)."[3]

Ziegler has not fared much better in the field of musicology, with only two articles presenting detailed considerations of Ziegler as cantata librettist: Wolfgang Herbst's "Ein Vergleich zwischen Joh. Seb. Bach und Chr. Mariane v. Ziegler"[4] and Sabine Ehrmann's "Johann Sebastian Bachs Textdichterin Christiane Mariane von

---

1   Columbia, SC, 1999.

2   *Daphnis* 19 (1990): 247–65.

3   In *"Der Buchstab tödt—der Geist macht lebendig": Festschrift zum 60. Geburtstage von Hans-Gert Roloff von Freunden, Schülern und Kollegen*, Vol. 2, ed. James Hardin and Jörg Jungmayr, 977–88 (Bern, 1992).

4   *Musik und Kirche* 30 (1960): 248–55.

Ziegler."[5] Herbst's article is highly critical of Ziegler, as his goal throughout seems to have been to elevate Bach by denigrating Ziegler and her texts. Furthermore, only two articles have been written on individual Ziegler cantatas set by Bach: Lothar and Renate Steiger's "J. S. Bach 'Es ist euch gut, daß ich hingehe' (BWV 108): Theologisch-musikalische Auslegung mit Anregungen für die Predigt und aufführungspraktischen Hinweisen"[6] and Ulrich Konrad's "Aspekte musikalisch-theologischen Verstehens in Mariane von Zieglers und Johann Sebastian Bachs Kantate *Bisher habt ihr nichts gebeten in meinem Namen* BWV 87."[7]

When Ziegler is mentioned elsewhere in the musicological literature, it is often in a somewhat negative light. While few authors (with the exception of Herbst) are directly critical of Ziegler, many tend to downplay her contribution to Bach's cantata output by stating that Bach or another librettist altered Ziegler's texts for Bach's setting of them and emphasizing that Bach never set any cantatas from the remainder of Ziegler's Jahrgang, the 64 sacred cantata texts published in her 1729 *Versuch in gebundener Schreib-Art, anderer und letzter Theil*. Granted, these authors are merely repeating what has been said about Ziegler in the Bach literature for decades, and I do not believe they are intentionally denigrating her work. However, in light of the fuller understanding of Ziegler, her writings, and Bach's settings of her cantata texts presented in this book, I feel the time has come for a reconsideration of our view of Ziegler. After reviewing the scholarly history of the claim that Bach or another librettist altered Ziegler's texts for their 1725 settings, I will present a re-interpretation of the evidence in this regard and argue for a revised understanding of Ziegler's importance as cantata librettist.

Text Changes in the Ziegler Cantatas: From Spitta to the Present[8]

The fact that Ziegler's texts set by Bach exist in two different versions is certainly a point of interest. We know surprisingly little about Bach's textual approach to cantata libretti, as the text sources for most of Bach's almost 200 extant sacred cantatas are unknown. In a number of cantatas for which the librettist is known, Bach's setting is itself the only source for the text with no published version existing. Therefore, the nine Ziegler cantatas are among a minority of pieces for which we are able to compare between cantata texts as they were published and as Bach set them. However, such a comparison is not in this case as straightforward as it first appears, since Bach was clearly not working from the published versions of the cantata texts. Ziegler published these nine texts in her *Versuch in gebundener Schreib-Art* of 1728, three years after Bach had set the texts in April and May of 1725.

---

5   *Beiträge zur Bachforschung* 9–10 (1991): 261–68.

6   In *Cantate: Eine Handreichung für Pfarrer und Kirchenmusiker zum Schütz- und Bach-Gedenkjahr 1985*, ed. Walter Blankenburg and Renate Steiger, 49–59 (Kassel, 1985).

7   *Archiv für Musikwissenschaft* 57 (2000): 199–221.

8   Material from this section first appeared in Mark Peters, "A Reconsideration of Bach's Role as Text Redactor in the Ziegler Cantatas," *BACH: Journal of the Riemenschneider Bach Institute* 36 (2005): 25–66. See article for a more detailed treatment of this topic.

Despite this chronology, most scholars have assumed that the texts Ziegler gave Bach in 1725 were identical to those she published in 1728 and that Bach or another librettist altered the texts for the 1725 settings. A significant source for the belief that Bach altered Ziegler's texts was Philip Spitta's chronology of the Bach cantatas from the late nineteenth century. Spitta had placed Bach's composition of the nine cantatas in the 1730s, well after Ziegler published the texts in her 1728 *Versuch in gebundener Schreib-Art*, and he therefore naturally assumed that Bach was working from the published versions.[9] Despite the "new" Bach chronology of the 1950s showing that the cantatas were actually first performed in 1725, three years before Ziegler published the texts, the belief that Bach altered Ziegler's texts persisted.

Wolfgang Herbst, writing in 1960, held Bach to be the originator of the differences between the two versions. In considering Bach's settings of Ziegler's texts, he stated:

> It is also remarkable how Bach treated the text models of Frau von Ziegler. Bach did not adopt a single one of the Ziegler texts unaltered. All were tightened up or revised, against their model, in reference to the theological message. Bach was further in the habit of making alterations to the text models without any consideration of poetic form when he held it to be factually necessary. So he shortened and altered the text without paying attention to the rhyme.[10]

Likewise, Friedrich Zander stated in 1968, "Bach freely altered the texts of none of his librettists as much as he did those of Mariane von Ziegler."[11]

More recent scholars have continued the trend of attributing the textual variants to Bach. In some cases, this is simply assumed without question, as in Lothar and Renate Steiger's 1985 discussion of BWV 108, which simply states that the cantata's text was slightly altered by Bach.[12] And Christoph Wolff writes in his 2000 Bach

---

9   Spitta himself speculated that the text differences originated from Ziegler's revision of her own 1728 texts for Bach's settings at what he believed to be a later date. See Philipp Spitta, "Über die Beziehungen Sebastian Bachs zu Christian Friedrich Hunold und Mariane von Ziegler," in *Historische und Philologische Aufsätze: Ernst Curtius zu seinem siebenzigsten Geburtstage am zweiten September 1884 gewidmet* (Berlin, 1884), 430–31.

10   "Bemerkenswert ist auch, wie Bach mit den Textvorlagen der Frau v. Ziegler umgegangen ist. Von den Ziegler-Texten hat Bach keinen einzigen unverändert übernommen. Alle sind gestrafft oder umgearbeitet worden, stets zu ihrem Vorteil, was die theologische Aussage anbetrifft. Bach war es außerdem gewohnt, ohne jede Rücksicht auf die poetische Form Änderungen an den Textvorlagen vorzunehmen, wenn er sie für sachlich notwendig hielt. So kürzt und ändert er den Text, ohne auf den Reim zu achten." Herbst, "Ein Vergleich zwischen Joh. Seb. Bach und Chr. Mariane v. Ziegler," 253.

11   "Bach freilich hat die Texte keines seiner Librettisten so stark verändert wie die der Mariane von Ziegler." Friedrich Zander, "Die Dichter der Kantatentexte Johann Sebastian Bachs," *Bach-Jahrbuch* 54 (1968): 25.

12   "[Der Text] lautet in der von Bach leicht veränderten Form: ..." Lothar and Renate Steiger, "J. S. Bach 'Es ist euch gut, daß ich hingehe' (BWV 108)," 51.

biography that the composer "chose to make some substantial changes to [Ziegler's] words."[13]

Other proponents of the view that Bach altered Ziegler's texts have considered the two versions more thoroughly, but always starting from the assumption that the 1728 published versions preceded the 1725 versions Bach set. Martin Petzoldt, for example, states, "Bach adopted no [Ziegler] text completely unaltered; it appears as though the alterations are theological corrections."[14] Hans-Joachim Schulze further states that the versions as Bach set them are theologically and poetically superior to the 1728 published versions. He argues that the 1728 texts are identical to those Ziegler gave Bach in 1725, and that Ziegler stubbornly refused to consider Bach's "corrections" of her texts and therefore printed her original versions instead without alteration:

> [Ziegler] supplied [Bach] with nine texts, all of which he set to music, however not completely. Rather, touch-ups are made in all kinds of places, which have been interpreted by theologians as especially relevant theologically, by literarily or musicologically oriented research more, at a glance, on impracticable or clumsy meters, unsingable word combinations, unnatural expressions. In 1728 Ziegler included the series of cantatas written for this specific purpose in her *Versuch in gebundener Schreib-Art*, evidently in their original forms, thereby also asserting herself against Bach's alterations.[15]

Despite the prevalence of this view, a number of scholars have recently begun to question, and at times challenge, the view that Bach altered Ziegler's texts, presenting the possibility that Bach set the texts as he received them in 1725 and that the variants between the two versions were a result of Ziegler's revision process three years later. Sabine Ehrmann, writing in 1991, cautiously states: "But whether Bach was this editor cannot be said, since the poet could also have revised the texts for

---

13   Christoph Wolff, *Johann Sebastian Bach: The Learned Musician* (New York, 2000), 279.

14   "Keinen Text übernimmt Bach völlig unverändert; es sieht so aus, als ob die Änderungen theologische Korrekturen sind." Martin Petzoldt, "Johann Sebastian Bach in theologischer Interaktion Persönlichkeiten in seinem beruflichen Umfeld," in *Über Leben, Kunst und Kunstwerke: Aspekte musikalischer Biographie Johann Sebastian Bach im Zentrum*, ed. Christoph Wolff (Leipzig, 1999), 159. See also Petzoldt's commentaries on the Ziegler cantatas in Martin Petzoldt, *Bach-Kommentar: theologisch-musikwissenschaftliche Kommentierung der geistlichen Vokalwerke Johann Sebastian Bachs*, Vol. 2, Die geistlichen Kantaten vom 1. Advent bis zum Trinitatisfest (Kassel, 2007).

15   "Dieser hat die ihm gelieferten neun Texte samt und sonders in Musik gesetzt, jedoch nicht mit Haut und Haar. Vielmehr sind an allerlei Stellen Retuschen angebracht worden, die von Theologen als theologisch besonders relevant gedeutet werden, von literarisch oder musikwissenschaftlich orientierten Forschern eher im Blick auf unbrauchbare oder ungeschickte Versmaße, unsingbare Wortverbindungen, gestelzte Wendungen. 1728 hat die Zieglerin die wohl ad hoc geschriebene Kantatenreihe in offenbar der ursprünglichen Gestalt in ihren *Versuch in gebundener Schreib-Art* aufgenommen, damit für sich selbst also ihren Kopf gegenüber Bachs Veränderungen durchgesetzt." Hans-Joachim Schulze, "Texte und Textdichter," in *Die Welt der Bach Kantaten*, Vol. 3, *Johann Sebastian Bachs Leipziger Kirchenkantaten*, ed. Christoph Wolff, 109–25 (Stuttgart and Kassel, 1999), 117–18.

her publication."[16] Hans Joachim Kreutzer, in 1992, further points out the problems inherent in the assumption that the versions Ziegler published in 1728 were identical to those she gave Bach in 1725:

[Ziegler's] printed texts have been criticized on the authority of Bach: he is said to have undertaken significant revisions. This is, from the viewpoint of textual criticism, a dubious assumption, as one continues to compare the cantata text with the published version. Yet we have absolutely no idea as to what versions Bach had received three years earlier.[17]

In his 2000 article on BWV 87, Ulrich Konrad addresses problems with assuming that the text variants originated with Bach rather than with Ziegler. He states:

The certainty with which it is constantly assumed and maintained in the literature that Bach appropriately arranged [the texts] for his needs is unfounded. It stands under the tacit assumption that Bach would have been, if he had only wished, his own best author, and that effected text alterations always mean qualitative improvement. The first of these assumptions is in high measure improbable, the second lacks the confirmation of fundamental, consciously methodical analysis. For the relationship between the text versions of our cantata [BWV 87] in any case allows for the consideration through-out of other variants. Thus the text set to music in its known version could also have originated from the quill of Mariane von Ziegler and later by her have been revised for publication. Moreover, it is possible that a third version intervened, and that either before the manuscript was available to Bach or after he had received it.[18]

---

16   "Zwischen den von Bach vertonten Texten und der 1728 veröffentlichten Version bestehen allerdings zum Teil beträchtliche Abweichungen. Gerade die von der Dichterin sehr knapp gehaltenen Rezitative (sie sind nur zwischen vier und sieben Zeilen lang) sind häufig gekürzt. Ob allerdings Bach dieser Bearbeiter gewesen ist, kann nicht gesagt werden, denn auch die Dichterin kann die Texte für ihre Publikation umgearbeitet haben." Ehrmann, "Johann Sebastian Bachs Textdichterin Christiane Mariane von Ziegler," 266.

17   Hans Joachim Kreutzer, "Bach and the Literary Scene in Eighteenth-Century Leipzig," in *Music and German Literature: Their Relationship since the Middle Ages*, ed. James M. McGlathery, 80–99 (Columbia, SC, 1992), 88.

18   "Wer hat den Text geschrieben, den Bach vertont hat? Eine in wichtigen Punkten stark von der Bachschen Vorlage abweichende Version der Dichtung steht bekanntlich in dem 1728 zu Leipzig gedruckten *Versuch In Gebundener Schreib=Art* der dem Gottschedkreis nahestehenden Autorin Christiane Mariane von Ziegler (1695–1760). Von dieser Publikation kann in Bezug auf Bachs drei Jahre zuvor entstandene Kantate füglicherweise nur gesagt werden, daß sie dem Komponisten nicht zur Verfügung gestanden hat. Die Gewißheit, mit der in der Literatur stets von diesem Druck ausgegangen und behauptet wird, Bach habe ihn seinen Bedürfnissen entsprechend eingerichtet, ist unbegründet. Sie steht unter den stillschweigenden Annahmen, Bach wäre, wenn er nur gewollt hätte, selbst sein bester Autor gewesen, und die vorgenommenen Textänderungen bedeuteten stets qualitative Verbesserungen. Die erste dieser Annahmen ist in hohem Maße unwahrscheinlich, der zweiten mangelt es zur Erhärtung an gründlichen, methodenbewußten Untersuchungen. Für die Beziehung zwischen den Textzeugen unserer Kantate lassen sich jedenfalls durchaus andere Varianten denken. So kann auch der vertonte Text in der bekannten Fassung aus Mariane von Zieglers Feder stammen und später von ihr für den Druck revidirt worden sein. Weiterhin ist es möglich, daß ein Dritter in die Textgestalt eingegriffen hat, und das entweder bevor Bach das Manuskript zugänglich war

Finally, Alfred Dürr, in his 2000 review of *Die Welt der Bach Kantaten*, urges that caution is necessary for those who would make it seem self-evident that Bach was responsible for particular text manipulations whose author cannot, in fact, be determined. In citing scholarly treatments of the Ziegler cantatas as an example of this, Dürr problematizes the belief that the 1725 versions are theologically or poetically superior to the 1728 texts:

> But Bach's versions are by no means all improvements, rather at times poetically clumsy (BWV 103/4 and frequently), at times even theologically hazy (for example, in BWV 87/2, printed version: "You have deliberately transgressed the Law," Bach's version: "… Law and Gospel …"—to most interpreters a subtle improvement, but in truth an error, since one can accept or reject a Gospel, but not "transgress" it). One would therefore ask here whether it was not the poet herself, who under the influence of her mentor Gottsched had polished some things in the three years leading up to the publication, whose clumsy early version is yet still celebrated today as Bach's stroke of genius.[19]

A Revised View and its Implications

The belief that Bach revised Ziegler's texts originated because of an error in chronology, since Spitta was working from the assumption that Bach composed these cantatas in the 1730s, several years after Ziegler published the texts in 1728. In considering the chronology of Bach's 1725 cantatas in relation to Ziegler's 1728 publication, it then seems natural to assume that the changes occurred at the later date. In this revised view, Ziegler gave Bach a version of the texts, which he set essentially as he received them. The texts then lay untouched for three years until Ziegler returned to them for inclusion in her 1728 *Versuch in gebundener Schreib-Art*. At that time, Ziegler modified certain of the movements in the cantatas, particularly with the goal of improving them poetically.

Such a view is in keeping with Ziegler's regular practices of revising texts for publication, as evidenced both from Ziegler's comments about her writings and from the writings themselves. In fact, not one of her poems which appears in two different venues is reproduced unchanged.

In the foreword to her *Versuch in gebundener Schreib-Art* of 1728 (the same publication in which the nine cantata texts set by Bach appear), Ziegler wrote in

---

oder nachdem er es erhalten hatte." Konrad, "Aspekte musikalisch-theologischen Verstehens in … BWV 87," 204.

19   "Nun sind aber Bachs Versionen keineswegs durchweg Verbesserungen, vielmehr zuweilen dichterisch ungelenk (BWV 103/4 und häufig), bisweilen sogar theologisch unscharf (z.B. in BWV 87/2, Druck: 'Ihr habet das Gesetz vorsätzlich übertreten,' Bach: '… Gesetz und Evangelium …'–nach den meisten Erklärern eine feinsinnige Verbesserung, in Wahrheit aber ein Fehler, denn ein Evangelium kann man annehmen oder ablehnen, aber nicht 'übertreten'). Hier wäre also zu fragen, ob es nicht die Dichterin selbst war, die unter dem Einfluß ihres Mentors Gottsched in den drei Jahren bis zur Drucklegung manches geglättet hat, dessen ungeschickte Frühversion heute noch immer als Bachscher Genieblitz gefeiert wird." Alfred Dürr, review of *Die Welt der Bach Kantaten*, 3 vols., ed. Christoph Wolff (Stuttgart and Kassel, 1999), *Theologische Rundschau* 65 (2000): 104.

reference to the poetic epistles contained therein, that those who received them initially should not be surprised to see that they appear now in altered form:

> [The original recipients] will probably not be surprised, when they find those letters somewhat altered which I formerly allowed myself to take the freedom of sending them. … [Since I] found that each day gives to humans with their endeavors and studies a new addition, I have in the same, by looking over and repeated reading through, altered one and another thing therein after my current taste, and through these lessons, if I may so flatter myself again, given substance to them, wherein they previously should have appeared poor.[20]

Ziegler expressed a similar thought in the foreword to her *Moralische und vermischte Send-Schreiben*, in regard to the prose letters in that volume. In describing her process of assembling the publication from earlier letters she had sent to friends, she stated that after choosing which letters to include, she "altered … one thing and another therein, since one is always of the opinion that one's depth of understanding increases from day to day, and this growth produces a noticeable alteration in one's thoughts."[21]

Furthermore, Ziegler's revision process in her poetry from the 1730s is clearly documented in her *Vermischete Schriften in gebundener und ungebundener Rede* (Göttingen, 1739). This volume represents the culmination of Ziegler's literary efforts in the 1730s and, as such, contains a number of poems that had been published previously over the course of the decade. Of the ten poems, one speech, and one dialogue that I have found published in earlier volumes (from 1732 to 1738), every one was altered or revised in some way for publication in the *Vermischete Schriften*. One example of this pattern of revision is Ziegler's "Ode. Auf das Absterben Ihro

---

20 "Diejenigen werthen Freunde und Freundinnen / mit welchen ich Briefe in dergleichen Schreib=Art zu wechseln die Ehre gehabt, und deren geschickte Feder mir bey meinen wenigen Dichten grossen Vortheil zu wege gebracht, werden sich vermuthl. nicht wundern, wenn sie diejenigen Briefe so ich ehemahls an sie abgehen zu lassen mir die Freyheit genommen, in etwas verändert finden; denn da ich selbige eines Theils noch bey denjenigen Stunden, als ich den Musen=Gott meine Erstlinge brachte, auch öffters in höchster Eyl wegen schleunigen Abgang der Posten niedergeschrieben, andern Theils aber von derjenigen Zeit an, da ich vor einigen Jahren von einen gewissen Freunde zu dieser edlen Kunst angeführet wurde, dessen Schrifften fleißig nachgelesen, und dergleichen Schreib=Art nachzufolgen mich bemühet, auch in der That befunden, daß jeder Tag dem Menschen bey seinen Bemühungen und Wissenschafften einen neuen Zusatz giebet, habe ich bey Übersehung und abermahliger Durchlesung derselbet, ein und andres nach meinen jetzigen Geschmack darinnen verändert, und ihnen durch diese Nachhülffe, wo ich mir anders damit schmeicheln darff, diejenige Gestalt gegeben, worinnen Sie vormahls billig hätten erscheinen sollen." Christiane Mariane von Ziegler, "Vorbericht" to *Versuch in gebundener Schreib-Art* (Leipzig, 1728), xix–xxi.

21 "… und änderte nach meinem Gutebefinden und jetziger wenigen Einsicht ein und anderes darinnen, massen der Mensch immer der Meynung ist, als verstärckten sich von Tage zu Tage die Kräffte seines Verstandes, welcher Zuwachs eine merckliche Veränderung der Gedancken zugleich mit würcket." Christiane Mariane von Ziegler, "Vorbericht" to *Moralische und vermischte Send-Schreiben, An einige Ihrer vertrauten und guten Freunde gestellt* (Leipzig, 1731), iv.

Hochfürstl. Durchl. Friderica Elisabetha, verwittw. Herz. zu Sachsen-Weissenfels," originally published in 1738, just one year prior to the *Vermischete Schriften*.[22] A comparison of the two versions of the poem's first stanza demonstrates Ziegler's process of revision for later publication:

1738	1739
Nein, Musen! heißt nur diesesmal	Nein, Musen! laßt dieses mal
Mich nicht nach Blat und Feder greifen.	Mich nicht den matten Kiel ergreifen,
Ich weis, ihr werdet meine Qual	Ich weis, ihr werdet meine Quaal
Und Schmerz dadurch unfehlbar häufen.	Und meinen Schmerz unfehlbar häufen.
Mein Herz hat ihn zu sehr gespürt;	Den Schmerz, den meine Seele spührt,
Ja Hand und Finger sind gerüh;rt,	Und der mich so empfindlich rührt,
Indem ich einer Post geglaubet,	Weil eine Post, die man kaum glaubet,
Die mir, und unsrer ganzen Stadt,	Mir und auch unsrer ganzen Stadt,
Die sie zugleich erschüttert hat,	Die sie zugleich erschüttert hat,
Vor Schrecken Muth und Geist geraubet.	Für Schrecken, Muth und Geist geraubet.

It is clear, then, that Ziegler was never content to simply reproduce her writings in a later publication without subjecting them to critical revision. Ziegler would surely have treated her nine sacred cantatas of 1725 in a similar fashion when preparing them for publication in 1728.[23] I believe, therefore, that Bach set Ziegler's texts as he received them in 1725 and that Ziegler herself revised the texts for her later publication.

What, then, are the implications of this revised understanding of Ziegler and Bach? I believe that scholars' hesitancy to reconsider Bach's role as text redactor in these works has been due in part to our veneration of Bach, our unwillingness to, in a sense, "take away" from something Bach may have done. However, an admission that Bach may not have made some rather minor textual changes in these cantatas in no way takes away from the compositional genius of their settings.

On the other hand, this revised understanding does contribute positively to our view of Ziegler as cantata librettist by removing a negative perception of her works. The statement that Bach or another librettist revised Ziegler's texts has conveyed, whether intentionally or not, Ziegler's inadequacy as a cantata librettist. It has communicated that Ziegler's texts were unacceptable for Bach's use until they had been edited by a man (whether Bach or another librettist). In recognizing that Bach set Ziegler's texts as he received them in 1725, we can acknowledge that Ziegler, as a woman, did indeed provide texts that were well-crafted and suitable for inclusion in the Leipzig liturgy. It further demonstrates Ziegler's literary astuteness through her critical reworking of her poetry for later publication.

---

22   In *Der Deutschen Gesellschaft in Leipzig: Oden und Cantaten in vier Büchern*, ed. Johann Christoph Gottsched (Leipzig, 1738), 41–45.

23   For further argument that many of Ziegler's changes in 1728 represent poetic or grammatical, and sometimes even theological, improvements, see Peters, "A Reconsideration of Bach's Role as Text Redactor in the Ziegler Cantatas," 37–46. This article also includes as an appendix the complete texts of both versions of the nine cantatas.

Ziegler's 1729 Cantata Texts

Although not as widely discussed, a second common misperception regarding Ziegler and Bach also requires reconsideration. This is the statement that Bach never again set another Ziegler text after their 1725 collaboration. The statement is, of course, true: although Ziegler published 64 sacred cantata texts in her 1729 *Versuch in gebundener Schreib-Art, anderer und letzter Theil*, there is no evidence that Bach set any of them. But the way such a statement is presented generally has negative implications once more: while Bach did set nine Ziegler texts, he did not see fit to set any more. But a consideration of chronology again clarifies this statement and further removes the negative stereotype assigned to Ziegler.

The fact that Bach did not set any of Ziegler's later cantata texts should not come as a surprise, since Bach clearly never intended to use Ziegler's texts for anything more than the completion of his second Jahrgang. This cycle came to a close on Trinity Sunday, 27 May 1725, with the final Ziegler/Bach cantata, BWV 176, *Es ist ein trotzig und verzagt Ding*. Beginning the next week with the first Sunday after Trinity, Bach appears to have either re-performed his own compositions or performed cantatas by other composers. And while Bach did briefly resume regular cantata composition at the beginning of the ensuing liturgical year (beginning with Christmas Day, 1725, which is generally understood as marking the start of Bach's third Leipzig Jahrgang), he continued the year instead by performing cantatas of his cousin Johann Ludwig Bach of Meiningen before returning to a somewhat regular schedule of cantata composition during the Trinity season of 1726.[24]

It cannot be known whether Bach ever considered requesting texts from Ziegler for his third Jahrgang. If such further collaboration between composer and poet was ever discussed, it was not realized. For this Jahrgang, Bach turned instead to earlier published cantata cycles, setting texts by Georg Christian Lehms from 1711 (BWV 110, 57, 151, 16, 32, 13, 35), by Salomo Franck from 1715 (BWV 72), and by Erdmann Neumeister from 1714 (BWV 28), as well as texts from a 1704 collection attributed to Duke Ernst Ludwig of Saxe-Meiningen (BWV 43, 39, 88, 187, 45, 102, 17).[25]

What exists of Bach's fourth cantata Jahrgang, the cycle beginning in December 1728, is known as his Picander Jahrgang. While only nine Bach cantatas are extant from this year, they are all to texts by Leipzig poet Christian Friedrich Henrici (1700–64), who published under the pseudonym Picander and is best known as the librettist of Bach's *Matthäus-Passion* (1727). Bach's cantata settings of 1728–29 are of texts Picander published in his 1728 *Cantaten auf die Sonn- und Fest-Tage durch das gantze Jahr*. In his foreword to this volume, Picander clearly indicated his hope that these texts would be set by Bach:

> I have undertaken such a project all the more willingly because I flatter myself that perhaps the lack of poetic charm might be compensated by the loveliness of the incomparable

---

24   For a summary and list of the cantatas of this period, see Alfred Dürr, *The Cantatas of J. S. Bach*, rev. and trans. by Richard D. P. Jones (Oxford, 2005), 36–39, and Wolff, *Johann Sebastian Bach*, 281–83.

25   Wolff, *Johann Sebastian Bach*, 283.

Capellmeister Mr Bach's music, and that these songs will be sung in the principal churches of devout Leipzig.[26]

While it appears that Bach never undertook the composition of Picander's entire Jahrgang, he did focus solely on Picander's texts in 1729. In the year when Ziegler's complete Jahrgang appeared, Bach was thus occupied already with the texts of another librettist.

After 1729, Bach composed fewer than 20 known sacred cantatas for the liturgical year (excluding those for special occasions, such as weddings or the installation of the Leipzig town council). Alfred Dürr explains thus the paucity of Bach cantatas from the final two decades of his life:

> We cannot say with certainty how great the losses are in these later Leipzig years. It is quite possible, however, that, having an adequate supply of church cantatas at his disposal, Bach's creative will moved in other directions. Thus during these years the four parts of the *Clavierübung* and the Missa (Kyrie and Gloria) in B minor originated; and, in particular, Bach devoted himself, evidently with newly awakened interest, to the student Collegium musicum which he directed from 1729 onwards.[27]

Dürr goes on to explain that those cantatas which Bach did compose in these later years owed their origins to particular circumstances: either Bach's completion of an earlier cantata cycle (for example, BWV 112, 140, 177, 14, and 9), his parodies of earlier occasional cantatas for new liturgical occasions (for example, BWV 157, 36, 30, and 34), or his exploration of the per versum chorale cantata (for example, BWV 112 and 177).[28]

Furthermore, it is clear from their publication that Ziegler did not write her cantata texts specifically for Bach and the Leipzig churches. Ziegler explained in the foreword to her 1729 collection that she had written the 64 sacred cantata texts contained therein just prior to their publication. As opposed to those texts she published in 1728, which had been written for Bach in 1725, Ziegler wrote her 1729 cantata texts specifically for her *Versuch in gebundener Schreib-Art, anderer und letzter Theil*. Ziegler stated in her foreword that the impetus for her second volume came from these sacred cantatas. She referred to a government official who wrote to her in response to her first volume, expressed his approval of it, and stated that he would like to see the poetic texts completing the liturgical year. It was at that point, after the publication of her 1728 volume, that Ziegler decided to write texts for the remainder of the church year, texts she then published in 1729.[29]

---

26 "Ich habe solches Vorhaben desto lieber unternommen, weil ich mir schmeicheln darf, daß vielleicht der Mangel der poetischen Anmuth durch die Lieblichkeit des unvergleichlichen Herrn Capell-Meisters *Bachs*, dürfte ersetzet, und diese Lieder in den Haupt-Kirchen des andächtigen Leipzigs angestimmet werden." German original and English translation qtd. in Dürr, *The Cantatas of J. S. Bach*, 40–41.

27 Dürr, *The Cantatas of J. S. Bach*, 41–42.

28 Dürr, *The Cantatas of J. S. Bach*, 42–43.

29 Christiane Mariane von Ziegler, "Vorbericht" to *Versuch in gebundener Schreib-Art, anderer und letzter Theil* (Leipzig, 1729), iii–iv.

Ziegler's 1729 texts, then, were written with no relation to Bach, during the year when Bach was focusing on Picander's texts and after which he composed very few sacred cantatas. That Ziegler envisioned for these cantatas an audience broader than Bach's Leipzig is further evidenced by the fact that she provided cantata texts for the entire liturgical year, including the Second, Third, and Fourth Sundays of Advent and the Sundays of Lent, occasions for which no cantata was performed in Leipzig. Therefore, to assert, however truly, that Bach never set any of Ziegler's 1729 texts is not especially relevant to our understanding of Ziegler and Bach.

Conclusion

In light of this reconsideration of the relationship between Ziegler and Bach, we must encounter their cantatas not in terms of text alterations or in relation to later non-existent settings, but on their own textual and musical merits. In considering these cantatas in such a light I would like to conclude by summarizing their significance for our understandings of Mariane von Ziegler and of J. S. Bach. For Mariane von Ziegler, these nine cantatas:

- represent the only known instance of a woman providing liturgical texts for the Lutheran church in eighteenth-century Germany;
- are part of the only known cantata Jahrgang published by a woman in eighteenth-century Germany;
- represent Ziegler's first public, albeit anonymous, poetic endeavors;
- provided Ziegler the opportunity to write cantata texts that were liturgically appropriate, theologically astute, and poetically engaging;
- provided Ziegler the opportunity to work together with Leipzig's town cantor, J. S. Bach, a collaboration significant not only for Ziegler's poetic endeavors but also her musical interests and training;
- contributed to Ziegler's later publications, since the texts were not only published in revised versions in her 1728 *Versuch in gebundener Schreib-Art* but also led to an additional 64 texts (completing a year-long liturgical cycle) which Ziegler published a year later in her *Versuch in gebundener Schreib-Art, anderer und letzter Theil.*

For J. S. Bach, these nine cantatas:

- represent his only compositions to texts by a female poet;
- filled a pressing need for nine liturgical occasions in the post-Easter season of 1725;
- represent the conclusion of his second Leipzig Jahrgang, as well as the culmination of his intensive compositional exploration of the cantata as a genre during his first two years as Leipzig town cantor;
- represent a particularly fertile period of compositional creativity, as evidenced by his Vox Christi settings, as well as his treatments of movement ordering, aria forms, recitative, and scoring;

- were valued by the composer in later years, as evidenced by the fact that he re-performed at least four of them (BWV 103, 108, 175, and 176) and that he considered two others, BWV 128 and 68, as part of his chorale cantata Jahrgang.

Through Mariane von Ziegler's sacred cantata texts, a woman's voice was heard in Leipzig's churches. It is my hope that the current study will help us to hear this voice in new ways in the present as well, as we reconsider the significance of these cantatas for our understanding of both Mariane von Ziegler and J. S. Bach.

Appendix A

An Annotated Bibliography of Ziegler's Works

Books

Versuch in gebundener Schreib-Art. Leipzig: Johann Friedrich Braun, 1728.

352 pages plus Dedication to Ernst Christoph von Manteufel (10 unnumbered pages) and "Vorbericht" (23 unnumbered pages). Contains 150 poems in a variety of genres, both sacred and secular, including cantatas, dialogues, poetic epistles, pastoral poems, mottos, epitaphs, arias, epigrams, and satirical poems. Contains revised versions of the nine sacred cantata texts set by Bach in 1725.

Versuch in gebundener Schreib-Art, anderer und letzter Theil. Leipzig: Johann Friedrich Braun, 1729.

443 pages plus "Vorbericht" (14 unnumbered pages). Contains 64 sacred cantatas (for liturgical occasions which, taken with her nine earlier cantatas, complete an entire Jahrgang) and 57 secular poems in various genres.

Moralische und vermischte Send-Schreiben, An einige Ihrer vertrauten und guten Freunde gestellt. Leipzig: Johann Friedrich Braun, 1731.

416 pages plus Dedication to Conrad Siegfried (8 unnumbered pages) and "Vorbericht" (14 unnumbered pages). Contains 100 prose letters on various topics to unnamed persons.

Vermischete Schriften in gebundener und ungebundener Rede. Göttingen: Universitäts-Buchhandlung, 1739.

611 pages plus "Vorrede" (10 unnumbered pages). Contains 118 poems (including odes, pastoral poems, humorous poems, poetic epistles, cantatas, fables, and miscellaneous poems), 34 prose selections (including speeches, dialogues, and fables), and three translations.

Translations

De Scudéry, Madeleine. *Scharffsinnige Unterredungen, von Dingen, Die zu einer wohlanständigen Aufführung gehören*. Leipzig: Bernhard Christoph Breitkopf, 1735.

456 pages plus Dedication to Eleanor von Damnitz (6 unnumbered pages) and Foreword (14 unnumbered pages) by Ziegler.

Meré, Herrn Chevalier de. "Abhandlung von dem rechtschaffnen Wesen." In *Der Deutschen Gesellschaft in Leipzig: Eigene Schriften und Übersetzungen in gebundener und ungebundener Schreibart*. Vol. 3. Edited by Johann Friedrich May, 371–412. Leipzig: Bernhard Christoph Breitkopf, 1739.

Title: "Abhandlung von dem rechtschaffnen Wesen aus dem Französischen des Herrn Chevalier de Meré übersetzt von Christianen Marianen von Ziegler." Addresses various themes related to learning, poetry, women, and the ancient Greeks and Romans.

Trublet, Abte. *Gedanken über verschiedene Sachen, welche zur Gelehrsamkeit und Sittenlehre gehören.* Greifswald and Leipzig: Johann Jacob Weitbrecht, 1744.
Part I, 214 pages plus Dedication to Friedrich von Reichenbach (4 unnumbered pages) and "Vorrede" (8 unnumbered pages) by Ziegler. Part II, 150 pages. Listed as forthcoming in Amaranthes's *Nutzbares, Galantes und curiöses Frauenzimmer-Lexicon* (1739), but did not appear until 1744.

Dialogue

"Gespräche von der wahren Freundschaft." In *Der Deutschen Gesellschaft in Leipzig: Eigne Schriften und Übersetzungen in gebundener und ungebundener Schreibart.* Vol. 2. Edited by Johann Christoph Gottsched, 308–19. Leipzig: Breitkopf, 1734. Rev. ed. in *Vermischete Schriften*, 456–66.

Speech

"Antrittsrede der Hoch=Wohlgebohrnen Frauen Christianen Marianen von Ziegler, geb. Romanus, aus Leipzig." In *Der Deutschen Gesellschaft in Leipzig Gesammlete Reden und Gedichte, Welche bey dem Eintritte und Abschiede ihrer Mitglieder pflegen abgelesen zu werden.* Edited by Johann Christoph Gottsched, 287–95. Leipzig: Bernhard Christoph Breitkopf, 1732. Rev. ed. in *Vermischete Schriften*, 381–89.
Followed by "Antwort aufs forhergehend von Carl Heinrich Frh. von Sehrrthoß" in *Der Deutschen Gesellschaft in Leipzig Gesammlete Reden und Gedichte, Welche bey dem Eintritte und Abschiede ihrer Mitglieder pflegen abgelesen zu werden.* Edited by Johann Christoph Gottsched, 296–301. Leipzig: Bernhard Christoph Breitkopf, 1732.

Individually Published Poems

"Gedicht auf die Doktor-Promotion des gelehrten Frauenzimmers Laura Maria Catharina Bassi zu Bologna." Leipzig, 1732. Reprint in *Neue Zeitungen von gelehrten Sachen* 18 (1732): 918–21. Rev. ed. in *Vermischete Schriften*, 56–60.

"Gedicht auf das Absterben Königs Friedrich August von Polen und Kurfürsten von Sachsen." Reprint in *Neue Zeitungen von gelehrten Sachen* 19 (1733): 261–64. Rev. ed. in *Vermischete Schriften*, 235–38.

"Ode, dem bischoffe Adam Adami zu Ehren gefertiget, als desselben *Relatio historica de Pacificatione Osnabrugo-Monasteriensi, Anno M. DCC XXXVII.*" Leipzig, 1737. Rev. ed. in *Vermischete Schriften*, 60–67. Reprint in Zedler, Johann Heinrich. "Christiane Mariane von Ziegler." In *Grosses vollständiges Universal-Lexicon*, Vol. 62, 580–84. Leipzig and Halle: Verlegts Johann Heinrich Zedler, 1749.

Poems in Contemporary Publications

"Vertheidigung unsers Geschlechts wider die Mannspersonen, in Ansehung der Fähigkeit zur Poesie." In *Die vernünftigen Tadlerinnen, erster Jahr-Theil 1725*. Edited by Johann Christoph Gottsched, 412–15. Halle: Johann Adam Spörl, 1725.
Published pseudonymously as "de Rose," 26 December 1725, with a letter of introduction addressed to the "Tadlerinnen." Written in response to a poetry contest announced on 4 July 1725 on the subject of "Vertheidigung des weiblichen Geschlechts gegen die Beschuldigungen der Mannspersonen" ("a defense of the female sex against the accusations of men").

"Anrede an Dero Verläumder." In *Anhang. Derjenigen Briefe So an die vernünftigen Tadlerinnen Im Jahr 1726 eingelauffen*. Edited by Johann Christoph Gottsched, 1–3. Halle: Johann Adam Spörl, 18 February 1726.
Published pseudonymously as "Clarimene von Lindenheim" and included as part of letter to the "Tadlerinnen."

"Vertheidigung des weiblichen Geschlechts wieder die Schmähschrifft Philanders von Sittewald." In *Anhang. Derjenigen Briefe So an die vernünftigen Tadlerinnen Im Jahr 1726. eingelauffen*. Edited by Johann Christoph Gottsched, 7–12. Halle: Johann Adam Spörl, 18 February 1726.
Published pseudonymously as "de Rose." Included as part of letter to the "Tadlerinnen."

"Es solte billig dir / was man nur weiblich heist." In Abraham Wiegner. *Eine treue Liebhaberin Jesu: Leichenpredigt für Johanna Charlotte von Gersdorf*, fol. 138. Lauban: Schillen, (1729).

"Der Sächsischen Unterthanen getreue Wünsche und frohe Hoffnung bey dem glücklichen Antritt des grossen Stuffen-Jahres Gr. Königl. Majest. in Pohlen und Churfürstl. Durchl. zu Sachsen." In *Zwo Schriften, welche In der Deutschen Gesellschaft zu Leipzig, auf das Jahr 1732. die Preise der Poesie und Beredsamkeit erhalten haben*. Leipzig: Breitkopf, 1732. Rev. ed. in *Vermischete Schriften*, 227–35.

"Die Zufriedenheit eines Landes, das nach einem schweren Kriege durch den Frieden wieder erfreuet wird." In *Zwo Schriften, welche In der Deutschen Gesellschaft zu Leipzig, auf das Jahr 1734. Die Preise der Poesie und Beredsamkeit erhalten haben*. Leipzig: Bernhard Christoph Breitkopf, 1734, 3–16. Rev. ed. in *Vermischete Schriften*, 28–38.

"Damons Klage über den Verlust und Abschied der Phyllis." In *Der Deutschen Gesellschaft in Leipzig: Eigene Schriften und Übersetzungen in gebundener und ungebundener Schreibart*. Vol. 2. Edited by Johann Christoph Gottsched, 247–54. Leipzig: Breitkopf, 1734. Rev. ed. in *Vermischete Schriften*, 254–61.

"Ode. Auf das Absterben der Frau Baumeisterinn Oertelinn in Leipzig." In *Der Deutschen Gesellschaft in Leipzig: Oden und Cantaten in vier Büchern*. Edited by Johann Christoph Gottsched, 371–74. Leipzig: Breitkopf, 1738. Rev. ed. in *Vermischete Schriften*, 47–50.

"Ode. An die Musen, warum sie wiederum Verse mache?" In *Der Deutschen Gesellschaft in Leipzig: Oden und Cantaten in vier Büchern*. Edited by Johann Christoph Gottsched, 475–78. Leipzig: Breitkopf, 1738. Rev. ed. in *Vermischete Schriften*, 102–06.

"Ode. Auf des Herrn von Klüx frühzeitigen Tod bey einem Scharmützel in Pohlen." In *Der Deutschen Gesellschaft in Leipzig: Oden und Cantaten in vier Büchern*. Edited by Johann Christoph Gottsched, 247–49. Leipzig: Breitkopf, 1738. Rev. ed. in *Vermischete Schriften*, 53–55.

"Ode. Auf das Absterben Ihro Hochfürstl. Durchl. Friderica Elisabetha, verwittw. Herz. zu Sachsen-Weissenfels." In *Der Deutschen Gesellschaft in Leipzig: Oden und Cantaten in vier Büchern*. Edited by Johann Christoph Gottsched, 41–45. Leipzig: Breitkopf, 1738. Rev. ed. in *Vermischete Schriften*, 39–42.

Poems in Modern Publications

"Was für ein schnelles Todesschrecken: Arnalda di Recas." In *Deutschlands Dichterinnen: Blüthen deutscher Frauenpoesie*. Vol. 1. Edited by Karl Wilhelm Bindewald, 19–20. Osterwieck/Harz: Zickfeld, (1896–97).

"Das männliche Geschlechte, im Namen einiger Frauenzimmer besungen." In *Deutsche Dichterinnen vom 16. Jahrhundert bis zur Gegenwart*. Edited with an introduction by Gisela Brinker-Gabler, 114–15. Frankfurt am Main: Fischer, 1978.

"Als sie ihr Bildnis schildern sollte." In *Deutsche Dichterinnen vom 16. Jahrhundert bis zur Gegenwart*. Edited with an introduction by Gisela Brinker-Gabler, 116. Frankfurt am Main: Fischer, 1978.

"Auf einen schönen und artigen Papagoy." In *Deutsche Dichterinnen vom 16. Jahrhundert bis zur Gegenwart*. Edited with an introduction by Gisela Brinker-Gabler, 116–17. Frankfurt am Main: Fischer, 1978.

"Ode: Zürne nicht, wenn ich dir sage." In *Deutsche Dichterinnen vom 16. Jahrhundert bis zur Gegenwart*. Edited with an introduction by Gisela Brinker-Gabler, 117–18. Frankfurt am Main: Fischer, 1978.

"Die Dichterin und die Musen." In *Deutsche Dichterinnen vom 16. Jahrhundert bis zur Gegenwart*. Edited with an introduction by Gisela Brinker-Gabler, 119. Frankfurt am Main: Fischer, 1978.

"Das männliche Geschlechte, im Namen einiger Frauenzimmer besungen" / "In Praise of the Male Sex, as Seen by Certain Females." In *The Defiant Muse: German Feminist Poems from the Middle Ages to the Present. A Bilingual Anthology*. Edited by Susan L. Cocalis, 16–19. New York: The Feminist Press, 1986.

"Das männliche Geschlechte, im Namen einiger Frauenzimmer besungen." In *Frauenliteratur*. Edited by Lydia Schieth, 162–63. Bamberg: C. C. Buchner, 1991.

"Die Dichterin und die Musen." In *Frauenliteratur*. Edited by Lydia Schieth, 141. Bamberg: C. C. Buchner, 1991.

Poems Set to Music

Johann Sebastian Bach [Ziegler 1728, 243–72]

- *Ihr werdet weinen und heulen* (BWV 103)
- *Es ist euch gut, daß ich hingehe* (BWV 108)
- *Bisher habt ihr nichts gebeten in meinem Nahmen* (BWV 87)
- *Auf Christi Himmelfahrt allein* (BWV 128)
- *Sie werden euch in den Bann tun* (BWV 183)
- *Wer mich liebet, der wird mein Wort halten* (BWV 74)
- *Also hat Gott die Welt geliebt* (BWV 68)
- *Er rufet seinen Schafen mit Namen* (BWV 175)
- *Es ist ein trotzig und verzagt Ding* (BWV 176)

Georg Philipp Telemann. In *Der getreue Music-Meister*. Hamburg, 1728.

- *Ich kann lachen, weinen, scherzen*. No. 56, pp. 74–75, 78–79 (Lessons 19 and 20). [Ziegler 1728, 212–13]

Johann Friedrich Gräfe. *Samlung verschiedener und auserlesener Oden zu welchen von den berühmtesten Meistern in der Music eigene Melodieyen verfertiget worden*. 4 vols. Halle, 1737–1743.

- Hurlebusch, *Angenehme grüne Zweige* (Vol. 2, 32). [Ziegler 1728, 219]
- Hurlebusch, *Du schattenreiche Fichte* (Vol. 3, 2). [Ziegler 1739, 111–12]
- Hurlebusch, *Ach dichte keine Klagen* (Vol. 3, 3). [Ziegler 1739, 112–13]
- Hurlebusch, *Ihr so schön und grünen Auen* (Vol. 3, 6). [Ziegler 1739, 114–15]
- Gräfe, *Zürne nicht wenn ich dir sage* (Vol. 3, 11). [Ziegler 1739, 116–17]
- de Giovannini, *Ach mein Schicksal laß mich wissen* (Vol. 3, 22). [Ziegler 1739, 119–21]
- C. P. E. Bach, *Eilt ihr Schäfer aus den Gründen* (Vol. 3, 33). [Ziegler 1739, 151–53]
- Hurlebusch/de Giovannini, *Zu dein und meiner Lust* (Vol. 3, 36). [Ziegler 1739, 173–76]
- Hurlebusch, *Saußt ihr Winde spielt ihr Aeste* (Vol. 4, 17). [Ziegler 1729, 394–96]

Works Published in Honor of Ziegler

Gottsched, Johann Christoph. "An die Frau von Ziegler bey Überschickung eines Gedichtes. Madgrigal." In *Versuch einer critischen Dichtkunst vor die Deutschen*. Leipzig: Bernhard Christoph Breitkopf, 1730, 495.

Exemplary poem for Part II, Ch. 7, "Von Sinn= und Schertz=Gedichten." Comes directly before poems addressed to Anna Marie Volckmann and Luise Kulmus in 1730 edition (first edition). Poem to Volckmann also praises Ziegler. Poems to Ziegler and to Volkmann not included in 1737 (2nd ed.) or in later editions.

Gottsched, Johann Christoph. "So nimm denn Ring und Lorber hin." *Neuen Zeitungen von gelehrten Sachsen*, Leipzig 19 (2. November 1733): 789–92. Reprint in *Sammlung der Schriften und Gedichte welche auf die Poetische Krönung Der Hochwohlgebohrnen Frauen, Frauen Christianen Marianen von Ziegler gebohrnen Romanus, verfertiget worden*. Edited by Jacob Friedrich Lamprecht. Leipzig: Bernhard Christoph Breitkopf, 1734. Reprint in Johann Heinrich Zedler. "Christiane Mariane von Ziegler." *Grosses vollständiges Universal-Lexicon*, Vol. 62, 577–79. Leipzig and Halle: Verlegts Johann Heinrich Zedler, 1749.
Written for Ziegler's coronation as poet laureate. In Lamprecht, author listed as "Die Deutsche Gesellschaft in Leipzig, durch Joh. Chr. Gottsched, P. P."

Gottsched, Luise Adelgunde Victorie. "Hochwohlgebohrne Frau! Du Wunder unsrer Zeit: Schreiben. An Fr. Christianen Marianen von Ziegler / geb. Romanus / in Leipzig / 1733." In *Sammlung der Schriften und Gedichte welche auf die Poetische Krönung Der Hochwohlgebohrnen Frauen, Frauen Christianen Marianen von Ziegler gebohrnen Romanus, verfertiget worden*. Edited by Jacob Friedrich Lamprecht, 35–37. Leipzig: Bernhard Christoph Breitkopf, 1734. Reprint in L. A. V. Gottsched. *Sämmtliche Kleinere Gedichte*. Edited by Johann Christoph Gottsched, 105–06. Leipzig: Breitkopf, 1763.

Köhler, Johann David. "Gedächtnüs-Müntze, auf die Poetische Krönung der vortrefflichen Frauen Christianen Marianen von Ziegler / gebohrnen Romanus, in Leipzig." *Historischer Münz-Belustigung* 9 (1737): 137–44.

Lamprecht, Jacob Friedrich, ed. *Sammlung der Schriften und Gedichte welche auf die Poetische Krönung Der Hochwohlgebohrnen Frauen, Frauen Christianen Marianen von Ziegler gebohrnen Romanus, verfertiget worden*. With Foreword by Jacob Friedrich Lamprecht. Leipzig: Bernhard Christoph Breitkopf, 1734.

MetRoPhiluS. "So laut? du Wunder unsrer Zeit!" In *Neuen Zeitungen von gelehrten Sachen* 19 (2 February 1733): 84–87.
In response to Ziegler's poem honoring Laura Bassi in the *Neuen Zeitungen von gelehrten Sachen* 18 (22 December 1732): 918–21.

Volckmann, Anna Helena. "An die Frau von Ziegler in Leipzig." In *Die erstlinge unvollkommene Gedichte*. Leipzig, 1736.

Zuverläßige Nachrichten von dem gegenwärtigen Zustande, Veränderung und Wachsthum der Wissenschaften, 2. Theil. Leipzig: Johann Friedrich Gleditsch, 1740.
Ziegler's picture appears opposite title page.

Works Dedicated to Ziegler

Gräfe, Johann Friedrich, ed. *Samlung verschiedener und auserlesener Oden zu welchen von den berühmtesten Meistern in der Music eigene Melodieyen verfertiget worden.* Vol. 1, 1st and 2nd eds. Halle, 1740 (1737).

Third edition (1743) dedicated not to Ziegler, but to Wilhelmine Ernestine von Plotho, geb. von Manteufel. Gräfe published four volumes under the same title, each containing 36 odes with melodies (1737, 1739, 1741, 1743). See "Poems Set to Music" above.

May, Johann Friedrich, trans. *Des berühmten Französischen Paters Poree Rede von der Schau-Spielen, Ob sie eine Schule guter Sitten sind, oder seyn können?* Leipzig: Bernhard Christoph Breitkopf, 1734.

With dedication and foreword by May. Announced in the Leipzig *Neuen Zeitungen von gelehrten Sachen* 20 (22 February 1734): 135.

Philippi, Johann Ernst, trans. *Marquis von Sable, Hundert vernünftige Maximen mit 366 moralischen Bildnissen.* Leipzig: Jacob Born, 1734.

Announced in the Leipzig *Neuen Zeitungen von gelehrten Sachen* 20 (17. May 1734): 352, which remarks that, due to its content, it is unusual to dedicate this book to a woman. On the relationship between Ziegler and Philippi, see Katherine Goodman, *Amazons and Apprentices*, 174–78, Columbia, SC: Camden House, 1999.

Appendix B

The Ziegler/Bach Cantatas, Complete Texts with Translations[1]

BWV 103, *Ihr werdet weinen und heulen*
Jubilate (Gospel, John 16:16–23)

1. [Chorus]

Ihr werdet weinen und heulen, aber die Welt wird sich freuen. Ihr aber werdet traurig sein. Doch eure Traurigkeit soll in Freude verkehret werden.

You will weep and wail, but the world will rejoice. You, however, will be sorrowful. Yet your sorrow will be transformed into joy.

2. Recitative (T)

Wer sollte nicht in Klagen untergehn,
Wenn uns der Liebste wird entrissen?
Der Seele Heil, die Zuflucht kranker Herzen
Acht' nicht auf unsre Schmerzen.

Who would not sink in lamentation,
When our beloved is torn from us?
The soul's salvation, the refuge of ailing hearts
Pays no heed to our sorrows.

3. Aria (A)

Kein Arzt ist außer dir zu finden,
Ich suche durch ganz Gilead;
Wer heilt die Wunden meiner Sünden,
Weil man hier keinen Balsam hat?
Verbirgst du dich, so muß ich sterben.
Erbarme dich, ach höre doch!
Du suchest ja nicht mein Verderben,
Wohlan, so hofft mein Herze noch.

No physician is to be found other than you,
Though I search all through Gilead;
Who will heal the wounds of my sins,
Since there is no balm here?
If you hide yourself, then I must die.
Have mercy, ah, hear me, please!
Surely you do not seek my ruin,
Well! Then my heart still has hope.

4. Recitative (A)

Du wirst mich nach der Angst auch wiederum
 erquicken;
So will ich mich zu deiner Ankunft schicken,
Ich traue dem Verheißungswort,
Daß meine Traurigkeit
In Freude soll verkehret werden.

You will also revive me after my anguish;

Therefore I will prepare myself for your arrival,
I trust the word of promise,
That my sorrow
Shall be transformed into joy.

---

1   Translations are my own, with reference to Melvin P. Unger, *Handbook to Bach's Sacred Cantata Texts* (Lanham, MD, 1996). I have included only the texts as Bach set them in 1725 without reference to changes made by Ziegler for publication in 1728. For an analysis of the two versions of the cantata texts with a side-by-side comparison of the texts, see Mark Peters, "A Reconsideration of Bach's Role as Text Redactor in the Ziegler Cantatas," *BACH: Journal of the Riemenschneider Bach Institute* 36 (2005): 25–66.

5. Aria (T)

Erholet euch, betrübte Sinnen,	Recover yourselves, distressed senses,
Ihr tut euch selber allzu weh.	You cause yourselves too much woe.
Laßt von dem traurigen Beginnen,	Leave off your sorrowful undertakings:
Eh ich in Tränen untergeh,	Ere I sink in tears,
Mein Jesus läßt sich wieder sehen,	My Jesus will again appear.
O Freude, der nichts gleichen kann!	O joy, which nothing can equal!
Wie wohl ist mir dadurch geschehen,	How greatly I benefit by this:
Nimm, nimm mein Herz zum Opfer an.	Receive, receive my heart as an offering.

6. Chorale

Ich hab dich einen Augenblick,	I have for a moment,
O liebes Kind, verlassen:	O dear child, forsaken you:
Sieh aber, sieh, mit großem Glück	Behold, however, behold, with great fortune
Und Trost ohn alle Maßen	And comfort beyond all measure
Will ich dir schon die Freudenkron	I will already the crown of joy
Aufsetzen und verehren;	Place upon you and honor you;
Dein kurzes Leid soll sich in Freud	Your brief suffering shall into joy
Und ewig Wohl verkehren.	And eternal well-being be transformed.

BWV 108, *Es ist euch gut, daß ich hingehe*
Kantate (Gospel, John 16:5–15)

1. [Aria] (B)

Es ist euch gut, daß ich hingehe; denn so ich nicht hingehe, kömmt der Tröster nicht zu euch. So ich aber gehe, will ich ihn zu euch senden.	It is good for you that I depart; for if I do not depart, then the Comforter will not come to you. But if I go, then I will send him to you.

2. Aria (T)

Mich kann kein Zweifel stören,	No doubt can deter me
Auf dein Wort, Herr, zu hören.	From hearkening to your word, Lord.
Ich glaube, gehst du fort,	I believe that if you go away,
So kann ich mich getrösten,	Then I can comfort myself
Daß ich zu den Erlösten	That I with the redeemed
Komm an gewünschten Port.	Will arrive at the desired port.

3. Recitative (T)

Dein Geist wird mich also regieren,	Your Spirit will so rule me,
Daß ich auf rechter Bahne geh;	That I will go on the right path;
Durch deinen Hingang kommt er ja zu mir,	Through your departure, he indeed comes to me,
Ich frage sorgensvoll: Ach, ist er nicht schon hier?	I ask anxiously: Ah, is he not yet here?

4. Chorus

Wenn aber jener, der Geist der Wahrheit, kommen wird, der wird euch in alle Wahrheit leiten. Denn er wird nicht von ihm selber reden, sondern was er hören wird, das wird er reden; und was zukünftig ist, wird er verkündigen.	But when he, the Spirit of truth, will come, he will lead you into all truth. For he will not speak of himself, but rather what he will hear, that will he speak; and what is in the future, he will proclaim.

5. Aria (A)

Was mein Herz von dir begehrt,	What my heart desires from you,
Ach, das wird mir wohl gewährt.	Ah, that will indeed be imparted to me.
Überschütte mich mit Segen,	Cover me with blessing,
Führe mich auf deinen Wegen,	Lead me upon your ways,
Daß ich in der Ewigkeit	So that I in eternity
Schaue deine Herrlichkeit!	Will behold your glory!

6. Chorale

Dein Geist, den Gott vom Himmel gibt,	Your Spirit, whom God gives from heaven,
Der leitet alles, was ihn liebt,	Leads all who love him
Auf wohl gebähntem Wege.	On well-paved paths.
Er setzt und richtet unsren Fuß,	He places and directs our foot,
Daß er nicht anders treten muß,	So that it does not tread elsewhere
Als wo man findt den Segen.	Than where one finds blessing.

BWV 87, *Bisher habt ihr nichts gebeten in meinem Namen*
Rogate (Gospel, John 16:23–30)

1. [Aria] (B)

Bisher habt ihr nichts gebeten in meinem Namen.	Until now you have asked nothing in my name.

2. Recitative (A)

O Wort, das Geist und Seel erschreckt!	O word, that alarms spirit and soul!
Ihr Menschen, merkt den Zuruf, was dahinter steckt!	You people, take note of his call, [and] what lies behind it!
Ihr habt Gesetz und Evangelium vorsätzlich übertreten,	You have deliberately transgressed Law and Gospel,
Und diesfalls möcht ihr ungesäumt	And therefore you should immediately
In Buß und Andacht beten.	In penitence and devotion pray.

3. Aria (A)

Vergib, o Vater, unsre Schuld	Forgive, O Father, our guilt
Und habe noch mit uns Geduld,	And have yet patience with us,
Wenn wir in Andacht beten	When we pray in devotion
Und sagen, Herr, auf dein Geheiß:	And say, Lord, upon your bidding:
Ach, rede nicht mehr sprüchwortsweis,	Ah, speak epigrammatically no more,
Hilf uns vielmehr vertreten!	Help us rather advocate!

4. Recitative (T)

Wenn unsre Schuld bis an den Himmel steigt,	When our guilt rises up to heaven,
Du siehst und kennest ja mein Herz, das nichts vor dir verschweigt;	You indeed see and know my heart, which conceals nothing before you;
Drum suche mich zu trösten!	Therefore seek to comfort me!

5. [Aria] (B)

In der Welt habt ihr Angst; aber seid getrost, ich habe die Welt überwunden.	In the world you have fear; but be of good cheer, I have overcome the world.

6. Aria (T)

Ich will leiden, ich will schweigen,	I would suffer, I would keep silent,
Jesus wird mir Hülf erzeigen,	Jesus will reveal his help to me,
Denn er tröst mich nach dem Schmerz.	For he comforts me after my suffering.
Weicht, ihr Sorgen, Trauer, Klagen,	Depart, you sorrows, mourning, lamentations,
Denn warum sollt ich verzagen?	For why should I despair?
Fasse dich betrübtes Herz!	Compose yourself, troubled heart!

7. Chorale

Muß ich sein betrübet?	Must I be troubled?
So mich Jesus liebet,	If Jesus loves me,
Ist mir aller Schmerz	All pain is to me
Über Honig süße,	Sweeter than honey,
Tausend Zuckerküsse	A thousand sweet kisses
Drücket er ans Herz.	He presses upon my heart.
Wenn die Pein sich stellet ein,	Whenever pain sets in,
Seine Liebe macht zur Freuden	His love turns into joy
Auch das bittre Leiden.	Even bitter suffering.

BWV 128, *Auf Christi Himmelfahrt allein*
Ascension (Gospel, Mark 16:14–20)

1. [Chorale]

Auf Christi Himmelfahrt allein	Upon Christ's ascension alone
Ich meine Nachfahrt gründe	I base my own ascension
Und allen Zweifel, Angst und Pein	And all doubt, fear, and pain
Hiermit stets überwinde;	Herewith ever conquer;
Denn weil das Haupt im Himmel ist,	For since the head is in heaven,
Wird seine Glieder Jesus Christ	Will Jesus Christ its members
Zu rechter Zeit nachholen.	Bring after in good time.

2. Recitative (T)

Ich bin bereit, komm, hole mich!	I am ready, come, get me!
Hier in der Welt	Here in the world
Ist Jammer, Angst und Pein;	Is misery, fear, and pain;
Hingegen dort, in Salems Zelt,	By contrast, there, in Salem's tent,
Werd ich verkläret sein.	I will be transfigured.
Da seh ich Gott von Angesicht zu Angesicht,	There I will see God face to face,
Wie mir sein heilig Wort verspricht.	As his holy Word promises me.

3. Aria and Recitative (B)

Auf, auf, mit hellem Schall	Rise up, rise up with bright sound
Verkündigt überall:	Proclaim everywhere:
Mein Jesus sitzt zur Rechten!	My Jesus sits at the right hand [of God]!
Wer sucht mich anzufechten?	Who seeks to attack me?
Ist er von mir genommen,	Though he is taken from me,
Ich werd einst dahin kommen,	I will one day come to that place,
Wo mein Erlöser lebt.	Where my Redeemer lives.
Meine Augen werden ihn in größter Klarheit schauen.	My eyes will see him in the greatest clarity.
O könnt ich im voraus mir eine Hütte bauen!	O, if I could only build a shelter for myself ahead of time!
Wohin? Vergebner Wunsch!	Whither? Useless wish!
Er wohnet nicht auf Berg und Tal,	He dwells not on hill and vale,
Sein Allmacht zeigt sich überall;	His omnipotence reveals itself everywhere;
So schweig, verwegner Mund,	So be silent, presumptuous mouth,
Und suche nicht dieselbe zu ergründen!	And do not seek to fathom it!

4. Aria (AT)

Sein Allmacht zu ergründen,	To fathom his omnipotence
Wird sich kein Mensche finden,	Will no human be able,
Mein Mund verstummt und schweigt.	My mouth falls dumb and becomes silent.
Ich sehe durch die Sterne,	I see through the stars,
Daß er sich schon von ferne	That he already in the distance
Zur Rechten Gottes zeigt.	Appears at God's right hand.

5. Chorale

Alsdenn so wirst du mich	Thereupon you will
Zu deiner Rechten stellen	Station me at your right hand
Und mir als deinem Kind	And upon me as your child
Ein gnädig Urteil fällen,	Pass a gracious judgement,
Mich bringen zu der Lust	And will bring me into that pleasure
Wo deine Herrlichkeit	Where your glory
Ich werde schauen an	I will behold
In alle Ewigkeit.	Through all eternity.

BWV 183, *Sie werden euch in den Bann tun*
Exaudi (Gospel, John 15:26–16:4)

1. [Recitative] (B)

Sie werden euch in den Bann tun, es kömmt aber die Zeit, daß, wer euch tötet, wird meinen, er tue Gott einen Dienst daran.	They will excommunicate you, there is indeed coming a time when whoever kills you will think he is doing God a service thereby.

2. Aria (T)

Ich fürchte nicht des Todes Schrecken,	I do not fear the terror of death,
Ich scheue ganz kein Ungemach.	I dread absolutely no hardship.
Denn Jesus' Schutzarm wird mich decken,	Since Jesus's guiding arm will cover me,
Ich folge gern und willig nach;	I follow after [him] gladly and willingly;
Wollt ihr nicht meines Lebens schonen	If you would not spare my life
Und glaubt, Gott einen Dienst zu tun,	And believe you are doing God a service,
Er soll euch selben noch belohnen,	He will yet reward you;
Wohlan, es mag dabei beruhn.	Well! It may rest therewith.

3. Recitative (A)

Ich bin bereit, mein Blut und armes Leben	I am prepared my blood and poor life
Vor dich, mein Heiland, hinzugeben,	To give up for you, my Savior;
Mein ganzer Mensch soll dir gewidmet sein;	My entire person will be dedicated to you;
Ich tröste mich, dein Geist wird bei mir stehen,	I console myself that your Spirit will stand by me,
Gesetzt, es sollte mir vielleicht zuviel geschehen.	If it should ever become too much for me.

4. Aria (S)

Höchster Tröster, Heilger Geist,	Highest comforter, Holy Spirit,
Der du mir die Wege weist,	You who show to me the paths
Darauf ich wandeln soll,	On which I am to walk,
Hilf meine Schwachheit mit vertreten,	Help my weakness with intercession,
Denn von mir selber kann ich nicht beten,	For I cannot pray by myself;
Ich weiß, du sorgest vor mein Wohl!	I know you care for my well-being!

5. Chorale

Du bist ein Geist, der lehret,	You are a Spirit who teaches
Wie man recht beten soll;	How one should truly pray;
Dein Beten wird erhöret,	Your praying is heard,
Dein Singen klinget wohl.	Your singing resounds well.
Es steigt zum Himmel an,	It rises to heaven,
Es steigt und läßt nicht abe,	It rises and does not cease
Bis der geholfen habe,	Until he has helped,
Der allein helfen kann.	Who alone can help.

BWV 74, *Wer mich liebet, der wird mein Wort halten*
Pentecost Sunday (Gospel, John 14:23–31)

1. [Chorus]

Wer mich liebet, der wird mein Wort halten, und mein Vater wird ihn lieben, und wir werden zu ihm kommen und Wohnung bei ihm machen.	Whoever loves me will keep my word, and my Father will love him, and we will come to him and make our abode with him.

2. Aria (S)

Komm, komm, mein Herze steht dir offen,	Come, come, my heart stands open to you,
Ach, laß es deine Wohnung sein!	Ah, let it be your dwelling!
Ich liebe dich, so muß ich hoffen:	I love you, so I must hope:
Dein Wort trifft itzo bei mir ein;	Your word will now be fulfilled in me;
Denn wer dich sucht, fürcht', liebt und ehret,	For whoever seeks, fears, loves, and honors you,
Dem ist der Vater zugetan.	To him the Father is devoted.
Ich zweifle nicht, ich bin erhöret,	I doubt not, I have been heard,
Daß ich mich dein getrösten kann.	So I can comfort myself in you.

3. Recitative (A)

Die Wohnung ist bereit.	The dwelling is prepared.
Du findst ein Herz, das dir allein ergeben,	You find a heart, that is surrendered to you alone,
Drum laß mich nicht erleben,	Therefore let me not experience,
Daß du gedenkst, von mir zu gehn.	That you should intend to go from me.
Das laß ich nimmermehr, ach, nimmermehr geschehen!	That I will never, ah, never allow!

4. Aria (B)

Ich gehe hin und komme wieder zu euch. Hättet ihr mich lieb, so würdet ihr euch freuen.	I go there and come again to you. If you had loved me, then you would have rejoiced.

5. Aria (T)

Kommt, eilet, stimmet Sait und Lieder	Come, hasten, tune strings and songs
In muntern und erfreuten Ton.	In lively and glad sound.
Geht er gleich weg, so kömmt er wieder,	Though he goes away, he will come again,
Der hochgelobte Gottessohn.	The highly exalted son of God.
Der Satan wird indes versuchen,	Satan will meanwhile attempt
Den Deinigen gar sehr zu fluchen.	Greatly indeed to curse your own.
Er ist mir hinderlich,	He is obstructive to me,
So glaub ich, Herr, an dich.	So I believe, Lord, in you.

6. Recitative (B)

Es ist nichts Verdammliches an denen, die in Christo Jesu sind.	There is nothing worthy of condemnation in those who are in Christ Jesus.

7. Aria (A)

Nichts kann mich erretten	Nothing can save me
Von höllischen Ketten	From hell's chains
Als, Jesu, dein Blut.	But, Jesus, your blood.
Dein Leiden, dein Sterben	Your passion, your dying
Macht mich ja zum Erben:	Makes me indeed an heir:
Ich lache der Wut.	I laugh at the fury.

8. Chorale

Kein Menschenkind hier auf der Erd	No human here on the earth
Ist dieser edlen Gabe wert,	Is worthy of this noble gift,
Bei uns ist kein Verdienen;	In us is no merit;
Hier gilt gar nichts als Lieb und Gnad,	Nothing at all is effective here but love and grace,
Die Christus uns verdienet hat	Which Christ has earned for us
Mit Büßen und Versühnen.	With his atonement and reconciliation.

BWV 68, *Also hat Gott die Welt geliebt*
Pentecost Monday (Gospel, John 3:16–21)

1. [Chorale]

Also hat Gott die Welt geliebt,	God has so loved the world,
Daß er uns seinen Sohn gegeben.	That he gave us his Son.
Wer sich im Glauben ihm ergibt,	Whoever gives himself to him in faith
Der soll dort ewig bei ihm leben.	Will live eternally there with him.
Wer glaubt, daß Jesus ihm geboren,	Whoever believes that Jesus was born for him
Der bleibet ewig unverloren,	Remains not lost eternally,
Und ist kein Leid, das den betrübt,	And no sorrow can grieve the one
Den Gott und auch sein Jesus liebt.	Whom God and also his Jesus loves.

2. Aria (S)

Mein gläubiges Herze,	My believing heart,
Frohlocke, sing, scherze,	Rejoice, sing, jest,
Dein Jesus is da!	Your Jesus is here!
Weg Jammer, weg Klagen,	Away misery, away lamentation,
Ich will euch nur sagen:	I would simply say to you:
Mein Jesus ist nah.	My Jesus is near.

3. Recitative (B)

Ich bin mit Petro nicht vermessen,	I am with Peter not mistaken,
Was mich getrost und freudig macht,	This consoles me and makes me joyful,
Daß mich mein Jesus nicht vergessen.	That my Jesus has not forgotten me.
Er kam nicht nur, die Welt zu richten,	He came not only to judge the world,
Nein, nein, er wollte Sünd und Schuld	No, no, he wanted sin and guilt
Als Mittler zwischen Gott und Mensch vor	To arbitrate at this time as mediator between
diesmal schlichten.	God and mankind.

4. Aria (B)

Du bist geboren mir zugute,	You are born for my benefit,
Das glaub ich, mir ist wohl zumute,	This I believe; I am in good spirits,
Weil du vor mich genug getan.	Since you have done enough for me.
Das Rund der Erden mag gleich brechen,	Should the circle of the earth break,
Will mir der Satan widersprechen,	Should Satan oppose me,
So bet ich dich, mein Heiland, an.	Then I will pray to you, my Savior.

5. Chorus

Wer an ihn gläubet, der wird nicht gerichtet;	Whoever believes in him will not be judged;
wer aber nicht gläubet, der ist schon gerichtet;	but whoever does not believe is already
denn er gläubet nicht an den Namen des einge-	judged; for he does not believe on the name
bornen Sohnes Gottes.	of the only begotten Son of God.

BWV 175, *Er rufet seinen Schafen mit Namen*
Pentecost Tuesday (Gospel, John 10:1–11)

1. [Recitative] (T)

Er rufet seinen Schafen mit Namen und führet sie hinaus.	He calls his sheep by name and leads them out.

2. Aria (A)

Komm, leite mich,	Come, lead me,
Es sehnet sich	Yearns
Mein Geist auf grüner Weide!	My spirit for green pastures!
Mein Herze schmacht',	My heart languishes,
Ächzt Tag und Nacht,	Groans day and night:
Mein Hirte, meine Freude.	My shepherd, my joy.

3. Recitative (T)

Wo find' ich dich? Ach, wo bist du verborgen?	Where do I find you? Ah, where are you hidden?
O! Zeige dich mir bald!	Oh, appear to me soon!
Ich sehne mich. Brich an, erwünschter Morgen!	I yearn [for you]. Break forth, desired morning!

4. Aria (T)

Es dünket mich, ich seh dich kommen,	It seems to me that I see you coming,
Du gehst zur rechten Türe ein.	You enter by the right door.
Du wirst im Glauben aufgenommen	You are received by faith
Und mußt der wahre Hirte sein.	And must be the true shepherd.
Ich kenne deine holde Stimme,	I recognize your gracious voice,
Die voller Lieb und Sanftmut ist,	Which is so full of love and gentleness,
Daß ich im Geist darob ergrimme,	That I am angered in my spirit at anyone
Wer zweifelt, daß du Heiland seist.	Who doubts that you are the Savior.

5. Recitative (AB)

Sie vernahmen aber nicht, was es war, das er zu ihnen gesaget hatte.	But they did not understand what it was that he had said to them.
Ach ja! Wir Menschen sind oftmals den Tauben zu vergleichen:	Ah, yes! We humans are often like deaf persons:
Wenn die verblendete Vernunft nicht weiß, was er gesaget hatte.	When our deluded reason does not understand what he has said.
O! Törin, merke doch,	Oh, fool, note indeed,
wenn Jesus mit dir spricht,	when Jesus speaks with you,
Daß es zu deinem Heil geschicht.	That it concerns your salvation.

6. Aria (B)

Öffnet euch, ihr beiden Ohren,	Open both your ears,
Jesus hat euch zugeschworen,	Jesus has sworn to you,
Daß er Teufel, Tod erlegt.	That he slays devil, death.
Gnade, Gnüge, volles Leben	Grace, plenty, abundant life
Will er allen Christen geben,	Would he give to all Christians
Wer ihm folgt, sein Kreuz nachträgt.	Who follow him, carry his cross.

7. Chorale

Nun, werter Geist, ich folge dir;	Now, dear Spirit, I follow you;
Hilf, daß ich suche für und für	Help that I would seek forever and ever,
Nach deinem Wort ein ander Leben,	At your word, a different life,
Das du mir willt aus Gnaden geben.	Which, out of grace, you desire to give me.
Dein Wort ist ja der Morgenstern,	Your word is indeed the morning star,
Der herrlich leuchtet nah und fern.	Which gloriously radiates near and far.
Drum will ich, die mich anders lehren,	Therefore I will eternally refuse to hear
In Ewigkeit, mein Gott, nicht hören.	Those who would teach me otherwise.
Alleluja, alleluja!	Alleluia, Alleluia!

BWV 176, *Es ist ein trotzig und verzagt Ding*
Trinity Sunday (Gospel, John 3:1–15)

1. [Chorus]

Es ist ein trotzig und verzagt Ding um aller Menschen Herze.

It is an obstinate and despondent thing about all human hearts.

2. Recitative (A)

Ich meine, recht verzagt,
Daß Nikodemus sich bei Tage nicht,
Bei Nacht zu Jesus wagt.
Die Sonne mußte dort bei Josua so lange stille stehn,
So lange bis der Sieg vollkommen war geschehn;
Hier aber wünschet Nikodem:
O säh ich sie zu Rüste gehn!

I think it was truly fainthearted,
That Nicodemus not by day,
[But only] by night ventured to Jesus.
The sun was forced with Joshua to stand still so long,
Until the victory had been fully accomplished;
But here Nicodemus wishes:
O that the sun would go to rest!

3. Aria (S)

Dein sonst hell beliebter Schein
Soll für mich umnebelt sein,
Weil ich nach dem Meister frage,
Denn ich scheue mich bei Tage.
Niemand kann die Wunder tun,
Denn sein Allmacht und sein Wesen,
Scheint, ist göttlich auserlesen,
Gottes Geist muß auf ihm ruhn.

Your beloved radiance, normally so bright,
Must be beclouded for me,
While I seek for the master,
For I am fearful by day.
No human could do such wonders,
For his omnipotence and his nature,
It appears, are divinely chosen:
God's Spirit must be resting upon him.

4. Recitative (B)

So wundre dich, o Meister, nicht,
Warum ich dich bei Nacht ausfrage!
Ich fürchte, daß bei Tage
Mein Ohnmacht nicht bestehen kann.
Doch tröst ich mich, du nimmst mein Herz und Geist
Zum Leben auf und an,
Weil alle, die nur an dich glauben, nicht verloren werden.

So do not wonder, Oh master,
Why I seek you by night!
I fear that by day
My weakness will not be able to stand the test.
Yet I comfort myself, that my heart and spirit
You admit and accept into life,
For all who will only believe in you will not be lost.

5. Aria (A)

Ermuntert euch, furchtsam und schüchterne Sinne,
Erholet euch, höret, was Jesus verspricht:
Daß ich durch den Glauben den Himmel gewinne.
Wenn die Verheißung erfüllend geschicht,
Werd ich dort oben
Mit Danken und Loben
Vater, Sohn und Heilgen Geist
Preisen, der dreinig heißt.

Rouse yourselves, fearful and timid senses,
Be renewed, hear what Jesus promises:
That I through faith will obtain heaven.
When the promise is fulfilled,
I will up there,
With thanks and praise
Father, Son, and Holy Spirit
Praise, who is called triune.

6. Chorale

Auf daß wir also allzugleich	So that we thus all together
Zur Himmelspforten dringen	To the gates of heaven may press
Und dermaleinst in deinem Reich	And hereafter in your kingdom
Ohn alles Ende singen,	Without end may sing,
Daß du alleine König seist,	That you alone are king,
Hoch über alle Götter,	High above all gods,
Gott Vater, Sohn und Heilger Geist,	God Father, Son, and Holy Spirit,
Der Frommen Schutz und Retter,	Refuge and Savior of godly people,
Ein Wesen, drei Personen.	One being, three persons.

Appendix C

The Cantatas of J. S. Bach's First Two Leipzig Jahrgänge

Jahrgang I (complete performance schedule)

Date	Liturgical occasion	BWV	Text incipit	Librettist
30 May 1723	Trinity 1	75	Die Elenden sollen essen	unknown
6 June 1723	Trinity 2	76	Die Himmel erzählen die Ehre Gottes	unknown
13 June 1723	Trinity 3	21[R]	Ich hatte viel Bekümmernis	unknown
20 June 1723	Trinity 4	24	Ein ungefärbt Gemüte	Neumeister
20 June 1723	Trinity 4	185[R]	Barmherziges Herze der ewigen Liebe	Franck
24 June 1724	John the Baptist	167	Ihr Menschen, rühmet Gottes Liebe	unknown
2 July 1723	Visitation of Mary	147[N]	Herz und Mund und Tat und Leben	Franck + unknown
11 July 1723	Trinity 7	186[N]	Ärgre dich, o Seele, nicht	Franck + unknown
18 July 1723	Trinity 8	136	Erforsche mich, Gott, und erfahre mein Herz	unknown
25 July 1723	Trinity 9	105	Herr, gehe nicht ins Gericht	unknown
1 Aug 1723	Trinity 10	46	Schauet doch und sehet	unknown
8 Aug 1723	Trinity 11	179	Siehe zu, daß deine Gottesfurcht	unknown
8 Aug 1723	Trinity 11	199[R]	Meine Herze schwimmt im Blut	Lehms
15 Aug 1723	Trinity 12	69a	Lobe den Herrn, meine Seele	Knauer
22 Aug 1723	Trinity 13	77	Du sollt Gott, deinen Herren, lieben	Knauer
29 Aug 1723	Trinity 14	25	Es ist nichts Gesundes an meinem Leibe	unknown
30 Aug 1723	Town Council	119	Preise, Jerusalem, den Herrn	unknown

Date	Liturgical occasion	BWV	Text incipit	Librettist
5 Sept 1723	Trinity 15	138	Warum betrübst du dich, mein Herz?	unknown
12 Sept 1723	Trinity 16	95	Christus, der ist mein Leben	unknown
3 Oct 1723	Trinity 19	48	Ich elender Mensch, wer wird mich erlösen	unknown
10 Oct 1723	Trinity 20	162^R	Ach! ich sehe, itzt, da ich zur Hochzeit gehe	Franck
17 Oct 1723	Trinity 21	109	Ich glaube, lieber Herr	unknown
24 Oct 1723	Trinity 22	89	Was soll ich aus dir machen, Ephraim?	unknown
31 Oct 1723	Trinity 23	163^R	Nur jedem das Seine	Franck
7 Nov 1723	Trinity 24	60	O Ewigkeit, du Donnerwort	unknown
14 Nov 1723	Trinity 25	90	Es reißet euch ein schrecklich Ende	unknown
21 Nov 1723	Trinity 26	70^N	Wachet! betet! betet! wachet!	Franck + unknown
28 Nov 1723	1 Advent	61^R	Nun komm der Heiden Heiland	Neumeister
25 Dec 1723	1 Christmas	63^R	Christen, ätzet diesen Tag	unknown
26 Dec 1723	2 Christmas	40	Darzu ist erschienen der Sohn Gottes	unknown
27 Dec 1723	3 Christmas	64	Sehet, welch eine Liebe	unknown
1 Jan 1724	New Year's Day	190	Singet dem Herrn ein neues Lied	unknown
2 Jan 1724	New Year 1	153	Schau, lieber Gott, wie meine Feind	unknown
6 Jan 1724	Epiphany	65	Sie werden aus Saba alle kommen	unknown
9 Jan 1724	Epiphany 1	154	Mein liebster Jesus ist verloren	unknown
16 Jan 1724	Epiphany 2	155^R	Mein Gott, wie lang, ach lange	unknown
23 Jan 1724	Epiphany 3	73	Herr, wie du willt, so schicks mit mir	unknown
30 Jan 1724	Epiphany 4	81	Jesus schläft, was soll ich hoffen?	unknown
2 Feb 1724	Purification of Mary	83	Erfreute Zeit im neuen Bunde	unknown

Date	Liturgical occasion	BWV	Text incipit	Librettist
6 Feb 1724	Septuagesima	144	Nimm, was dein ist, und gehe hin	unknown
13 Feb 1724	Sexagesima	181	Leichtgesinnte Flattergeister	unknown
13 Feb 1724	Sexagesima	18^R	Gleichwie der Regen und Schnee	Neumeister
20 Feb 1724	Estomihi	22^R	Jesus nahm zu sich die Zwölfe	unknown
20 Feb 1724	Estomihi	23^R	Du wahrer Gott und Davids Sohn	unknown
25 Mar 1724	Annunciation of Mary	—	[Siehe eine Jungfrau ist schwanger]	
25 Mar 1724	Annunciation of Mary	182^R	Himmelskönig, sei willkommen	unknown
9 Apr 1724	Easter Sunday	31^R	Der Himmel lacht	Franck
9 Apr 1724	Easter Sunday	4^R	Christ lag in Todesbanden	(chorale)
10 Apr 1724	Easter Monday	66^P	Erfreut euch, ihr Herzen	unknown
11 Apr 1724	Easter Tuesday	134^P	Ein Herz, das seinen Jesum lebend weiß	unknown
16 Apr 1724	Quasimodogeniti	67	Halt im Gedächtnis Jesum Christ	unknown
23 Apr 1724	Misericordias Domini	104	Du Hirte Israel, höre	unknown
30 Apr 1724	Jubilate	12^R	Weinen, Klagen, Sorgen, Zagen	unknown
7 May 1724	Kantate	166	Wo gehest du hin?	unknown
14 May 1724	Rogate	86	Wahrlich, wahrlich, ich sage euch	unknown
18 May 1724	Ascension	37	Wer da gläubet und getauft wird	unknown
21 May 1724	Exaudi	44	Sie werden euch in den Bann tun	unknown
28 May 1724	Pentecost Sunday	172^R	Erschallet, ihr Lieder	Franck
28 May 1724	Pentecost Sunday	59^R	Wer mich liebet, der wird mein Wort halten	Neumeister
29 May 1724	Pentecost Monday	173^P	Erhöhtes Fleisch und Blut	unknown
30 May 1724	Pentecost Tuesday	184^P	Erwünschtes Freudenlicht	unknown

Date	Liturgical occasion	BWV	Text incipit	Librettist
4 June 1724	Trinity Sunday	194[R]	Höchsterwünschtes Freudenfest	unknown
4 June 1724	Trinity Sunday	165[R]	O heilges Geist- und Wasserbad	Franck

[R] Reperformance of pre-Leipzig work, in some cases with minor changes
[N] New version of pre-Leipzig work
[P] Parody

Jahrgang II

Date	Liturgical occasion	BWV	Text incipit	Librettist
11 June 1724	Trinity 1	20	O Ewigkeit, du Donnerwort	unknown
18 June 1724	Trinity 2	2	Ach Gott, vom Himmel sieh darein	unknown
24 June 1724	John the Baptist	7	Christ unser Herr zum Jordan kam	unknown
25 June 1724	Trinity 3	135	Ach Herr, mich armen Sünder	unknown
2 July 1724	Visitation of Mary	10	Meine Seel erhebt den Herren	unknown
9 July 1724	Trinity 5	93	Wer nur den lieben Gott läßt walten	unknown
23 July 1724	Trinity 7	107	Was willst du dich betrüben	unknown
30 July 1724	Trinity 8	178	Wo Gott der Herr nicht bei uns hält	unknown
6 Aug 1724	Trinity 9	94	Was frag ich nach der Welt	unknown
13 Aug 1724	Trinity 10	101	Nimm von uns, Herr, du treuer Gott	unknown
20 Aug 1724	Trinity 11	113	Herr Jesu Christ, du höchstes Gut	unknown
3 Sept 1724	Trinity 13	33	Allein zu dir, Herr Jesu Christ	unknown
10 Sept 1724	Trinity 14	78	Jesu, der du meine Seele	unknown
17 Sept 1724	Trinity 15	99	Was Gott tut, das ist wohlgetan	unknown
24 Sept 1724	Trinity 16	8	Liebster Gott, wenn werd ich sterben	unknown

Date	Liturgical occasion	BWV	Text incipit	Librettist
29 Sept 1724	Michael's Day	130	Herr Gott, dich loben alle wir	unknown
1 Oct 1724	Trinity 17	114	Ach, lieben Christen, seid getrost	unknown
8 Oct 1724	Trinity 18	96	Herr Christ, der einge Gottessohn	unknown
15 Oct 1724	Trinity 19	5	Wo soll ich fliehen hin	unknown
22 Oct 1724	Trinity 20	180	Schmücke dich, o liebe Seele	unknown
29 Oct 1724	Trinity 21	38	Aus tiefer Not schrei ich zu dir	unknown
5 Nov 1724	Trinity 22	115	Mache dich, mein Geist, bereit	unknown
12 Nov 1724	Trinity 23	139	Wohl dem, der sich auf seinen Gott	unknown
19 Nov 1724	Trinity 24	26	Ach wie flüchtig, ach wie nichtig	unknown
26 Nov 1724	Trinity 25	116	Du Friedefürst, Herr Jesu Christ	unknown
3 Dec 1724	1 Advent	62	Nun komm, der Heiden Heiland	unknown
25 Dec 1724	1 Christmas	91	Gelobet seist du, Jesu Christ	unknown
26 Dec 1724	2 Christmas	121	Christum wir sollen loben schon	unknown
27 Dec 1724	3 Christmas	133	Ich freue mich in dir	unknown
31 Dec 1724	Christmas 1	122	Das neugeborne Kindlein	unknown
1 Jan 1725	New Year's Day	41	Jesu, nun sei gepreiset	unknown
6 Jan 1725	Epiphany	123	Liebster Immanuel, Herzog der Frommen	unknown
7 Jan 1725	Epiphany 1	124	Meinen Jesum laß ich nicht	unknown
14 Jan 1725	Epiphany 2	3	Ach Gott, wie manches Herzeleid	unknown
21 Jan 1725	Epiphany 3	111	Was mein Gott will, das g'scheh allzeit	unknown
28 Jan 1725	Septuagesima	92	Ich hab in Gottes Herz und Sinn	unknown
2 Feb 1725	Purification of Mary	125	Mit Fried und Freud ich fahr dahin	unknown

Date	Liturgical occasion	BWV	Text incipit	Librettist
4 Feb 1725	Sexagesima	126	Erhalt uns, Herr, bei deinem Wort	unknown
11 Feb 1725	Estomihi	127	Herr Jesu Christ, wahr' Mensch und Gott	unknown
25 Mar 1725	Annunciation of Mary	1	Wie schön leuchtet der Morgenstern	unknown
2 Apr 1725	Easter Tuesday	6	Bleib bei uns, denn es will Abend werden	unknown
8 Apr 1725	Quasimodogeniti	42	Am Abend aber desselbigen Sabbaths	unknown
15 Apr 1725	Misericordias Domini	85	Ich bin ein gutter Hirt	unknown
22 Apr 1725	Jubilate	103	Ihr werdet weinen und heulen	Ziegler
29 Apr 1725	Kantate	108	Es ist euch gut, daß ich hingehe	Ziegler
6 May 1725	Rogate	87	Bisher habt ihr nichts gebeten	Ziegler
10 May 1725	Ascension	128	Auf Christi Himmelfahrt allein	Ziegler
13 May 1725	Exaudi	183	Sie werden euch in den Bann tun	Ziegler
20 May 1725	Pentecost Sunday	74	Wer mich liebet, der wird mein Wort halten	Ziegler
21 May 1725	Pentecost Monday	68	Also hat Gott die Welt geliebt	Ziegler
22 May 1725	Pentecost Tuesday	175	Er rufet seinen Schafen mit Namen	Ziegler
27 May 1725	Trinity Sunday	176	Es ist ein trotzig und verzagt Ding	Ziegler

Select Bibliography

This bibliography is divided chronologically as follows: sixteenth- to eighteenth-century sources, nineteenth-century sources, and twentieth- and twenty-first-century sources. Within each section, citations are arranged alphabetically by author.

Ziegler's own writings are not included in this bibliography, but are listed in Appendix A above, "An Annotated Bibliography of Ziegler's Works."

Sixteenth- to Eighteenth-century Sources

Amaranthes [Gottlieb Siegmund Corvinus]. *Nutzbares, galantes und curiöses Frauenzimmer-Lexicon*, revised and expanded edition. Leipzig: Johann Friedrich Gleditsch, 1739 (1715).

Amsterdam. "Nouvelles Literaires." *Bibliothèque germanique, ou histoire littéraire de l'Allemagnge* 28 (1734): 137–98 (180).

Brockes, Barthold Heinrich. *Irrdischen Vergnügens in Gott*. Vol. 2. Hamburg: Kissner, 1727.

Deutschen Gesellschaft in Leipzig, ed. *Beyträge zur Critischen Historie der Deutschen Sprache, Poesie und Beredsamkeit*. 8 vols. Leipzig: Bernhard Christoph Breitkopf, 1732–42. (Reprint, Hildesheim: Georg Olms, 1970.)

Finauer, Peter Paul. *Allgemeines Historisches Verzeichniß gelehrter Frauenzimmer*. Munich: Johann Christoph Mayr, 1761.

Göttingsche Zeitungen von gelehrten Sachen. Göttingen, 1739–52. [1 (1739): 293–94; 6 (1744): 352].

Gottsched, Johann Christoph, ed. *Die Vernünftigen Tadlerinnen, erster Jahr-Theil 1725*. Halle: Johann Adam Spörl, 1725. (Reprint, Hildesheim: Georg Olms, 1993.)

Gottsched, Johann Christoph, ed. *Die Vernünftigen Tadlerinnen, andrer Jahr-Theil 1726*. Leipzig: Johann Friedrich Braun, 1727. (Reprint, Hildesheim: Georg Olms, 1993.)

Gottsched, Johann Christoph, ed. *Anhang. Derjenigen Briefe So an die Vernünftigen Tadlerinnen Im Jahr 1726. eingelauffen*. Halle: Johann Adam Spörl, 18 February 1726. (Reprint, Hildesheim: Georg Olms, 1993.)

Gottsched, Luise Adelgunde Victorie. *Der Frau Luise Adelgunde Victoria Gottschedinn, geb. Kulmus, sämmtliche Kleinere Gedichte*. Edited by Johann Christoph Gottsched. Leipzig: Bernhard Christoph Breitkopf, 1763.

Gottsched, Luise Adelgunde Victorie. *Briefe der Frau Luise Adelgunde Victorie Gottsched gebohrne Kulmus*. Edited by Dorothee Henriette von Runckel. 3 vols. Dresden: Harpeter, 1771–72.

Gottsched, Luise Adelgunde Victorie. *Pietism in Petticoats and Other Comedies*. Translated with an introduction by Thomas Kerth and John R. Russel. Columbia, SC: Camden House, 1994.

[Gräf, Sophie Regina.] *Eines andächtigen Frauenzimmers S. R. G. Ihrem JESU im Glauben dargebrachte Liebes-Opffer, d. i. Poetische Applicationes derer Sonn- und Fest-täglichen Evangelien zu Ihrer eigenen Erbauung und Vergnügung Ihrer Seelen abgefasset, Und Ohne Dero Wissen zum Druck befördert von N. N.* Leipzig: Johann Christian Martini, 1715.

Gräfe, Johann Friedrich. *Samlung verschiedener und auserlesener Oden zu welchen von den berühmtesten Meistern in der Music eigene Melodieyen verfertiget worden.* Vol 1. Halle, 1737.

Hallische Beyträge zu der Juristischen Gelehrten Historie. Vol. 3, part 10. Halle: Renger, 1758.

Hamburgische Berichte von neuen gelehrten Sachen. Hamburg, 1733–58. [(1733): 750–51; (1734): 50–51; (1741): 840].

Knauer, Johann Oswald. *Gott=geheiligtes Singen und Spielen des Friedensteinischen Zions, nach allen und jeden Sonn= und Fest=Tags=Evangelien, vor und nach der Predigt / angestellet Vom Advent 1720. bis dahin 1721.* Gotha: Johann Andreas Reiher, 1720.

Köhler, Johann David. "Gedächtnüs-Müntze, auf die Poetische Krönung der vortrefflichen Frauen Christianen Marianen von Ziegler/gebohrnen Romanus, in Leipzig." *Historischer Münz-Belustigung* 9 (1737): 137–44.

Lamprecht, Jacob Friedrich, ed. *Sammlung der Schriften und Gedichte welche auf die Poetische Krönung Der Hochwohlgebohrnen Frauen, Frauen Christianen Marianen von Ziegler gebohrnen Romanus, verfertiget worden.* With Foreword by Jacob Friedrich Lamprecht. Leipzig: Bernhard Christoph Breitkopf, 1734.

Lehms, Georg Christian. *Teutschlands Galante Poetinnen Mit Ihren sinnreichen und netten Proben: Nebst einem Anhang Ausländischer Dames, So sich gleichfalls durch Schöne Poesien Bey der curieusen Welt bekannt gemacht, und einer Vorrede, Daß das Weibliche Geschlecht so geschickt zum Studieren, als das Männliche.* Frankfurt am Main: Anton Heinscheidt, 1715.

Lehms, Georg Christian. *Lob-Rede des Frauenzimmers in gebundener Rede.* Leipzig: Johann Christian Martini, 1716.

Leipziger Kirchen-Staat. Leipzig: Friedrich Groschuff, 1710.

Liscow, Joachim Friedrich, ed. *Hamburger Correspondenten.* [22 December 1734, 29 January 1735].

Luther, Martin. "Deutsche Messe und Ordnung Gottesdiensts, 1526." In *D. Martin Luthers Wercke.* Vol. 19, 44–113. Weimar: Hermann Böhlaus, 1897.

Luther, Martin. "Ein Brief D. Mart. Luthers Von den Schleichern und Winkelpredigern, 1532." In *D. Martin Luthers Wercke,* Vol. 30, 510–27. Weimar: Hermann Böhlaus, 1910. English translation as "Infiltrating and Clandestine Preachers, 1532," in *Luther's Works, American Edition,* Vol. 40. Translated and edited by Conrad Bergendoff, 379–94. Philadelphia: Muhlenberg Press, 1958.

Luther, Martin. *The Complete Sermons of Martin Luther.* 7 vols. Grand Rapids: Baker Books, 2000.

Menantes [Christian Friedrich Humbold]. *Die Edle Bemühung müssiger Stunden / In Galanten, Verlibten / Sinn= und Schertz= und Satyrischen Gedichten.* Hamburg: Gottfried Liebernickel, 1702.

Mencke, Johann Burchard, ed. *Acta Eruditorum* 156. Leipzig: Johann Friedrich Gleditsch, 1732.

Neuen Zeitungen von gelehrten Sachen. Leipzig, 1715–84. [14 (1728): 31–32; 15 (1729): 359–60; 16 (1730): 712, 816; 17 (1732): 567–68; 18 (1732): 464–65, 529–30, 918–21; 19 (1733): 84–87, 261–64, 789–92, 830–31; 20 (1734): 135, 352, 439, 894–95; 21 (1735): 52, 544; 23 (1737): 240, 682–83; 25 (1739): 818].

Olearius, Johann. Biblische *Erklärung*. 5 vols. Leipzig: Tarnov, 1678–81.

Olearius, Johann. *Evangelischer Glaubens-Sieg der Kinder Gottes wider ihre Hauptfeinde Welt, Sünde, Tod, Teufel u. Hölle, auß d. ordentlichen Sonn- u. Fest-tags Evangelien gezeiget.* Leipzig: Frommann, 1672.

Philippi, Johann Ernst. "Sottises galantes, oder Galante Thorheiten, angezeiget in einem Sendschreiben an . . . Gottsched . . . von Carl Gustav." Lübeck, 1733. 3rd ed. In *Cicero: Ein großer Wind=Beutel, Rabulist, und Charletan; Zur Probe aus Dessen übersetzter Schutz=Rede*, 327–56. Halle: Jacob Born, 1735.

Picander [Christian Friedrich Henrici]. "Cantaten auf die Sonn= und Fest=Tage durch das gantze Jahr, Leipzig 1729." In *Picanders Ernst=Schertzhaffte und Satÿrische Gedichte*, Vol. 3, 79–188. Leipzig: Boetius, 1732.

R., M. *Der Genealogische Archivarivs, auf das Jahr 1733.* Leipzig: Joh. Sam. Heinsius, 1734.

Riegerin, Magdalenen Sibyllen. *Versuch einiger Geistlichen und Moralischen Gedichte.* Frankfurt am Main: Franz Varrentrapp, 1743.

Schurman, Anna Maria van. *Whether a Christian Woman Should Be Educated and Other Writings from Her Intellectual Circle.* Edited and translated by Joyce L. Irwin. Chicago: University of Chicago Press, 1998.

Schwabe, Johann Joachim, ed. *Belustigungen des Verstandes und des Witzes.* Vol. 2. Leipzig: Bernhard Christoph Breitkopf, 1742.

Sperontes [Johann Sigismund Scholze]. *Singende Muse an der Pleiße.* Leipzig, 1736.

Stolle, Gottlieb. *Zusätze und Ausbesserungen der Historie der Philosophischen Gelahrheit.* Jena: Johann Meyer, 1736.

Telemann, Georg Philipp. *Der getreue Music-Meister.* Hamburg, 1728.

Telemann, Georg Philipp. *Tafelmusik*, Teil III. Edited by Johann Philipp Hinnenthal. Musikalische Werke. Vol. 14. Kassel: Bärenreiter, 1963.

Triller, Daniel Wilhelm. "Vorrede" to Magdalenen Sibyllen Riegerin. *Versuch einiger Geistlichen und Moralischen Gedichte.* Frankfurt am Main: Franz Varrentrapp, 1743.

Weidlich, Christoph. *Geschichte der jetztlebenden Rechts=Gelehrten in Teutschland.* Vol. II. Merseburg: Johann Gottlob Schubarth, 1749.

Weidlich, Christoph. *Zuverläßige Nachrichten von denen jetzlebenden Rechtsgelehrten.* Vol. 4. Halle: Carl Christian Kümmel, 1760.

Zäunemann, Sidonia Hedwig. *Poetische Rosen in Knospen.* Erfurt: Johann Heinrich Nonne, 1738.

Zäunemann, Sidonia Hedwig. *Die von denen Faunen gepeitschte Laster.* Frankfurt and Leipzig: Brönner, 1739.

Zedler, Johann Heinrich. "Christiane Mariane von Ziegler." In *Grosses vollständiges Universal-Lexicon.* Vol. 62, 575–84. Leipzig and Halle: Verlegts Johann Heinrich Zedler, 1749.

Ziegler, Christiane Mariane von. See Appendix A, "An Annotated Bibliography of Ziegler's Works."
Zuverläßige Nachrichten von dem gegenwärtigen Zustande, Veränderung und Wachsthum der Wissenschaften. Vol. 2. Leipzig: Johann Friedrich Gleditsch, 1740.

Nineteenth-century Sources

Ditsel, Theodor. "Zur Biographie der Dichterin Marianne von Ziegler." *Archiv für Litteraturgeschichte* 14 (1886): 103–05.

Einert, E. "Eine vergessene Dichterin." In *Aus den Papieren eines Rathauses*, 183–96. Arnstadt: Emil Frotscher, 1892.

Goedeke, Karl. *Grundriß zur Geschichte der deutschen Dichtung aus den Quellen.* 2nd ed. Vol. 3. Dresden: Ehlermann, 1887.

Große, Karl. *Geschichte der Stadt Leipzig von der ältesten bis auf die neueste Zeit.* Vol. 2. Leipzig: C. B. Polet, 1842.

Gross, Heinrich. *Deutschlands Dichterinen und Schriftstellerinen: Eine literarhistorische Skizze.* 2nd ed. Wien: Carl Gerold, 1882.

Hanstein, Adelbert von. *Die Frauen in der Zeit des Aufschwunges des Deutschen Geisteslebens.* Vol. 1 of *Die Frauen in der Geschichte des deutschen Geistesleben des 18. und 19. Jahrhunderts.* Leipzig: Freund und Wittig, 1899.

Klemm, Gustav. *Die Frauen: Culturgeschichtliche Schilderungen des Zustandes und Einflusses der Frauen in den verschiedenen Zonen und Zeitaltern.* Vol. 6. Dresden: Arnold, 1859.

Maltzahn, Wendelin von, ed. *Deutscher Bücherschatz des sechszehnten, siebenzehnten und achtzehnten bis um die Mitte des neunzehntet Jahrhunderts.* Jena: Friedrich Mauke, 1875.

Meiern, Johann Gottfried von. *Acta Pacis Westphalicae Publica: Oder = Westphälische Friedens-Handlungen und Geschichte.* Hannover: Joh. Christ. Ludoph Schultzen, 1734–36.

Spitta, Philipp. *Johann Sebastian Bach.* 3 vols. New York: Dover, 1951 (original German version 1873, 1879–80).

Spitta, Philipp. "Über die Beziehungen Sebastian Bachs zu Christian Friedrich Hunold und Mariane von Ziegler." In *Historische und Philologische Aufsätze: Ernst Curtius zu seinem siebenzigsten Geburtstage am zweiten September 1884 gewidmet*, 403–34. Berlin: A. Asher & Co, 1884. Section on Ziegler republished as "Mariane von Ziegler und Johann Sebastian Bach." In *Zur Musik. Sechzehn Aufsätze*, 95–118. Berlin: Gebrüder Paetel, 1892. (Reprint, Hildesheim: Georg Olms, 1976.)

Spitta, Philipp. "Sperontes' 'Singende Muse an der Pleiße': Zur Geschichte des deutschen Hausgesanges im achtzehnten Jahrhundert." *Musikgeschichtliche Aufsätze.* Berlin: Gebrüder Paetel, 1894. (Reprint, Hildesheim: Georg Olms, 1976.)

Weber, Karl von, ed. *Archiv für die Sächsische Geschichte.* Vol. 5. Leipzig: Bernhard Tauchnitz, 1867.

Wolff, Eugen. *Gottscheds Stellung im deutschen Bildungsleben.* Kiel & Leipzig: Lipsius & Tischer, 1897.

Wustmann, Gustav. *Aus Leipzigs Vergangenheit: Gesammelte Aufsätze*. Leipzig: Friedrich Wilhelm Grunow, 1885.

Wustmann, Gustav. *Bilderbuch aus der Geschichte der Stadt Leipzig*. Leipzig: Reprintverlag, 1990 (1897).

Wustmann, Gustav. "Der Bürgermeister Romanus." In *Quellen zur Geschichte Leipzigs: Veröffentlichungen aus dem Archiv und der Bibliothek der Stadt Leipzig*. Vol. 2. Edited by Gustav Wustmann, 263–352. Leipzig: Duncker & Humblot, 1895.

Twentieth- and Twenty-first-century Sources

Baader, Renate. "Die verlorene weibliche Aufklärung: Die französische Salonkultur des 17. Jahrhunderts und ihre Autorinnen." In *Frauen Literatur Geschichte: Schreibende Frauen vom Mittelalter bis zur Gegenwart*. Edited by Hiltrud Gnüg and Renate Möhrmann, 58–82. Stuttgart: J. B. Metzler, 1985.

Bach-Archiv Leipzig, ed. *Bachs Nachbarn: Die Familie Bose*. Kabinettausstellung im Bach-Museum Leipzig vom 1. September 2005 bis 11. Januar 2006. Leipzig: Thomas Druck, 2005.

Baron, Carol, ed. *Bach's Changing World: Voices in the Community*. Rochester: University of Rochester Press, 2006.

Becker-Cantarino, Barbara. "Leben als Text: Briefe als Ausdrucks- und Verständigungsmittel in der Briefkultur und Literatur des 18. Jahrhunderts." In *Frauen Literatur Geschichte: Schreibende Frauen vom Mittelalter bis zur Gegenwart*. Edited by Hiltrud Gnüg and Renate Möhrmann, 83–103. Stuttgart: J. B. Metzler, 1985.

Becker-Cantarino, Barbara. *Der lange Weg zur Mündigkeit: Frau und Literatur (1500–1800)*. Stuttgart: J. B. Metzler, 1987.

Bennholdt-Thomsen, Anke and Alfredo Guzzoni. "Gelehrte Arbeit von Frauen: Möglichkeiten und Grenzen im Deutschland des 18. Jahrhunderts." *Querelles: Jahrbuch für Frauenforschung* 1 (1996): 48–76.

Blackall, Eric A. *The Emergence of German as a Literary Language: 1700–1775*. 2nd ed. Ithaca: Cornell University Press, 1978.

Blackwell, Jeannine and Susanne Zantop. *Bitter Healing: German Women Writers 1700–1830. An Anthology*. Lincoln: University of Nebraska Press, 1990.

Bolduan, Miriam F. "The Significance of the *Viola Pomposa* in the Bach Cantatas." *BACH: Journal of the Riemenschneider Bach Institute* 14 (1983): 12–17.

Boringhieri, Gustavo. "A Proposito del "Violoncello Piccolo" di Bach." *Rivista Italiana di Musicologia* 8 (1973): 113–31.

Boyd, Malcolm. *Bach*. Oxford: Oxford University Press, 2000.

Bragg, Marvin. *From Gottsched to Goethe: Changes in the Social Function of the Poet and Poetry*. New York: Peter Lang, 1984.

Brinker-Gabler, Gisela, ed. *Deutsche Dichterinnen vom 16. Jahrhundert bis zur Gegenwart*. Introduction by Gisela Brinker-Gabler. Frankfurt am Main: Fischer, 1978.

Brinker-Gabler, Gisela. "Das weibliche Ich: Überlegungen zur Analyse von Werken weiblicher Autoren mit einem Beispiel aus dem 18. Jahrhundert: Sidonia Hedwig Zäunemann." *Die Frau als Heldin und Autorin: Neue kritische Ansätze zur deutschen Literatur.* Edited by Wolfgang Paulsen, 55–65. Bern: Francke, 1979.

Brinker-Gabler, Gisela, ed. *Vom Mittelalter bis zum Ende des 18. Jahrhunderts.* Vol. 1 of *Deutsche Literatur von Frauen.* 2 vols. München: C. H. Beck, 1988.

Catling, Jo. "Introduction" to *A History of Women's Writing in Germany, Austria and Switzerland.* Edited by Jo Catling, 1–10. Cambridge: Cambridge University Press, 2000.

Cocalis, Susan L. "Der Vormund will Vormund sein: Zur Problematik der weiblichen Unmündigkeit im 18. Jahrhundert." In *Gestaltet und Gestaltend: Frauen in der deutschen Literatur.* Edited by Marianne Burkhard, 33–55. Amsterdamer Beiträge zur Neuen Germanistik 10. Amsterdam: Rodopi, 1980.

Cocalis, Susan L., ed. *The Defiant Muse: German Feminist Poems from the Middle Ages to the Present. A Bilingual Anthology.* New York: Feminist Press, 1986.

Crist, Stephen A. "Aria Forms in the Vocal Works of J. S. Bach, 1714–24." Ph.D. diss., Brandeis University, 1988.

Dadelsen, Georg von. *Beiträge zur Chronologie der Werke Johann Sebastian Bachs.* Tübinger Bach–Studien 4/5. Trossingen: Hohner, 1958.

Dahlqvist, Reine. "Taille, Oboe da Caccia and Corno Inglese," *Gaplin Society Journal* 26 (1973): 58–71.

Davis, Natalie Zemon. *Women on the Margins: Three Seventeenth-Century Lives.* Cambridge, MA: Harvard University Press, 1995.

Debes, Dietmar. Foreword to *Bibliotheca Societatis Teutonicae Saeculi XVI–XVIII: Katalog der Büchersammlung der Deutschen Gesellschaft in Leipzig.* Edited by Ernst Kroker. 2 vols. Munich: Kösel-Verlag, 1971, vii–xiv.

Döring, Detlef. *Johann Christoph Gottsched in Leipzig: Ausstellung in der Universitätsbibliothek Leipzig zum 300. Geburtstag von J. Chr. Gottsched.* Stuttgart & Leipzig: S. Hirzel, 2000.

Douglass, Jane Dempsey. "The Image of God in Women in Luther and Calvin." In *The Image of God: Gender Models in Judaeo-Christian Tradition.* Edited by Kari Elisabeth Børresen, 236–66. Minneapolis: Fortress Press, 1991.

Dreyfus, Laurence. *Bach's Continuo Group: Players and Practices in His Vocal Works.* Cambridge, MA: Harvard University Press, 1987.

Drüner, Ulrich. "Violoncello piccolo und Viola pomposa bei Johann Sebastian Bach: Zu Fragen von Identität und Spielweise dieser Instrumente." *Bach-Jahrbuch* 73 (1987): 85–112.

Dulong, Claude. "Conversation to Creation." In *A History of Women in the West. III. Renaissance and Enlightenment Paradoxes.* Translated by Arthur Goldhammer. Edited by Natalie Zemon Davis and Arlette Farge, 395–419. Cambridge, MA: Belknap Press, 1993.

Dürr, Alfred. *Zur Chronologie der Leipziger Vokalwerke J. S. Bachs*, 2nd ed. Kassel: Bärenreiter, 1976. Revision of "Zur Chronologie der Leipziger Vokalwerke J. S. Bachs," *Bach-Jahrbuch* 44 (1957): 5–162.

Dürr, Alfred. Review of *Studi sui testi delle cantate sacre di J. S. Bach*, by Luigi Ferdinando Tagliavini (Padua, 1956). *Die Musikforschung* 12 (1959): 104–07.

Dürr, Alfred. *Kritischer Bericht* to *Johann Sebastian Bach: Neue Ausgabe Sämtlicher Werke* I/35. Kassel: Bärenreiter, 1964.

Dürr, Alfred. *Johann Sebastian Bach: Die Kantaten*, 7th ed. Kassel: Bärenreiter, 1999 (1971).

Dürr, Alfred. "Bachs Kantatentexte: Probleme und Aufgaben der Forschung." *Bach-Studien* 5. Edited by Rudolf Eller & Hans-Joachim Schulze, 49–61. Leipzig: Breitkopf & Härtel, 1975.

Dürr, Alfred. "Philologisches zum Problem Violoncello piccolo bei Bach." In *Festschrift Wolfgang Rehm zum 60. Geburtstag*, 45–50. Kassel: Bärenreiter, 1989.

Dürr, Alfred. Review of *Die Welt der Bach Kantaten*, 3 vols., edited by Christoph Wolff (Stuttgart: J. B. Metzler and Kassel: Bärenreiter, 1999), *Theologische Rundschau* 65 (2000): 102–09.

Dürr, Alfred. *The Cantatas of J. S. Bach*. Revised and translated by Richard D. P. Jones. Oxford: Oxford University Press, 2005.

Ehrmann, Sabine. "Johann Sebastian Bachs Textdichterin Christiane Mariane von Ziegler," *Beiträge zur Bachforschung* 9–10 (1991): 261–68.

Eigler, Friederike and Susanne Kord. *The Feminist Encyclopedia of German Literature*. London: Greenwood Press, 1997.

Florstedt, Renate. "Dementi für unsere Schwester in Apollo." In *Ich muß mich ganz hingeben können: Frauen in Leipzig*. Edited by Friderun Bodeit, 9–19. Leipzig: Verlag für die Frau, 1990.

Fox-Genovese, Elizabeth. "Women and the Enlightenment." In *Becoming Visible: Women in European History*. 2nd ed. Edited by Renate Bridenthal, Claudia Koonz, and Susan Stuard, 251–77. Boston: Houghton Mifflin, 1987.

Frevet, Ute, Heide Wunder, and Christina Vanja. "Historical Research on Women in the Federal Republic of Germany." In *Writing Women's History: International Perspectives*. Edited by Karen Offen, Ruth Roach Pierson, and Jane Rendall, 291–331. Bloomington: Indiana University Press, 1991.

Friedrichs, Elisabeth. *Die deutschsprachigen Schriftstellerinnen des 18. und 19. Jahrhunderts*. Repertorien zur Deutschen Literaturgeschichte. Vol. 9. Edited by Paul Raabe. Stuttgart: J. B. Metzler, 1981.

Geck, Martin. "Die *vox-Christi*-Sätze in Bachs Kantaten." In *Bach und die Stile*. Edited by Martin Geck, 79–101. Dortmund: Klangfarben Musikverlag, 1999.

Gnüg, Hiltrud and Renate Möhrmann, eds. *Frauen Literatur Geschichte: Schreibende Frauen vom Mittelalter bis zur Gegenwart*. Stuttgart: J. B. Metzler, 1985.

Gössmann, Elisabeth. "Rezeptionszusammenhänge und Rezeptionsweisen deutscher Schriften zur Frauen-gelehrsamkeit." In *Res Publica Litteraria: Die Institutionen der Gelehrsamkeit in der frühen Neuzeit*. Vol. 2. Edited by Sebastian Neumeister and Conrad Wiedemann, 589–601. Wiesbaden: Harrassowitz, 1987.

Gössmann, Elisabeth, ed. *Das wohlgelahrte Frauenzimmer*. Archiv für philosophie- und theologiegeschichtliche Frauenforschung. Vol. 1. 2nd ed. Munich: Iudicium, 1998 (1984).

Goodman, Katherine R. *Amazons and Apprentices: Women and the German Parnassus in the Early Enlightenment*. Columbia, SC: Camden House, 1999.

Goodman, Katherine R. "'Ich bin die deutsche Redlichkeit': Letters of Christiane Mariane von Ziegler to Johann Ernst Philippi." *Daphnis* 29 (2000): 307–54.

Goodman, Katherine R. "From Salon to *Kaffeekranz*: Gender Wars and the *Coffee Cantata* in Bach's Leipzig." In *Bach's Changing World: Voices in the Community*. Edited by Carol K. Baron, 190–218. Rochester: University of Rochester Press, 2006.

Gray, Marion W. *Productive Men, Reproductive Women: The Agrarian Household and the Emergence of Separate Spheres during the German Enlightenment*. New York: Berghahn Books, 2000.

Häfner, Klaus. "Picander, der Textdichter von Bachs viertem Kantatenjahrgang: ein neuer Hinweis." *Die Musikforschung* 35 (1982): 156–62.

Herbst, Wolfgang. "Ein Vergleich zwischen Joh. Seb. Bach und Chr. Mariane v. Ziegler." *Musik und Kirche* 30 (1960): 248–55.

Heuser, Magdalene. "Das Musenchor mit neuer Ehre zieren: Schriftstellerinnen zur Zeit der Frühaufklärung." In *Vom Mittelalter bis zum Ende des 18. Jahrhunderts*. Vol. 1 of *Deutsche Literatur von Frauen*. Edited by Gisela Brinker-Gabler, 293–313. Munich: C. H. Beck, 1988.

Huff, Steven R. "Christiane Mariane von Ziegler's *Versuch in gebundener Schreib=Art* (Volume I, 1728)." In *"Der Buchstab tödt–der Geist macht lebendig": Festschrift zum 60. Geburtstage von Hans-Gert Roloff von Freunden, Schülern und Kollegen*. Vol. 2. Edited by James Hardin and Jörg Jungmayr, 977–88. Bern: Peter Lang, 1992.

Hufton, Olwen. "Women, Work, and Family." In *A History of Women in the West. III. Renaissance and Enlightenment Paradoxes*. Edited by Natalie Zemon Davis and Arlette Farge, 15–45. Cambridge, MA: Belknap Press, 1993.

Hunt, Margaret, Margaret Jacob, Phyllis Mack, and Ruth Perry, eds. *Women and the Enlightenment*. New York: The Haworth Press, 1984.

Joeres, Ruth-Ellen Boetcher. "The German Enlightenment (1720–1790)." In *The Cambridge History of German Literature*. Edited by Helen Watanabe-O'Kelly, 147–210. Cambridge: Cambridge University Press, 1997.

Killy, Walther, ed.. *Literatur Lexikon: Autoren und Werke deutscher Sprache*, 12 vols. Gütersloh: Bertelsmann, 1992.

Kleinau, Elke and Claudia Opitz, ed. *Geschichte der Mädchen und Frauenbildung*. Vol. 1, Vom Mittelalter bis zur Aufklärung. Frankfurt am Main: Campus, 1996.

Kock, Hermann. *Genealogisches Lexicon der Familie Bach*. Bearbeitet und Aktualisiert von Ragnhild Siegel. Gotha: Kunstverlag, 1995.

Konrad, Ulrich. "Aspekte musikalisch-theologischen Verstehens in Mariane von Zieglers und Johann Sebastian Bachs Kantate *Bisher habt ihr nichts gebeten in meinem Namen* BWV 87." *Archiv für Musikwissenschaft* 57 (2000): 199–221.

Kord, Susanne. "Die Gelehrte als Zwitterwesen in Schriften von Autorinnen des 18. und 19. Jahrhunderts." *Querelles: Jahrbuch für Frauenforschung* 1 (1996): 158–189.

Kord, Susanne. *Sich einen Namen machen: Anonymität und weibliche Autorschaft 1700–1900*. Stuttgart: J. B. Metzler, 1996.

Kreutzer, Hans Joachim. "Johann Sebastian Bach und das literarische Leipzig der Aufklärung." *Bach-Jahrbuch* 77 (1991): 7–31.

Kreutzer, Hans Joachim. "Bach and the Literary Scene in Eighteenth-Century Leipzig." In *Music and German Literature: Their Relationship since the Middle Ages*. Edited by James M. McGlathery, 80–99. Columbia, SC: Camden House, 1992.

Kroker, Ernst, ed. *Bibliotheca Societatis Teutonicae Saeculi XVI–XVIII: Katalog der Büchersammlung der Deutschen Gesellschaft in Leipzig.* 2 vols. Munich: Kösel-Verlag, 1971.

Krull, Edith. "Das Wirken der Frau im frühen deutschen Zeitschriftenwesen." Ph.D. diss., Friedrich-Wilhelms-Universität, Berlin, 1939.

Krummacher, Friedhelm. *Bachs Zyklus der Choralkantaten: Aufgaben und Lösungen.* Göttingen: Vandenhoeck & Ruprecht, 1995.

Küster, Konrad. "Die Frankfurter und Leipziger Überlieferung der Kantaten Johan Ludwig Bachs." *Bach-Jahrbuch* 75 (1989): 65–106.

Küster, Konrad. *Bach Handbuch.* Kassel: Bärenreiter, 1999.

Küster, Konrad. "Christiane Mariane von Ziegler (*née* Romanus)." In *J. S. Bach*, Oxford Composer Companions. Edited by Malcolm Boyd, 535. Oxford: Oxford University Press, 1999.

Leaver, Robin A. *Bachs Theologische Bibliothek / Bach's Theological Library*, Beiträge zur theologischen Bachforschung 1. Neuhausen-Stuttgart: Hänssler-Verlag, 1983.

Leaver, Robin A. "Theological Consistency, Liturgical Integrity, and Musical Hermeneutics in Luther's Liturgical Reforms." *Lutheran Quarterly* 9 (1995): 117–38.

Lehmstedt, Mark. "'Es steckt dem weiblichen Geschlecht kein Spinngeweb in dem Gehirne': Christiana Mariana von Ziegler." *Leipziger Blätter* 38 (2001): 68–69.

Littler, Margaret, ed. *Gendering German Studies: New Perspectives on German Literature and Culture.* Oxford: Blackwell, 1997.

Ludolphy, Ingetraut. "Die Frau in der Sicht Martin Luthers," in *Vierhundertfünfzig Jahre lutherische Reformation, 1517–1967.* Edited by Helmar Junghans, Ingetraut Ludolphy, and Kurt Meier, 204–21. Göttingen: Vandenhoeck & Ruprecht, 1967.

Martens, Wolfgang. *Die Botschaft der Tugend: Die Aufklärung im Spiegel der deutschen Moralischen Wochenschriften*, 2nd ed. Stuttgart: Metzler, 1971.

Melamed, Daniel R. *J. S. Bach and the German Motet.* Cambridge: Cambridge University Press, 1995.

Mitchell, P. M. *Johann Christoph Gottsched (1700–1766): Harbinger of German Classicism.* Columbia, SC: Camden House, 1995.

Möbius, Helga. *Woman of the Baroque Age.* Translated by Barbara Chruscik Beedham. Montclair, NJ: Abner Schram, 1982.

Mühne, Christian. "Die weltlichen Solokantaten Georg Philipp Telemanns als Gelegenheitswerke." In *Telemanns Auftrags- und Gelegenheitswerke-Funktion, Wert und Bedeutung.* Edited by Wolf Hobohm, Carsten Lange, and Brit Reipsch, 181–89. Telemann-Konferenzberichte 10. Oschersleben: dr. ziethen, 1997.

Müller, Michael and Ulla Heisl. *Das Romanushaus in Leipzig.* Leipzig: Das Stadtkabinett, 1990.

Neumann, Werner, ed. *Sämtliche von Johann Sebastian Bach vertonte Texte.* Leipzig: VEB Deutscher Verlag für Musik, 1974.

Neumann, Werner. *Handbuch der Kantaten Johann Sebastian Bachs*, 5th ed. Wiesbaden: Breitkopf & Härtel, 1984.

Niemeyer, Beatrix. "Ausschluss oder Ausgrenzung?: Frauen im Unkreis der Universitäten im 18. Jahrhundert." In *Geschichte der Mädchen und Frauenbildung.* Vol. 1, Vom Mittelalter bis zur Aufklärung. Edited by Elke Kleinau and Claudia Opitz, 275–94. Frankfurt am Main: Campus, 1996.

Nörtemann, Regina. "Schwache Werkzeuge als öffentliche Richterinnen: Zur fiktiven weiblichen Herausgeber- und Verfasserschaft in Moralischen Wochenschriften des 18. Jahrhunderts." *Archiv für Kulturgeschichte* 72 (1990): 381–403.

Offen, Karen. *European Feminisms 1700–1951: A Political History*. Stanford: Stanford University Press, 2000.

Osthoff, Helmuth and Rufus Hallmark. *Kritischer Bericht* to *Johann Sebastian Bach: Neue Ausgabe Sämtlicher Werke* I/23. Kassel: Bärenreiter, 1984.

Peters, Mark. "Christiana Mariana von Ziegler's Sacred Cantata Texts and Their Settings by Johann Sebastian Bach." Ph.D. diss., University of Pittsburgh, 2003.

Peters, Mark. "A Reconsideration of Bach's Role as Text Redactor in the Ziegler Cantatas." *BACH: Journal of the Riemenschneider Bach Institute* 36 (2005): 25–66.

Petschauer, Peter. "Eighteenth-Century German Opinions about Education for Women." *Central European History* 19 (1986): 262–92.

Petzoldt, Martin. *'Texte zur Leipziger Kirchen=Music': Zum Verständnis der Kantatentexte Johann Sebastian Bachs*. Jahresgabe 1992/1993 der Internationalen Bach-Gesellschaft Schaffhausen. Leipzig: Breitkopf & Härtel, 1993.

Petzoldt, Martin. "Johann Sebastian Bach and His Vocal Works: Their Meaning for Liturgy and Worship in the Lutheran Church." In *Incarnation and Creativity: St. Olav Conference on Theology and Music*. Edited by Øystein Bjørdal, 83–98. Trondheim: Tapir, 1997.

Petzoldt, Martin. "Bachs Prüfung vor dem Kurfürstlichen Konsistorium zu Leipzig." *Bach-Jahrbuch* 84 (1998): 19–30.

Petzoldt, Martin. "Johann Sebastian Bach in theologischer Interaktion Persönlichkeiten in seinem beruflichen Umfeld." In *Über Leben, Kunst und Kunstwerke: Aspekte musikalischer Biographie Johann Sebastian Bach im Zentrum*. Edited by Christoph Wolff, 133–59. Leipzig: Evangelische Verlagsanstalt, 1999.

Petzoldt, Martin. *Texthefte zur Kirchenmusik aus Bachs Leipziger Zeit*. Stuttgart: Carus, 2000.

Petzoldt, Martin. *Bach-Kommentar: theologisch-musikwissenschaftliche Kommentierung der geistlichen Vokalwerke Johann Sebastian Bachs*. Vol. 1, Die geistlichen Kantaten des 1. bis 27. Trinitatis-Sonntages. Vol. 2, Die geistlichen Kantaten vom 1. Advent bis zum Trinitatisfest. Kassel: Bärenreiter, 2004, 2007.

Predeek, Albert. "Ein vergessener Freund Gottscheds [Christian Gabriel Fischer]." In *Beiträge zur Deutschen Bildungsgeschichte: Festschrift zur Zweihundertjahrfeier der Deutschen Gesellschaft in Leipzig 1727–1927*, 109–23. Leipzig: Alfred Lorentz, 1927.

Rifkin, Joshua and Konrad Küster. "Ziegler, Christiane Mariane von." In *The New Grove Dictionary of Music and Musicians*, 2nd ed. Vol. 27. Edited by Stanley Sadie, 820. London: Macmillan, 2001.

Sagarra, Eda and Peter Skrine. *Companion to German Literature: From 1500 to the Present*. Oxford: Blackwell Publishers, 1997.

Scheide, William H. "Johann Sebastian Bachs Sammlung von Kantaten seines Vetters Johann Ludwig Bach." *Bach-Jahrbuch* 46 (1959): 52–94; 48 (1961), 5–24; 49 (1962): 5–32.

Scheide, William H. "Bach und der Picander-Jahrgang–Eine Erwiderung." *Bach-Jahrbuch* 66 (1980): 47–51.

Scheide, William H. "Eindeutigkeit und Mehrdeutigkeit in Picanders Kantatenjahrgangs– Vorbemerkung und im Werkverzeichnis des Nekrologs auf Johann Sebastian Bach." *Bach-Jahrbuch* 69 (1983): 109–13.

Schering, Arnold. *Johann Sebastian Bach und das Musikleben Leipzigs im 18. Jahrhundert.* Vol. 3 of *Der Musikgeschichte Leipzigs.* Leipzig: Kistner & Siegel, 1941.

Schieth, Lydia. *Frauenliteratur.* Bamberg: C. C. Buchner, 1991.

Schneider, Susanne. "Lebensgeschichte und literarisches Werk als Wechselbeziehung: Zur Frage der Geschlechter in den Texten der Dichterin Christiana Mariana von Ziegler (1695–1760)." Master's thesis: Universität Gesamthochschule Kassel, 1997.

Schneider, Wolfgang. *Leipzig: Dokumente und Bilder zur Kulturgeschichte.* Leipzig and Weimar: Kiepenheuer, 1990.

Schrammek, Winfried. "Viola pomposa und Violoncello piccolo bei Johann Sebastian Bach." In *Bericht über die Wissenschaftliche Konferenz zum III. Internationalen Bachfest der DDR, Leipzig, 1975.* Edited by Werner Felix, Winfried Hoffmann, and Armin Schneiderheinze, 345–54. Leipzig: VEB Deutscher Verlag für Musik, 1977.

Schulze, Hans-Joachim. "Neuerkenntnisse zu einigen Kantatentexten Bachs auf Grund neuer biographischer Daten." In *Bach-Interpretationen.* Edited by Martin Geck, 22–28. Göttingen, 1969.

Schulze, Hans-Joachim. "Texte und Textdichter." In *Die Welt der Bach Kantaten.* Vol. 3, *Johann Sebastian Bachs Leipziger Kirchenkantaten.* Edited by Christoph Wolff, 109–25. Stuttgart: J. B. Metzler and Kassel: Bärenreiter, 1999.

Schulze, Hans-Joachim. *Die Bach-Kantaten: Einführungen zu sämtlichen Kantaten Johann Sebastian Bachs.* Leipzig: Evangelische Verlagsanstalt, 2006.

Schumann, Sabine. "Das 'lesende Frauenzimmer:' Frauenzeitschriften im 18. Jahrhundert." In *Die Frau von der Reformation zur Romantik: Die Situation der Frau vor dem hintergrund der Literatur- und Sozialgeschichte.* Edited by Barbara Becker-Cantarino, 138–69. Bonn: Herbert Grundmann, 1980.

Schweitzer, Albert. *J. S. Bach.* Translated by Ernest Newman. 2 vols. New York: Dover, 1966 (1911).

Siegele, Ulrich. "Bach's Ort in Orthodoxie und Aufklärung." *Musik und Kirche* 51 (1981): 11.

Simon, Sunka. "'Als sie ihr Bildness schildern sollte:' Die sprachliche Struktur der Innen- und Aussenporträts in der Lyrik Christiana Mariana von Zieglers." *Daphnis* 19 (1990): 247–65.

Smith, Mark M. "Joh. Seb. Bachs Violoncello piccolo: Neue Aspekte—offene Fragen." *Bach-Jahrbuch* 84 (1998): 63–81.

Sonnet, Martine. "A Daughter to Educate." In *A History of Women in the West. III. Renaissance and Enlightenment Paradoxes.* Translated by Arthur Goldhammer. Edited by Natalie Zemon Davis and Arlette Farge, 101–31. Cambridge, MA: Belknap Press, 1993.

Starke, Werner. *Das Romanushaus in Leipzig.* Leipzig: VEB E. A. Seemann, 1976.

Steiger, Lothar and Renate Steiger. "J. S. Bach 'Es ist euch gut, daß ich hingehe' (BWV 108): Theologisch-musikalische Auslegung mit Anregungen für die Predigt und aufführungspraktischen Hinweisen." In *Cantate: Eine Handreichung für Pfarrer und Kirchenmusiker zum Schütz- und Bach-Gedenkjahr 1985.* Edited by Walter Blankenburg and Renate Steiger, 49–59. Kassel: Merseburger, 1985.

Stiller, Günther. *Johann Sebastian Bach and Liturgical Life in Leipzig*. Translated by Herbert J. A. Bouman, Daniel F. Poellot, and Hilton C. Oswald. Edited by Robin A. Leaver. St. Louis: Concordia Publishing House, 1984.

Targiel, Ralf-Rüdiger. "Zum 300. Geburtstag von Wolf Balthasar Adolph von Steinwehr." *Uni on* 44 (November 2004): 23.

Unger, Melvin P. *Handbook to Bach's Sacred Cantata Texts*. Lanham, MD: Scarecrow Press, 1996.

Voigt, Heinz. "Christiane Marianne von Ziegler, eine Dichterin der Bachzeit." Manuscript, Leipzig, 1984 (Bach-Archiv Leipzig, Sig. P-SM 3/10).

Watanabe-O'Kelly, Helen. "What Difference Does Feminism Make to the Study of German Literature?" In *Gendering German Studies: New Perspectives on German Literature and Culture*. Edited by Margaret Littler, 2–11. Oxford: Blackwell, 1997.

Wiesner, Merry E. *Women and Gender in Early Modern Europe*. Cambridge: Cambridge University Press, 1993.

Witkowski, Georg. *Geschichte des literarischen Lebens in Leipzig*. Leipzig and Berlin: B. G. Teubner, 1909. (Reprint Munich: K. G. Saur, 1994.)

Wolff, Christoph. "Ein Gelehrten-Stammbuch aus dem 18. Jahrhundert mit Einträgen von G. Ph. Telemann, S. L. Weiß und anderen Musikern." *Die Musikforschung* 26 (1973): 217–24.

Wolff, Christoph, ed. *Die Welt der Bach Kantaten*. Vol. 3, *Johann Sebastian Bachs Leipziger Kirchenkantaten*. Stuttgart: J. B. Metzler and Kassel: Bärenreiter, 1999.

Wolff, Christoph. *Johann Sebastian Bach: The Learned Musician*. New York: W. W. Norton, 2000.

Wolter, Christine. *Mariane: oder, die Unsterblichkeit*. Leipzig: Faber & Faber, 2004.

Woods, Jean M. "Das 'Gelahrte Frauenzimmer' und die deutschen Frauenlexika 1631–1743." In *Res Publica Litteraria: Die Institutionen der Gelehrsamkeit in der frühen Neuzeit*. Vol. 2. Edited by Sebastian Neumeister and Conrad Wiedemann, 577–87. Wiesbaden: Otto Harrassowitz, 1987.

Wunder, Heide. *He Is the Sun, She Is the Moon: Women in Early Modern Germany*. Translated by Thomas Dunlap. Cambridge, MA: Harvard University Press, 1998. Originally published as *"Er ist die Sonn', sie ist der Mond": Frauen in der Frühen Neuzeit*. Munich: C. H. Beck, 1992.

Wunder, Heide. "Gender Norms and Their Enforcement in Early Modern Germany." In *Gender Relations in German History: Power, Agency, and Experience from the Sixteenth to the Twentieth Century*. Edited by Lynn Abrams and Elizabeth Harvey, 39–56. Durham, NC: Duke University Press, 1997.

Zander, Friedrich. "Die Dichter der Kantatentexte Johann Sebastian Bachs." *Bach-Jahrbuch* 54 (1968): 9–64.

Zophy, Jonathan W. "We Must Have the Dear Ladies: Martin Luther and Women." In *Pietas et Societas: New Trends in Reformation Social History*. Edited by Kyle C. Sessions and Phillip N. Beff, 141–50. Kirksville, MO: Sixteenth Century Journal Publishers, 1985.

Index of Bach's Compositions

General Index

Date Due